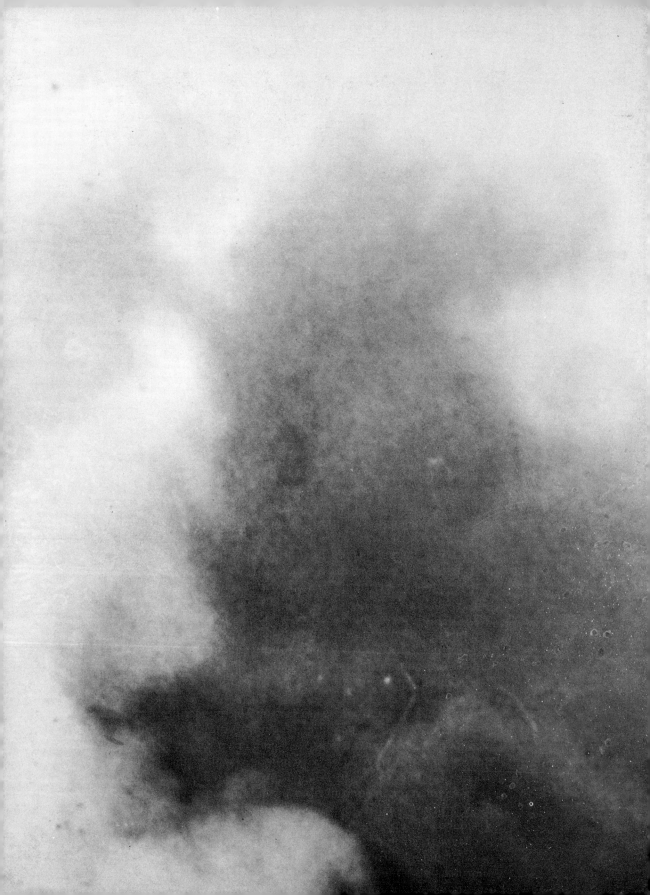

DUNKIRK
The Great Escape

A. J. Barker

J. M. Dent & Sons Ltd
London   Toronto   Melbourne

ALSO BY A. J. BARKER

Military History
The March on Delhi
Suez: The Seven Day War
Eritrea 1941
The Neglected War: Mesopotamia 1914–1918
Townshend of Kut.
The Civilizing Mission
The War Against Russia
Fortune Favours the Brave
Behind Barbed Wire
Short History of The East Yorkshire Regiment
Short History of the West Yorkshire Regiment

Weapons
Principles of Small Arms
German Infantry Weapons of World War II
British and American Infantry Weapons of
    World War II
Russian Infantry Weapons of World War II
    (with John Walter)
Mortars of the World

For Young Adults
Weapons and Armour
Famous Military Battles
Redcoats

First published 1977
© A. J. Barker
All rights reserved. No part of this publication
may be reproduced, stored in a retrieval
system, or transmitted, in any form or by any
means, electronic, mechanical, photocopying,
recording or otherwise, without the prior
permission of J. M. Dent & Sons Ltd.

Made in Great Britain
Printed by Butler & Tanner Ltd
Frome and London
for
J. M. Dent & Sons Ltd
Aldine House, Albemarle Street, London
This book is set in 11/12 pt Baskerville 169

ISBN 0 460 12020 4

British Library Cataloguing in Publication Data

Barker, Arthur J
    Dunkirk: the great escape.
    1. Great Britain. Army. British Expeditionary
    Force 2. Dunkirk, France, Battle of, 1940
    I. Title
    940.54′21   D756.5.D8
    ISBN 0–460–12020–4

Contents

	Acknowledgements	6
	Prologue	7
1	War Shadows	10
	1918–40	
2	Countdown	20
	September 1939 – May 18 1940	
3	Retreat and Collapse	40
	May 18 – 25	
4	Dunkirk Bridgehead	62
	May 25 – 27	
5	The Most Compelling Hour	80
	7 – 8 p.m. May 26	
6	Hell's Delight	102
	Midnight May 26 – 8 a.m. May 30	
7	Within the Perimeter	126
	May 28 – June 1	
8	Destroyers, Trawlers and Tugs	148
	May 28 – June 2	
9	Enterprise and Courage	166
	May 30 – June 1	
10	Final Phase	186
	June 1 – 2.30 p.m. June 4	
11	Aftermath	206
	June 4 – July 6	
	Epilogue	224
	Appendix 1	232
	Composition of the British Expeditionary Force in France	
	Appendix 2	234
	Summary of Ships taking part in Operation Dynamo	
	Allied Troops evacuated from Dunkirk	
	French Troops evacuated from Dunkirk	
	Bibliography	237
	Index	239

Acknowledgements

The backbone of information for this book came from men who were at Dunkirk in 1940; without their help the story would have lacked human interest. Very many people told me their stories and supplied documentation and details from diaries, letters and carefully preserved reports, maps and snapshots. Unfortunately, for a variety of reasons—mainly duplication, lack of corroboration and sheer bulk—not every personal story or experience could be included. I hope that the many contributors will understand.

It is difficult to know where to begin in naming all the individuals who have helped me to reconstruct the story of what is still one of the greatest dramas of contemporary European history. But I am especially grateful to those Dunkirk Veterans who now live in southern Africa and whose stories have not been solicited previously by other historians. Of these I wish particularly to thank the following: The Mayor of Salisbury, Rhodesia, H. Douglas Tanner Esq.; Major M. E. Few T.D., F. J. Lomath Esq., The Venerable E. Aldington-Hunt, S. Payne Esq., R. V. L. Worsdale Esq., G. H. Bryan Esq., S. J. Porter Esq., Mrs D. McF Reid; Lt-Col. J. C. Paterson, H. Hunt Esq., H. J. Leach Esq., Captain E. A. R. Lang.

Thanks must also be expressed to the following other D.V.A. contributors: Major C. K. Lewis, H. Jubb Esq., Captain A. Alexander, F. D. Williams Esq., J. A. Bambury Esq., S. Proest Esq., Lt-Col. Longden, Captain A. Purvis and J. Mannion Esq.

For their help in locating veterans I am indebted to the Editor of *Soldier* magazine, H. Robinson Esq., M.B.E., the Hon. Secretary of the Dunkirk Veterans' Association; and L. Taplin Esq., Chairman of the Portsmouth Branch of the Association. Many thanks in this respect are also due to Major H. N. Grieve, M.B.E., and Lt-Col. C. J. Robinson, M.B.E., both of my own old regiment.

On the German side I am indebted to my old friend Generalmajor H. J. Löser who was himself an active participant in *Operation Sichelschnitt*, and to the Bundesarchiv Koblenz.

Of the many others whose support and assistance helped to make this book possible I must single out my wife, Alexandra, who—besides controlling the domestic aspects of our lives—translated, interpreted, typed and generally helped to organize and collate research.

And, finally, my thanks are due to Geoffrey Wadsley for drawing the excellent maps in the book.

The author and publishers wish to thank the following for permission to reproduce photographs in their possession: Associated Press, pp. 54 (left), 62–3, 131, 145 (bottom), 148–9, 191 (left), 194, 200; Barnaby's Picture Library, pp. 126–7; Mr Chaz Bowyer, pp. 31, 34, 174 (top), 178; Bundesarchiv, Koblenz, pp. 203, 206–7, 211, 212, 215, 216 (top); Camera Press, p. 219 (bottom); Daily Mail, p. 183; Etablissement Cinématographique et Photographique des Armées, Fort D'Ivry, France, pp. 55, 191 (right); Fox, pp. 120–1, 132 (bottom); Robert Hunt Library, pp. 17, 220–1; Imperial War Museum, pp. 10–11, 13, 15, 26–7, 37, 40–1, 44–5, 46, 48, 50, 54–5, 58–9, 66–7, 70–1, 72, 73, 77, 78, 80–1, 88, 91 (top), 94 (top), 97, 98, 100, 102–3, 106, 117, 118, 120, 135, 141, 145 (top), 152, 161, 163, 174 (bottom), 177, 186–7, 195, 197, 204, 216 (bottom), 219 (top); Kent Messenger, pp. 122–3, 155; Keystone Press, pp. 20–1; National Railway Museum, York, pp. 111, 114; Mr S. Payne, pp. 91 (bottom), 93, 110; Paul Popper Ltd, pp. 24, 86; Mr R. J. Slack, p. 74; Sport and General, p. 94 (bottom); Times Newspapers, pp. 136–7, 166–7; Topix, 132 (top), 170, 173; World Ship Photo Library, p. 84.

6

Prologue

'Dear God, be good to me; the sea is so wide
and my boat is so small.'

An old fisherman's prayer

Dunkirk (*Dunkerque*), France's fourth port, is an ancient city with a
colourful history of war. In Oliver Cromwell's time it was ceded to the
English, who quickly sold it back to the French. Forty years later it
was the base from which Jean Bart and other French corsairs preyed
on English shipping. Because of this the English insisted that its fortifications be demolished and its harbour filled up before they would sign
the peace treaty at Utrecht in 1713. After another eighty years Dunkirk
was once again the focal point in a war between Britain and Revolu-
tionary France. This time the English lost, when the gallant Duke of
York—famed for his march up a hill and down again—was defeated
at Hondschoote. In World War I—during which it was for most of the
time a mere thirty kilometres behind the Allied line—Dunkirk was
heavily damaged. At the nearby village of La Panne, King Albert of
the Belgians set up his headquarters and in the churchyard there lies
the body of a Belgian lady who was one of the victims of the sinking
of the *Lusitania*.

The city itself lies inside a ring of old ramparts, amid a network of
canals west and south of the port. Outside it the coast stretches away,
east-north-east towards the Belgian frontier and Nieuwpoort. Rosendael
and St Pol-sur-Mer are suburbs on the east and west sides of the town
respectively; the seaside resort of Malo-les-Bains lies some three kilometres north-east of the city's ramparts.

Between Dunkirk and Nieuwpoort, twenty-six kilometres away,
the coast does not vary a great deal. Near the sea there is a broad shelv-
ing expanse of sand which in summer months is generally thronged
with bathers. Brick sea-walls known as 'digues' separate the beach from
the rolling sand-dune country which is covered with sea-grass and criss-
crossed with innumerable drainage channels. Beyond the dunes there
is a stretch of more solid terrain—scrub and bush country.

In times of peace holidaymakers have flocked to the Dunkirk beaches

7

in ever-increasing numbers since the turn of the century. But while the coast may seem alluring to summer visitors it can also be very treacherous. The tidal streams are very strong, and a northerly wind will raise a dangerous sea on the beaches and across the harbour entrance whenever it comes against a tide, while an easterly gale will create an awkward sea at the harbour entrance. When a surf is running it breaks some distance from the shore, and is much more evil than it looks.

On the north side of Dunkirk harbour the ramparts are shut from the sea by a canal mouth fenced with a stone causeway about 1500 metres long. This is known as the Promenade de la Digue and in 1940 a wooden pier, about 2250 metres long, ran north-north-west into the sea from the Promenade's seaward end. From the beaches up to La Panne, from this long pier, and from the jetty to the west of the harbour, the British Expeditionary Force and thousands of French troops were lifted to safety in the last week of a German campaign which ended with the fall of France.

Nearly four decades have elapsed since the tragedy, and the triumph, of what is simply referred to as 'Dunkirk'. A generation to whom the event can be no more than a matter of hearsay is now approaching middle age; and children asked what Dunkirk is, or was, will usually say they do not know. Their ignorance can be excused, for there have been many other tragedies and triumphs in the years which have passed since 1940. Yet, to those who survived the campaign and were lifted to safety under the very noses of the Germans, the year of 'Dunkirk' still seems very close.

The narrative which follows seeks to recapture a little of the spirit of that time as well as to recount the story of a remarkable enterprise. The men themselves are proud to be known as Dunkirk Veterans and to have taken part in the operation which marked the real beginning of Britain's long war with Nazi Germany. But many regret that their efforts are passing into historical oblivion without due recognition. In other wars, campaign veterans were awarded medals as symbols of their services. The men of the 1914 British Expeditionary Force were presented with the 'Mons Star', and their sons who served with the second B.E.F. are still hoping that the authorities will award a special medal or a commemorative bar to enhance the status of their 1939–1945 Star. In the past, however, there have been no stars or commemorative ribbons for those who have lost a battle, no matter how great their sacrifice or how arduous their efforts. And the battle of Dunkirk was won by the enemy. The evacuation has been variously described as a 'triumph' and a 'miracle', but as Winston Churchill reminded the House of Commons on 4 June 1940: 'We must be very careful not to assign to this deliverance the attributes of a victory. Wars are not won by evacuations.'

Yet if the evacuation was a triumph or a miracle it would be fitting to heed the Dunkirk Veterans' plea for recognition. The B.E.F. won no battle and when the men who returned from France merged into the armies which ultimately were to bring victory, the trials of Dunkirk were already more than half forgotten. But now, with the victory itself already a memory, let them be remembered as the first British soldiers, sailors and airmen in a war which is now won. For they were—in the words of a psalm written for a special service commemorating the Old Contemptibles of 1914, which might have been written for the B.E.F. of 1940—

'Worthy of the men who died to gain time.'

Cape Town   A. J. Barker
1977

Over the page
The Panzers were Hitler's élite troops, and their methods lacked the formality traditionally associated with the German Army's operations. Tank crews in their distinctive black uniforms and berets are seen here being briefed by a battalion commander prior to the launching of Sichelschnitt.

1. War Shadows

1918–40

'Today is Trinity Sunday. Centuries ago words were written to be a call and a spur to the faithful servants of Truth and Justice: "Arm yourselves, and be ye men of valour, and be in readiness for the conflict: for it is better for us to perish in battle than to look upon the outrage to our nation and our altar. As the Will of God is in Heaven, even so let it be."'

From an address, broadcast by Winston Churchill, 19 May 1940

Munich, capital of Bavaria, fourth largest town in the German Reich, birthplace and headquarters of Adolf Hitler's National Socialist Party, is famed for its beer and the Oktoberfest. The name of the town is also a byword of appeasement, for it was here, in 1938, that Neville Chamberlain bowed to Hitler's demands, and postponed a war that was inevitable.

Since 1914 there had, in fact, been no real peace in Europe, for the armistice signed on 11 November 1918 was essentially without meaning. The guns were silent, millions of men had returned to civilian life and vast cemeteries had been created to honour the dead. But the very nature of the conditions imposed on the vanquished carried the seeds of another conflict, and in the 1920s plans were laid for a new, redemptive war to avenge Germany's defeat. The trend of events in Germany, Italy and Japan provided plenty of indications of the changes ahead. Until hard facts compelled it to do so however, the British Government chose to disregard the possibility of war.

Thanks to a system by which obsolescent ships were retained and relegated to a reserve instead of being broken up, and to the fact that the obsolescence of ships was slower than that of aircraft, the Royal Navy managed to retain a strength adequate—though barely so—to the needs of war in 1940. The Royal Air Force also managed to stand up to the Luftwaffe in 1940 although, the speed of aircraft production being what it was, this was touch and go. When Chamberlain faced Hitler at Munich he did so with the knowledge that, except for a handful of new Hurricanes, Britain's fighter squadrons were inferior to those of Germany. When he returned to London waving his scrap of paper and rashly declaring 'Peace in our time', he had not saved his country from war but he had bought time—time to prepare Britain for what was an eventual certainty. Unfortunately the year's grace that was gained was largely wasted and the postponement of hostilities was of greater material and moral value to the Germans than to the British, the French, or the Poles.

Britain's army was in poor shape. Constrained by manpower, money and equipment, the British—like the French—had trained for a war

Concert parties were a feature of the Phoney War in France. Here Gracie Fields is 'having a cuppa' before a concert at Valenciennes.

like that of 1914–18. A few of the more far-sighted senior officers had seen the possibilities of tank warfare, and during the manœuvres of 1938 and 1939 experimental armoured vehicles clanked across Salisbury Plain. These vehicles were of very advanced design, but they were only prototypes; the financial starvation imposed on the army restricted the purchase of any reasonable quantity of such vehicles, with the result that the British Army had no tank force capable of taking the field when the war clouds gathering over Europe finally burst. Meanwhile the Germans were evolving the new philosophy of warfare—*Blitzkrieg*—which in 1940 would enable the Panzer forces to smash through to the Channel coast, and to victory.

That the Germans knew of Britain's weakness there can be little doubt. In the summer of 1939 the German military attaché visited Sandhurst and saw all the officer cadets engaged in making a commercial film on the orders of the War Office. Whatever impression he got from that must have been confirmed by what he saw on manœuvres that same summer, with infantrymen carrying lengths of gas piping stuck into pieces of wood to represent anti-tank rifles and blue flags denoting the vehicles they were supposed to have but did not. Unfortunately the problems were not limited merely to deficiencies in equipment, shortage of men or outmoded tactical doctrines. In September 1938 nobody in Whitehall knew quite where the British Army was going to fight. Tentative arrangements had been made to transfer the impressive total of two divisions to France if it should be deemed necessary, but at that time there was no plan for their employment. An 'Advanced Air Striking Force' of light bombers was also scheduled to go to France—not to help the French Army, or the British Army, but to get within range of German industry. Like the two divisions of troops, however, nobody had decided quite how the bomber squadrons were to be used.

Remembering the slaughter of World War I, British and French politicians could not visualize an Allied offensive in another war with Germany. Without Russia they could not see how Britain and France could possibly raise and maintain the huge armies to fight the war of attrition they assumed would occur again if either side were to attack. Moreover the French were obsessed with the myth of the 'inviolable front'. Believing that however badly it had been battered the French front line had never really been broken in World War I, they had built an 'impregnable' line of defences far stronger than the old forts around Verdun which had proved so crucial in 1916. In France and Britain alike it was popularly believed that this 'Maginot' line extended from the Swiss frontier to the North Sea, whereas it actually stopped at Luxembourg. Blissfully unaware of this fact or blithely unconscious of its significance, strategists in France dreamed of German offensives battering themselves to pieces against 'Le Maginot', and on the other side of the Channel experts in Britain speculated on a naval blockade to bring Germany to her knees.

In effect the great majority of people in both countries gave such matters little thought, and those who did were gloomy and unenthusiastic. Apart from expecting a new war to bring a repetition of the depressing story of the land fighting of 1914–18, they had plenty of reasons for believing that another war would be even more unpleasant. Civilians as well as soldiers, it seemed, were to be slaughtered on a vast scale. As soon as another war began, they had been told, the sky would be black with bomber aircraft, wing-tip to wing-tip, and death would rain down. From Stanley Baldwin's statement, 'The bomber will always get through', to the terrifying estimate of the Imperial Defence Committee that London could expect sixty days of air attacks starting on Day One of hostilities, with 600,000 people killed and twice that many injured, the proverbial man on the Clapham bus and his counterpart on the Paris Metro had been left with few illusions about what would happen to them if their governments declared war on Germany. In Britain during the summer of 1939 thousands of cardboard coffins were stacked in public swimming baths which had been requisitioned and 'closed for repairs'; a million burial forms had been printed; and thousands of hospital beds had been earmarked for the injured. Across the Channel Parisians panicked two days before the war began when they learned of similar precautions—on a less grandiose scale—being taken in the French capital. The French built public shelters, prepared posters and notices about the danger of bombing, tested air raid sirens

Lord Gort, Commander-in-Chief of the British Expeditionary Force, photographed in 1939. It was his prompt decision in May 1940 that saved the B.E.F. from death or captivity.

and, like the British, prepared schemes to evacuate children and others from the large cities.

All this produced a very pessimistic outlook. Yet at the beginning of August 1939 the news that Parliament was adjourning for the summer recess lifted British morale. If MPs could go away for that long, surely things could not be too bad, people concluded. 'Parliament is taking a holiday—why not you?' said an advertisement in the *Daily Express* before the August Bank Holiday weekend. 'Visit the Belgian coast where everyone is happy, peaceful and smiling.' It was a glorious sunny weekend and a record number of people took the *Express*'s advice and did go away. Ironically many were able to do so only because the prospect of war had brought material benefits. The wheels of industry had started to turn, and men who had spent years on the dole were able to take their families to the seaside—some for the first time. By mid-August however it was becoming clear that the gloomy predictions of a fortnight before seemed likely to prove correct. Regular Army reservists and members of the Territorial Army were quietly called up 'for training', and the barrage balloon crews practised flying the great ungainly gas bags that would ring the big towns and, hopefully, scare away low-flying raiders. It was rough on the reservists, many of whom had only just found themselves jobs in civilian life. All of them—except perhaps for those who had been recently relegated to the reserve—found that the army to which they returned was not the army they had known before. Much of the equipment was different; so too was the organization. The Bren had replaced the old Lewis gun, and one marched in threes instead of the time-honoured fours; the Army, opined many disgustedly, had gone to the dogs.

On August 21, when it was announced from Moscow and Berlin that Russia and Germany were concluding a non-aggression Pact, the politicians in Westminster and the Quai D'Orsay finally gave up hope of snatching peace from the fire; meanwhile the men in Berlin were completing their preparations for war. The Pact meant that Germany no longer had to worry about a Russian attack from the rear, and Hitler's commanders-in-chief foregathered at Obersalzberg on August 22 to finalize plans for an attack on Poland. Poland was at last where he wanted her, the Führer told the generals. Living space in the East must be acquired while Germany was still guided by his own unique self, Italy by Mussolini, Spain by Franco and Britain and France by 'no one more significant' than the 'miserable worms' he had seen at Munich. France, Hitler assured his audience, lacked men, arms and stomach for war; as for Britain, her navy was in a sorry state, her army was limited to a field force of three divisions and only 150 anti-aircraft guns were available to defend the whole of the British Isles. 'We need not be afraid of a blockade,' he continued, 'the Russians will supply us with grain, cattle, coal, lead and zinc.... I am only afraid that at the last minute some *Schweinehund* will propose mediation....'

German infantry spearheaded the advance of Guderian's Panzers to secure bridgeheads across the Meuse. An infantry assault boat is seen here at one such crossing.

16

Although the German armies did not in fact invade Poland until the morning of September 1, the heat was promptly turned on as Goebbels's incident-fabrication experts went into action. Reports of ficticious atrocities by the Poles against the German minorities multiplied in the German press, and the Poles—in no mood for giving way—ordered a general mobilization. Tension steadily mounted, the Poles were presented with an ultimatum and finally—at 4.45 on the morning of 1 September 1939—the leading tanks of Generalleutnant Heinz Guderian's 6th Panzer Division rolled across the East Prussian border into Poland.

By the following night these tanks were fifty miles into Poland, and German bombers were raiding Warsaw, Gdynia and Lwow. Yet Britain—pledged to come to Poland's aid—had still not declared war on Germany. Neville Chamberlain was waiting to deliver a joint ultimatum with France, and both countries were dithering and pleading for time.

Finally, at 11.15 a.m. on September 3, Neville Chamberlain spoke to the British nation over the B.B.C. As Germany had failed to respond to an Anglo-French ultimatum to withdraw from Poland, he said in a thin and sadly plaintive voice, Britain and Germany were at war. Twenty minutes later the air raid sirens in London wailed, and people braced themselves for the ordeal they had feared. But it did not come; the sirens sounded the all-clear a quarter of an hour later and, although there were other false alarms, the long winter which followed was one of anti-climax. In this winter of what came to be known by the British as the 'Phoney War', by the French as *drôle de guerre* and by the Germans as the *Sitzkrieg*, only the Poles suffered. After being bombed and ravished their country was parcelled out between Germany and the Soviet Union. The campaign in Poland lasted only a few weeks and there were many lessons to be learned from the German victory. As with the warnings of the years before, however, Britain and France took little heed of the techniques and nature of the *Blitzkrieg*. They were totally committed to a defensive war, confident in the power of the Royal Navy ultimately to bring Germany to her knees by economic blockade. So with neither side making any offensive move on land the era of the Phoney War and the air of unreality dragged on.

Only the Royal Navy found there was nothing phoney about the war in that bitterly cold winter of 1939–40. Within a few weeks its pride had been dented by a daring U-boat raid on Scapa Flow which cost the Navy the battleship *Royal Oak*. And that particular humiliation was only alleviated when the pocket-battleship *Graf Spee*—after a dramatic running battle—was trapped off the coast of Uruguay and put out of action for good. Meantime German U-boats were creating havoc among British shipping and Britain's warships were kept fully occupied in a pitiless struggle to keep the shipping lanes open.

Meantime the war leaders in London and Paris were living in a wonderland of illusion, for the relative fierceness of the war at sea contrasted sharply with the absence of activity in the air, as well as on the ground. When the Luftwaffe remained silent after Poland, the British and French showed no disposition to begin hostilities. The French urged restraint because they feared reprisals on targets in France; both the British and French were reluctant to start bombing for fear of alienating the sympathies of the neutral United States. So instead of bombs the R.A.F. was sent out on 'truth raids', dropping some 18,000,000 propaganda leaflets on German cities in the first month of the war.

In the spring of 1940, however, the situation underwent a dramatic change when the Germans invaded Denmark and Norway—launching their attack at a moment when Neville Chamberlain was actually claiming that 'Hitler has missed the bus'. With Chamberlain and his minions in Whitehall issuing statements of such fatuous optimism the British public confidently expected the Germans to be thrown back into the sea. By the end of April, however, it was all too clear that the Norwegian campaign was going badly and that it would be the British troops sent to Norway who would be thrown back into the sea. The campaign continued after the Norwegians capitulated on 3 May, but it was now clear that defeat was looming and a hitherto complacent Parliament finally turned on the Prime Minister and his administration. Following two days of hectic debate Mr Amery, a leading critic of the Government, electrified the House of Commons on the evening of 8 May by pointing at Neville Chamberlain and exhorting him in Cromwell's words to 'go in the name of God'. Britain no longer wanted the man with the umbrella; the nation was looking for a man with a pole-axe. Winston Spencer Churchill might well be described as such a man, and it was he who was to set the tone for a new age.

Meanwhile, even as Parliament was debating Chamberlain's inept prosecution of the war, Hitler's armies were again on the march. At first light on May 10 columns of German troops streamed across the frontiers of Holland and Belgium and the Luftwaffe bombed French, Belgian and Dutch airfields. The third and most impressive demonstration of the *Blitzkrieg* had begun. It was to end on the North Sea beaches at the ancient sea-port of Dunkirk.

Over the page
Howitzers of a German field artillery regiment in action during the first phase of Operation Sichelschnitt.

2. Countdown

September 1939 – May 18 1940

'It is no mere territorial conquest that our enemies are seeking. It is the overthrow, complete and final, of this Empire and of everything for which it stands—and after that the conquest of the world.

It is the issue of life or death for us all. The Germans used the word 'Imperialism' against us, but the free peoples of the Empire cast that word back in their teeth.... Keep your hearts proud and your resolve unshaken...with God's help we shall not fail.'

King George VI, in a message to the Empire,
24 May 1940

Hitler had hoped that as soon as the 'Polish question' was settled to his satisfaction Britain and France would come to their senses, and peace could be patched up. When, by the end of September, it was clear that this was not going to happen, Germany's Supreme Commander decided that he would have to force the issue by attacking France and the General Staff was ordered to produce its plan for such an event.

As those who had worked out the contingency plans between the wars had been schooled in the pre-*Blitzkrieg* type of warfare and had little faith in the feasibility of an invasion of France, what emerged from the files was to say the least, uninspiring. The main attack was to be directed through Belgium towards the Channel coast, with subsidiary attacks on Holland and—north of the allegedly impassable terrain of the Ardennes—towards Namur. Certainly nobody had ever thought of carving up the Allied front and cutting off British and French armies fighting in Flanders.

The date for the attack was originally set by Hitler as November 12, and although preparations went ahead with this date in mind the Wehrmacht was in no condition to undertake another offensive. From Warsaw the Panzers had limped into the repair shops—out of fuel and breaking down in large numbers; the infantry had suffered heavy losses. Panzer and infantry divisions all needed to be re-equipped and re-trained. Meanwhile the generals who would have to execute the plan for the attack on the west were arguing about its merits and certain improvements which Hitler had 'suggested'. Aircraft and tanks operating in massed formations to achieve surprise were already a feature of the revised contingency plan. What the Führer now proposed was that paratroops and glider-borne infantry should be used in conjunction with the mechanized columns to facilitate a crossing of the Meuse north of Liège. Another 'suggestion' was that there should be an attack across the Meuse south of Liège, followed by an advance towards Rheims and Amiens.

Up to this point the plan still relied on the weight of the offensive in northern Belgium being delivered by General Fedor von Bock's

22

Army Group B. Then Hitler suggested that the gap in the Belgian Ardennes (along a line from Arlon through Tintigny to Forenville) behind neutral Luxembourg might be a route to the French frontier town of Sedan on the upper Meuse. General Gerd von Rundstedt, the commander of the German Army Group A, on the southern sector facing the Ardennes, and his brilliant Chief of Staff, General Erich von Manstein, had been thinking on similar lines. Both had complained that as it stood 'Plan Yellow' (the contingency plan for the attack on France) was unlikely to bring victory, since it did not provide for the rapid destruction of the enemy's forces in the north; in their view the plan lacked 'penetration and versatility'. As an alternative they proposed that Army Group A should be made strong enough to cross the Meuse south of Namur. Once across the river its mechanized divisions would drive across France south of the Allied armies—which were expected to have moved into Belgium to deal with von Bock's offensive, sweeping through towards Arras and Boulogne on the Channel coast. At this time the proposal got no further than the commander-in-chief, Field Marshal Walther von Brauchitsch, who rejected it out of hand. Thus Hitler did not hear of it; nor were Rundstedt and Manstein aware of Hitler's 'suggestion' to the o.k.w.*

During November 1939 the weather compelled Hitler to agree to a series of postponements, and it was mid-December before better weather made a January D-Day seem possible. Meantime General Kurt Student, commander of Germany's airborne forces, had persuaded Hitler to agree that his paratroops and glider-borne commandos should concentrate on objectives in Holland where it was thought the British might establish air bases from which they could bomb the Ruhr. Then the weather took another change for the worse, and when a German staff officer's plane, carrying details of 'Plan Yellow', force-landed in Belgium, a further postponement was ordered. It was feared the operation had been compromised—though in actual fact the papers were burned before the officer was captured, and little was disclosed. Nevertheless enough information had by now filtered back to French Intelligence to convice the Allied High Command that, as in 1914, the main German blow was going to fall on Belgium. If the Germans had planned a great deceptive manoeuvre they could not have achieved more. Meanwhile von Rundstedt and Manstein were continuing to press their plan for an encircling move through the Ardennes, and pleading for more divisions with which to carry it out. Brauchitch refused either to change the order of battle or to submit their plan to Hitler, although his Chief-of-Staff, General Franz Halder, had concluded that von Rundstedt's Group A needed to be reinforced anyway. The matter was resolved in February when Manstein, during a routine

* *Oberkommando der Wehrmacht*, the supreme command of all German armed forces.

23

interview with the Führer, took the opportunity to expound his ideas with professional clarity and detail. Because they coincided so closely with his own views Hitler was delighted and next day recited the von Rundstedt-Manstein plan—as if it were his own—and von Brauchitch was told to get on with it. At von Brauchitch's headquarters Hitler's instructions were translated into detailed orders and directives. Based on Manstein's 'left hook' proposal, the final plan was for Army Group A to push down through the Forest of Ardennes, cross the Meuse at Sedan, then swing round south of the Allied armies in Belgium and trap them there. Special airborne operations would secure some of the initial objectives such as bridges and the Meuse crossings would be spear-headed by seven of the Wehrmacht's ten Panzer divisions. From its original twenty-two divisions Army Group A escalated to forty-five divisions, while von Bock's Army Group B in the north dwindled from forty-three to twenty-nine divisions. On February 24 the revised plans were complete and the operation was renamed *Sichelschnitt*—the sweep of a scythe.

Far left
General Gamelin,
Commander-in-Chief of the
Allied Armies in France.
From Lord Gort, in charge of
one of five armies in French
Army Group I, the chain of
command ran through Army
Group Commander (General
Billotte), and Commander
North-Eastern Front
(General Georges), to
Gamelin.

Left
General Billotte. He died in a
car accident at a critical time
in the campaign.

All was now ready, when Operation *Weserübung*—the invasion of Denmark and Norway—suddenly acquired priority. Hitler was anxious to secure Germany's flank against any threat developing from the Soviet-Finnish war, and to safeguard Germany's import of iron ore. So the attack on the West was postponed yet again—till May.

☆

The order to execute *Sichelschnitt* was finally issued on May 9, and that night long columns of vehicles, nose to tail, left their camouflaged concentration areas in the woods and began to move down the roads leading to the German frontier. By dawn on May 10 135 German divisions were on the move. The first German scout cars crossed the Luxembourg frontier at 5.30 a.m., and the convoys that came after them ran with their headlights full on. Under the impact of surprise such opposition as there was simply fell to pieces. In some places the defenders were literally caught napping by infiltrators dressed in civilian clothes who had gone ahead as 'tourists' to neutralize demolition devices and save bridges and defiles from destruction. Working alongside the tank and infantry battle groups were the assault engineers whose job it was to remove and demolish those road blocks which still stood. Everywhere the advance flowed smoothly and on schedule; by nightfall the Panzers were well inside Belgian territory. Meantime paratroops and gliders had descended on objectives in both Holland and Belgium at first light, while the Luftwaffe was bombing Dutch, Belgian and Allied airfields, railways and key supply points, in an effort to disrupt communications.

The Dutch were soon overwhelmed. They had always refused to co-operate in advance with the Allies on plans to meet a German invasion of their country, and although they fought bravely, they were unable to dislodge the German paratroops who had landed on Waalhaven air-field and at the great Moerdijk bridge—the key to 'Fortress Holland'. Simultaneously punched in the face and stabbed in the back, the struggle was all too brief. By the evening of May 13 the Dutch airforce had been virtually annihilated, Queen Wilhelmina was aboard a British destroyer, and the position everywhere in Holland was desperate. Whether it was to speed the Dutch admission of defeat or whether the whole horrific operation was due to a misunderstanding, Rotterdam was systematically bombed during the afternoon of May 14—the Luft-waffe showing the same mastery of the art of reducing undefended cities to a heap of rubble as it had exhibited at Warsaw eight months earlier. Within minutes the old town was a raging inferno; 20,000 buildings were destroyed, 78,000 people rendered homeless and nearly 1000 were killed. The greater part of the Dutch Army was still intact but on the morning of May 15 its men were ordered to lay down their arms.

If the timing of the German attack surprised the Allies, its general

25

direction was certainly not unexpected, and the necessary orders to execute the neatly formulated plans for dealing with the situation were issued almost at once. The predetermined riposte of the Allied armies, if the circumstances appeared favourable, was the so-called Plan 'D'. Pivoting on the Maginot line, the whole of the Allied forces drawn up along the Franco-Belgian frontier would advance into Belgium to the River Dyle, a few miles east of Brussels. The advantage of the plan, its organizers claimed, was that it ensured Belgium's co-operation and added sixteen Belgian divisions to the Allied fighting strength. As it turned out no plan could have suited the Germans better, for it placed the Allied armies in the north exactly where they wanted them. 'I could have wept with joy,' Hitler said later when he heard that the British Expeditionary Force and the French 7th Army, under its dashing General Henri Giraud, were racing forward into Belgium at a veritable *pas de galop*.

The British Expeditionary Force was one of five Armies in the Allied Army Group I under the command of General Gaston Billotte—the other four being the First, Second, Seventh and Ninth French Armies. General Billotte's immediate superior was General Jacques Georges, the commander of the North-Eastern Front, who was in turn responsible to the Commander-in-Chief Allied Forces, General Maurice Gamelin. Since September 1939 the strength of the B.E.F. had increased to a nominal thirteen divisions—including one which was on duty in the Maginot line and three partially equipped and half trained second line Territorial formations. The latter had been sent to France to build airfields and in common with the first line divisions they had spent most of the 'Bore War' digging and wiring. Indeed all the British troops were utterly sick and tired of building defences, and when the order came for the whole B.E.F. to abandon their defences and move forward in line with the French armies on either flank there was exhilaration that the sitting war was over at last. By special permission conducted parties of the British troops had been taken to gaze with awe at the fortifications against which Hitler's troops were expected to hurl themselves. And they had been impressed by the intricate galleries, the powerful guns and other equipment in the vast underground fortresses of the Maginot Line. Some of the infantry had even been permitted to man selected sections of the Line's outer defences during the bitterly cold winter months. But the French did not encourage offensive tactics. Their policy was one of 'live and let live'; shooting was thought to be anti-social and the cold was generally more of a hazard than the enemy. The plain truth was that the French had no stomach for *la guerre*. In World War I the best part of a generation had been exterminated, France's richest industrial region laid waste and other vast areas

Above
General Giraud, then commander of a crack French mechanized division, watches a French v. British Army rugby match at Arras at the beginning of May 1940.

Above right
Air Chief Marshal Sir Hugh Dowding. His refusal to commit the R.A.F. fighter squadrons to the Battle of France probably changed the course of history.

reduced to rubble or turned into a morass of shell-holes. The British had also suffered acutely, but their country had not been invaded and very few bombs had fallen on their soil. They had not wanted war either, but now that they were in it, they appeared to the French to regard the business of fighting as good fun—an attitude that was apt to irritate the French, who do not regard war as sport.

Commander of the B.E.F. was General John Standish Surtees Prendergast Vereker, 6th Viscount Gort, V.C., D.S.O. and two bars, M.V.O., M.C. A big burly man, no one could ever question Gort's qualities as a fighting soldier. He had won his Victoria Cross with the Grenadier Guards in the trenches of World War I, and his ideas had been irrevocably conditioned by trench warfare. At the age of fifty-three he did not disguise his liking for the excitement of war. But Gort expected war to be conducted in the military style to which he was accustomed and he was ill prepared for the fast-moving armoured combat of the German Panzers. His responsibilities as a Commander-in-Chief also lay especially heavily on him. To the British he was simply

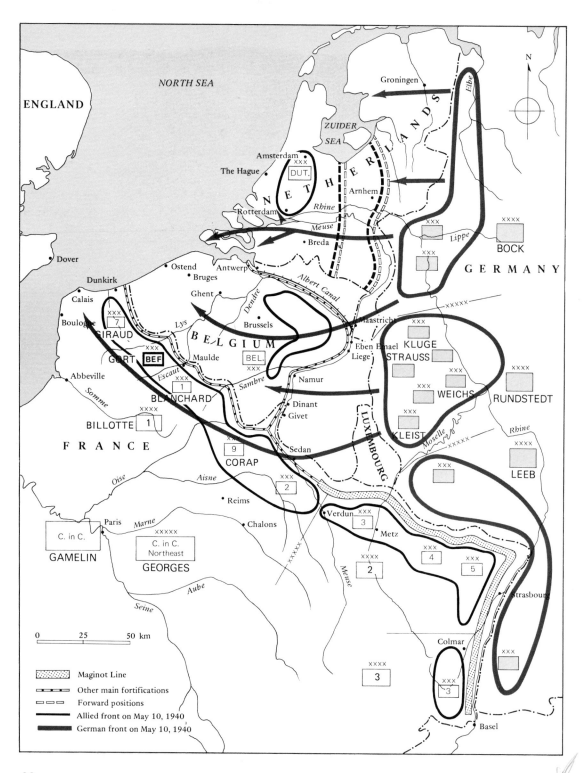

NORTH SEA

ENGLAND

Groningen

ZUIDER SEA

Amsterdam

The Hague

N E T H E R L A N D S

DUT.

Arnhem

Rotterdam

Rhine

Meuse

Breda

Dover

Lippe

BOCK

G E R M A N Y

Ostend
Bruges

Antwerp

Albert Canal

Calais

Dunkirk

Ghent

Dendre

Brussels

Maastricht

KLUGE
STRAUSS

Boulogne

GIRAUD

7

Lys

B E L G I U M

Maulde

BEL.

Eben Emael
Liege

WEICHS

RUNDSTEDT

Abbeville

GORT

BEF

Escaut

Sambre

Namur

Somme

BLANCHARD

1

Dinant

KLEIST

Moselle

Rhine

BILLOTTE

1

Givet

LEEB

F R A N C E

9

CORAP

Sedan

L U X E M B O U R G

Oise

Aisne

2

Reims

Verdun

3

Paris

Marne

Chalons

Metz

C. in C.

GAMELIN

C. in C.
Northeast

GEORGES

2

4

5

Aube

Meuse

Strasbourg

Seine

Colmar

0   25   50 km

3

3

Basel

Maginot Line

Other main fortifications

Forward positions

Allied front on May 10, 1940

German front on May 10, 1940

28

the C-in-C, responsible to the King, the British Government, and the British people for the safety of the British Expeditionary Force. To the French, however, he was simply the commander of a single army in a group of armies. Photographs published in British newspapers of Gort and Gamelin standing side by side convey the impression that the two men were on an equal footing. They were not. Gort was not even directly subordinate to Gamelin—between them, in the chain of command, came Billotte the Army Group commander and then General Georges, the Commander North-East front. Nevertheless more than 336,000 soldiers—French and British—had good cause to thank God that Gort's judgment was sound when it fell to him—deprived of instructions, outnumbered and outgunned—to take a prompt decision which saved the B.E.F. from death or incapacity.

While the British and French High Commands focused their attention on the attack they had been expecting in the north, von Rundstedt's Panzers and the Wehrmacht's crack infantry divisions were stealthily motoring along the narrow roads of the Ardennes—through what the French had maintained was 'impenetrable' forest—towards the 'impassable' barrier of the Meuse. The Germans encountered little opposition, quickly dispersing a few startled groups of French cavalry which emerged from the woods as from another age of warfare. Their worst worry was the close-packed columns of vehicles stretching back a hundred miles from head to tail. A few well-placed bombs on the roads would have brought chaotic delays to the armoured onslaught. But the Allied bombers were busy over Holland and the Panzer columns were protected by a massive umbrella of fighter aircraft.

The first Germans crossed the Meuse on the night of May 11–12 and the Panzers followed. It was all too simple; the French troops which had been rushed up to reinforce the river lines were of indifferent quality and poorly equipped. They had very few anti-aircraft guns and most of their artillery was horse-drawn. Consequently when two hundred Ju 87s screeched down on them the troops went to ground, the horses were killed, the guns stood fast and in a few hours the German tanks were across the river. So began the partition of the Allied armies and the German drive towards the Channel.

On the northern front the French had counted on the Belgians delaying the German advance while General Billotte's five armies—including the B.E.F.—moved into position along the River Dyle. At 6.15 a.m. on May 10 the order to advance went simultaneously to all five armies. From the end of the Maginot Line at Longuyon, in the foothills of the

Ardennes on the Luxembourg frontier, to the Channel coast, fifty-one divisions totalling some 800,000 men prepared to swing forward into Belgium in order to hold the banks of the River Meuse as far as Namur, and from there a line stretching northwards through Wavre, Louvain and Malines to Antwerp. The pivot of the swing was to be at Mezières-Charleville, a few miles from Sedan (the nodal point, in fact, of von Rundstedt's armoured assault).

Northwards from there General Corap's Ninth Army would take up positions along the Meuse; Corap's divisions consisted mainly of reservists and troops of inferior quality but as the French High Command maintained the Ardennes was impenetrable they were supposedly safe from attack. Next in line, north of the River Sambre, was General Georges Blanchard, commanding some of France's best troops in the First Army. Blanchard's force was expected to bear the brunt of the expected attack by the German Panzers, and so it included a force of some 400 tanks. North of the First Army came the B.E.F. and between them and the sea was Giraud's Seventh Army—whose troops were supposedly on a par with those of the First Army.

Armoured cars of the 12th Royal Lancers, followed by vehicles and guns of the Royal Artillery's 1st Anti-Aircraft Regiment, crossed the Belgian frontier at 1 p.m. on May 10, and by the afternoon a long column of British trucks and Bren-carriers was moving through Brussels. By the same evening Gort's advance units were taking up their positions along the Dyle in front of Louvain. The British troops were given a rapturous welcome, and wherever their vehicles stopped girls rushed up to embrace the delighted soldiers, shower gifts of beer, cigarettes and food on them, and decorate the trucks with flowers. Surprisingly, though, there was no sign of Goering's aircraft during the first day of the advance. The explanation, according to Gort's staff, was that the Luftwaffe could not bomb everywhere all the time, and presumably it was fully occupied with targets in Holland and northern Belgium. The idea that the Germans might not wish to deter the Allied armies from moving forward apparently did not occur to anyone.

Fairey Battle light bomber—an antiquated aircraft that was no match for the German fighters over north-west Europe.

Even before the 12th Lancers sighted the Dyle, men of General Walther von Reichenau's Sixth Army had crossed the Albert Canal, German armour was pouring across the undemolished bridges, and the Belgian forces were recoiling in headlong retreat. But none of this news reached the B.E.F. until next day, when the leading British infantry brigades were deploying in their battle positions. And by then two of Blanchard's cavalry divisions on the B.E.F's right flank were striving desperately to stem the onslaught of von Reichenau's Panzers. Further south, Guderian's tanks were emerging from the forests of the Ardennes and Marshal Hugo Sperrle's Stuka squadrons were hammering the positions occupied by the Second and Ninth French Armies.

Gamelin, already out of his depth, decided on May 12 to confer with King Leopold. General Georges, the North East Front commander, travelled with his supremo, and messages were sent to Billotte and Gort, telling them to rendezvous at Mons. As Gort was away from his headquarters touring the B.E.F. front, and there was no means of getting in touch with him, General Pownall, his Chief of Staff, went to the meeting instead. In the event the only decision of any importance to emerge from this meeting was that Billotte would take over some of Georges's responsibilities for 'co-ordinating' the activities of the First and Seventh French Armies and the B.E.F.

If they had known about it most of the B.E.F. would have seen this shift of responsibilities as nothing more than a change of emphasis, of little concern to them. As yet there was no sense of urgency, and the fact that company commanders of the 2nd Bn of the Durham Light Infantry were told that they would probably have ten to fourteen days to prepare their defences when they were shown their allotted areas is a true indication of the pre-*Blitzkrieg* mentality of the whole British Army. So far as the men on the Dyle were concerned, however, this outlook began to change on the morning of May 13 when von Reichenau's advance guard clashed with British patrols east of the river. By nightfall it was clear that the Germans were thrusting towards Louvain at the northern end of the line, and the situation was looking grim.

British airmen in France had been blitzed into action already, and their casualties were escalating. The original concept of the 'Advanced Air Striking Force'—the A.A.S.F. for short—had been extended, and

an air component which would cater solely for the requirements of the B.E.F. had been grafted on to it. Now known grandiosely as 'The British Air Forces in France' the A.A.S.F. consisted of twenty-five squadrons of fighters, light bombers and Lysanders, under the overall command of Air Marshal Sir Arthur Barratt—popularly known as 'Ugly'. Thirteen squadrons in direct support of the B.E.F.—slow-flying Lysanders for tactical co-operation, Blenheim light-bombers for strategical reconnaissance as far as the Rhine, and four squadrons of Hurricanes for the protection of the B.E.F's bases and the reconnaissance aircraft—made up one component of Barratt's force. The other, the A.A.S.F. proper, consisted of ten squadrons of Battle and Blenheim bombers supported by two squadrons of Hurricanes. The role of the bombers had been laid down at the beginning of the war: if and when the Germans launched an offensive, they were to attack the advancing enemy columns—preferably at natural bottlenecks such as bridges and road junctions. The Hurricanes were there to protect the bombers and to help defend the airfields around Rheims where the Air Striking Force was based.*

Hurricanes of No. 73 Squadron, a unit which had already sharpened its claws in action against German fighters over the France-German border, were the first of Barratt's force to go into action. Between dawn and dusk on May 10 the pilots of this and the other British fighter squadrons were almost continuously in the air fighting off Luftwaffe attacks directed against the airfields occupied by the R.A.F. Pilots of the Hurricanes of 501 Squadron, which flew out to reinforce them during the morning, found themselves in combat with forty Heinkel He 111s within an hour of arriving in France.

Meantime Barratt was awaiting orders to unleash his bombers against the German columns. But Gamelin was obstinately clinging to the hope that a 'bombing war' could somehow be avoided. So by midmorning when no word had come, Barratt took matters into his own hands and at 3 p.m. on May 10, eight of the obsolete Battles took off '. . . to attack', in the casual words of the official communiqué, 'troops advancing through Luxembourg'. Three of the eight were shot down before they reached the target area; the other five struggled back to base but were so severely shot up that they were beyond repair. Other Battles which were sent up that afternoon to 'finish the job' suffered a similar fate, and of the thirty-two Battles participating in the operation thirteen were lost and all the rest damaged. It was a high price to pay for operations whose effect on the German advance was negligible and also one that might have been anticipated, for soon after the

* Luftwaffe strength in May 1940 was some 3500 aircraft, of which about 1400 heavy bombers, 400 dive bombers and 1200 fighters—including about 800 of the superb Messerschmidt 109s—were deployed in the assault on the West. The Luftwaffe was then at the peak of its efficiency, its pilots having gained valuable experience in Poland.

outbreak of war four out of five Battles had been shot down by Me 109s while on a simple reconnaissance mission near the Franco-German border.

Meanwhile the French—judging the situation in Holland to be the most critical—saw the German advance through Maastricht as the greatest threat to ground operations, and on May 12 General Georges told Barratt that he wanted the British bombers to concentrate on its eradication. It was a suicidal task. Of nine Blenheims of 139 Squadron which took off to attack a German column reportedly marching along the Brussels road near Maastricht only two returned to base.

The antiquated Battles fared even worse. No. 12 Squadron—the R.A.F's 'Dirty Dozen'—was ordered to destroy two of the bridges across the Albert Canal which the Belgians had failed to demolish. Volunteer crews were called for and five aircraft eventually took off— two to attack the concrete bridge at Vroenhoven, and the other three the metal bridge at Veldwezelt. One bridge, that at Veldwezelt, was finally destroyed—by a Battle which crashed headlong on it. Nobody had appreciated the relative ineffectiveness of 250 lb H.E. bombs on massive structures such as these bridges; nor had anybody appreciated the speed with which the Germans would deploy their mobile anti-aircraft units around crucial targets. The pilot of one of the aircraft, who survived by baling out at very low level, found himself not merely captured, but soundly ticked off by a German officer for having acted suicidally. 'You British are mad,' said this officer with full Teutonic solemnity. 'We capture the bridge early Friday morning. You give us all Friday and Saturday to get our *flak* guns up in circles round the bridge, and then on Sunday you come along with three aircraft and try to blow the thing up.' The British pilot did not feel inclined to argue. Two posthumous Victoria Crosses were awarded to the twenty-one-year-old flying officer and the observer of the Battle which destroyed the bridge; they were the first tokens of supreme recognition to be awarded to the R.A.F. during the war.

On May 10 the A.A.S.F. had 135 bombers; forty-eight hours later there were only seventy-two, all of which needed servicing and whose crews equally needed rest. The French wanted the British to go on bombing bridges and columns of troops, but at the rate Barratt was losing aircraft and aircrews a prolonged bombing programme was just not possible. Throughout May 13 he rested his bombers, and it was while they took the day off that Guderian's Panzers broke through the French line along the Meuse and began their joy-ride through France. The news reached Barratt in the late evening and by midnight the squadrons of the A.A.S.F. knew that the following day would probably be their last. There can be little doubt that the events of May 14 determined the future of both the 'Royal Air Force in France' and the B.E.F.

In the early morning, Battles of 103 and 150 Squadrons pinpointed the German pontoon bridges which the engineers of the *Grossdeutschland*

Regiment had thrown across the Meuse near Sedan. They attacked them without loss, and when the French demanded an all-out effort in support of the counter-attack they were proposing in the area, Barratt decided to launch the whole of his bombers against the Sedan bridgehead. Shortly after 2 p.m. the seventy-one remaining Battles and Blenheims of the A.A.S.F. took off to attack the bridges. But the Me 109s which had failed to show up when the Battles attacked that morning were now on guard. The result was that forty bombers, and 120 of the 213 young men who had set out in bright sunshine never returned from the raid. When 'Ugly' Barratt heard the news it is said he covered his face and sobbed. This was the biggest daylight bombing raid made by the R.A.F. for many years to come and it showed the highest percentage of casualties of any air raid of its size in the whole war.

While the bombers were committing suicide Barratt's fighter squadrons were doing the same. During the Phoney War period they had had a comparatively easy time, but when the balloon went up on May 10 the fighters came briefly into their own. During that first day of the assault, Nos 1 and 72 Squadrons shot down sixteen German aircraft without loss, and in one interception a single patrol destroyed five Me 109s. But they too suffered heavy casualties.

It would be impossible to recount every desperate encounter that took place in the three weeks that followed, if only because in so many

*ristol Blenheim IV
mber—the mainstay of the
itish bombing offensive in
'40, before and after
unkirk.*

cases there were no survivors. Suffice to say, the R.A.F. in France fought against staggering odds. Indeed, when the Battle of Britain reached its height weeks later the odds were no greater. In his account of another epic—the evacuation from Greece—Winston Churchill has pointed out that, while in Greece the Luftwaffe was supreme, the R.A.F. at least controlled the air over Dunkirk, however little this fact was apparent to the men of the B.E.F.

Barratt's six squadrons of Hurricanes were reinforced and the campaign was not many hours old before the A.A.S.F. had absorbed the best part of twelve squadrons. But they were still far too few to cope with the Luftwaffe, and both Barratt and Gort asked for more. Then when the full extent of the disaster on the Meuse became clear, there came an urgent plea from the French Prime Minister, Paul Reynaud: 'You were kind enough to send us four squadrons,' he said on the telephone to Churchill, '. . . but if we are to win this battle, which might be decisive for the whole war, it is necessary to send at once—if possible today—ten more squadrons.'

Apart from the fact that immediate compliance with this request was impractical, 'never reinforce failure' is one of the oldest, most fundamental military maxims. The difficulty, of course, comes in recognizing failure before it has turned into utter defeat, and in refusing an ally's appeal for reinforcement. In this instance Air Chief Marshal Sir Hugh Dowding, C-in-C of the R.A.F's Fighter Command, had no illusions and on May 16 he sat down and penned a letter to the Secretary of State for Air which may have changed the course of history: 'I hope and believe that our Armies may yet be victorious in France and Belgium,' he wrote, *'but we have to face the fact that they may be defeated . . .'* However great the need on the Continent, he argued, and however tempting the opportunity to send our fighters where there were certainly large numbers of German bombers to be shot down, Hurricanes abroad could not fight as effectively as Hurricanes at home. Moreover, if the drain on fighters to France continued, Dowding could see his forces 'being bled white and in no condition to withstand the bombing attack which will inevitably be made on this country as soon as our powers of resistance fall below a level to which we are already perilously close'.

Summoned to a meeting of the War Cabinet to explain his views, Dowding's arguments prevailed: no more Hurricanes were to be sent to France.

☆

Dowding's fears for what might happen in the air were more than justified by what was happening on the ground. On May 14 a seemingly endless line of Belgian soldiers, some in boots and some in carpet slippers, a few—but very few—still clutching their rifles, streamed westwards through Brussels leaving a great gap on the B.E.F. left flank. As the next ten days were to show, there were still some brave and determined Belgian units resisting the German advance, but most of the Belgian Army could only be seen as a rabble in retreat.

Disasters had also occurred in the south. But communications between the B.E.F. Headquarters and Billotte's 1st Army Group Headquarters were already difficult and intermittent. Consequently although Gort learned that the Germans had crossed the Meuse at Sedan, the full extent of the catastrophe which followed did not reach him until the French Ninth Army had been routed, and the rot had spread to Blanchard's troops on the B.E.F's immediate right flank. In Paris and at Billotte's Army Group Headquarters where communications were better, however, there was consternation as worse news flowed in. Billotte, who had just been made responsible for co-ordinating the activities of the French, British and Belgians in the north, was completely bewildered, and his attention and that of his staff was focused on events to the south and east at the very time it should have been concerned with events in the north.

The situation was, if anything, worse at Blanchard's First Army Headquarters, and Captain Miles Reid, the British liaison officer appointed by Gort, was virtually driven to desperation by the administrative chaos which grew steadily worse as the situation deteriorated. Meantime demoralized soldiers from Corap's Ninth Army, fleeing from the battle zone, were looting villages and British base installations on the roads back to Paris. Officers and N.C.Os who tried to stop them were shot, and the tales these deserters told of thousands of German tanks and thousands of paratroops landing everywhere just behind them added to the demoralization they were themselves spreading. In relation to the size of the French forces in the field there were not many of them, but reports filtering back to the B.E.F. over the next few days did little to bolster the already weakening British confidence in their allies. More important at this stage was the fact that with Corap's Army no longer in position, Blanchard's right flank crumbling, and the gap created by the Belgians on the left not closed, the B.E.F. was almost isolated on the Dyle.

Plans were made to move Giraud's Seventh Army south, behind the B.E.F., in order to reinforce the shattered remains of Corap's Ninth Army, but Georges's efforts to transfer some reserve divisions—which had no motor transport, and which had been ill-advisedly positioned by Gamelin behind the Maginot Line—were thwarted by the Germans, who bombed the rolling stock and railway lines which were to carry them to the northern front. Meantime a highly rated North African division in the First Army suddenly crumbled, opening a new 5000-metre gap on the B.E.F's right. Gort, who was now beginning to have serious misgivings about the fighting qualities of the French troops, offered to send Blanchard a British brigade to help fill the gap, but

Lord Gort with Air Marsh A. S. ('Ugly') Barratt (right), commander of the 'British Air Forces in France'. When Barratt hea the news of the decimation his bombers at the Sedan bridgehead, May 14, it is said that he covered his fac and sobbed.

he was told that it had been decided to pull the First Army back to a new line. Gort, already disturbed by the absence of orders, was in a quandary. If the First Army pulled back both the British and the Belgians would be left out on a limb—with the B.E.F. committed to the defence of an untenable salient in front of Louvain. Clearly this was a case for the co-ordinator to co-ordinate, and Gort sent a senior officer to tell Billotte that he would appreciate some instructions. Billotte responded by ordering the whole Allied line to move back, first to the River Senne, then to the River Dendre, and finally, on Saturday night, May 17, to the Scheldt, where all the armies would stand and fight. It was a desperate attempt by the French High Command to stabilize the situation—just how desperate may be judged from the fact that it meant abandoning Brussels. But it was already too late. By the time the B.E.F. had withdrawn behind the Senne, the Dutch Army had surrendered and Guderian's Panzers were pouring through a gap a hundred kilometres wide where Corap's Army had disintegrated.

During the nights between May 16 and May 19 as the Allied armies fell back towards the Scheldt—pressed just strongly enough by von Bock's troops to keep them engaged—Guderian's Panzers raced around the south to cut them off. On the 17th the Panzers were across the Oise, and reported to be approaching St Quentin and the Canal du Nord, where Gort had won his V.C. almost exactly twenty-three years before. From Georges's headquarters came a brusque signal ordering the B.E.F. to send a brigade from the 23rd Division to hold fifteen miles of the Canal du Nord. French troops would hold the remainder of the canal, Georges said in his signal; but there were no signs of them when the unfortunate 23rd arrived—nor, indeed, subsequently.

Fortunately the traditional British ability to improvise now came into its own. The 23rd Division was one of three half-trained, under-strength territorial divisions which had been sent to France to work on the B.E.F's defences, not to fight. It had only six battalions, no artillery whatsoever, only a skeleton signal organization, and hardly any transport. But morale was high, and somehow a few guns were scraped up—forty in all, field, anti-tank and anti-aircraft—slightly more than two per mile of front. About ten miles in front of the British positions lay Cambrai, of bloody memory, and an unknown number of Panzers. On the afternoon of May 17 the clatter of tracks announced their approach.

By this time Major-General Richard Petre, the commander of the 12th Division, had been appointed to command the British force on the Canal du Nord. Like the 23rd, Petre's own 12th Division was under-trained and under-equipped. Nevertheless the men of the two divisions, now designated 'Petreforce', were in the words of Gort's subsequent despatch 'to fight and march continuously for a fortnight and to prove, if proof were needed, that they were composed of soldiers who despite their inexperience and lack of equipment could hold their own with a better and more numerous enemy'.

Over the next few days other improvised forces mushroomed within the B.E.F.—not all of them being formed on Gort's direct orders. Most were made up of men normally employed on administrative duties, who now had nothing to do or whose work was of dwindling importance. The lucky ones, designated as 'useless mouths', were sent off to Boulogne. The rest, who for various reasons had to stay, were formed into a scratch collection of fighting units, and from one such collection, plus an infantry brigade from the 42nd Division, the 1st Army Tank Brigade, and a regiment of field artillery, 'MacForce' was created, commanded by Gort's Director of Military Intelligence, Major-General Noel Mason-MacFarlane, whose task was to protect the B.E.F's right flank.

Another irregular force which came into being on May 19 was created when Gort realized that Dieppe, Le Havre and Rouen were threatened. A large proportion of the B.E.F's supplies passed through Dieppe or Le Havre, and vital B.E.F. installations had been established in or near all three towns. So 'Vickforce' was formed to protect them. Organized into five weak battalions, its 1700 men fought a delaying action for no less than a month and, although it is anticipating events, its story is worth recording here.

Vickforce took up a position along the river Béthune on May 19; to the north the Germans had reached the Somme, where the 51st Highland Division was fighting alongside the French. Once the Germans broke through on the Somme—and judging from the dismal experience of the past week there was every likelihood of their doing so—only Vickforce stood between them and Rouen. Bridges across the Béthune were mined, defences were sited, dug and wired. And as 1700 men could not cover a twelve-mile front, an elaborate subterfuge was attempted. 'Men' were manufactured from sandbags and sacking, topped with steel-helmets and armed with poles. These dummy warriors, it was hoped, might deceive the enemy as to the real strength of the Vickforce defences. British patrols said they looked realistic enough but there is no record of the Germans being deceived.

By June 7 French resistance on the Somme had collapsed, and the Highlanders of the 51st Division were ordered to fight their way back to St Valery, south of Dieppe. Meantime the evacuation from Dunkirk had been completed and broken French units were streaming, in utter disorder, through the positions held by Vickforce—now known as the Beauman Division or 'Beauforce'. Hard on the heels of the shattered French forces came the Germans, and as it was clear that it would not be possible to hold the Béthune line, Beauforce was ordered to withdraw. Having blown the bridges across the Béthune the men pulled out in text-book style, and on the morning of June 19 the rearguard marched on to the Quai Normandie at Cherbourg to embark in the destroyer which had been sent to fetch them home.

Over the page
Louvaine during the B.E.F. retreat—a sapper plunges
home a detonator to blow up a bridge. Some bridges
were demolished successfully, others left until it was
too late.

39

3. Retreat and Collapse

May 18–25

'Let me now state the sequence of events. At the call of the King of the Belgians, the British Expeditionary Force advanced into Belgium and took up its position on the River Dyle. The advance lasted several days. Through events it could not control our Army had to come back in less than half that time. It did so with little confusion and with few losses. Seventy-five miles forward, a fight at the end of the advance, and seventy-five miles back, fighting all the way, all in the space of ten days.'

From a broadcast by Anthony Eden, Secretary of State for War,
2 June 1940

On May 18 the whole Allied line was moving back in what was supposed to be a staged withdrawal and, in accordance with Billotte's orders, the B.E.F. had fallen back on the River Senne. The next stage would take it west of Brussels to the River Dendre; from there Gort's men would pull back to the Scheldt. But now the French began to have second thoughts about the retreat.

During the morning Billotte signalled Gort saying that he thought the B.E.F. ought really to stay on the Senne and protect Brussels. This message was quickly followed by one with contradictory instructions from Georges's headquarters further afield. Then Billotte changed his mind again. Responding to frantic appeals from Blanchard—first to delay the withdrawal because the French First Army troops were exhausted, and then to speed it up because they could no longer resist German pressure on the First Army front—Billotte decided not to stop at the Dendre but to pull straight back to the Scheldt. From this confusion of orders Gort concluded that the safety of the B.E.F. was now at stake and that in its interest he might well have to disregard his French superiors. To Billotte's signals he replied to the effect that changes in the original plan were quite out of the question.

This message seems to have had a salutary effect on Billotte, for early next morning, Sunday, May 19, he arrived at Gort's headquarters. After giving Gort an account of the catastrophes in the south he confessed that he had no idea how to cope with them, no reserves and very little hope. '*Je suis crevé de fatigue*,' he said despondently, '...*et contre ces Panzers je ne peux rien faire.*' If Gort had had any doubts before he knew now that the campaign was as good as lost, and that he might well be faced with a retreat to the coast and the evacuation of the B.E.F.

Meantime the Germans, thundering towards the sea far to the south of the main force of the B.E.F., had reached Amiens. To cover the hundred kilometres from the Meuse to the Sambre had taken them four days. Now the Panzers advanced eighty kilometres in a single day and, at Amiens on the evening of the 18th, they were only fifty kilometres from the coast. Here they halted to await reinforcements, although there was in fact nothing to stop them driving straight on, and really no need for caution.

Five German armoured divisions now lay across the lines of communications linking the B.E.F. with Le Havre, Nantes, Cherbourg and Brest. Fortunately for the B.E.F. however, as soon as Gort's staff appreciated the extent of the break-through on Corap's Ninth Army front no time had been lost in switching the B.E.F's main channel of supply from the railway running through Amiens to Arras. This was becoming uncomfortably close to the advancing enemy, and the line running further to the west through Eu and Abbeville to Béthune seemed a safer alternative. An emergency programme to shift as much material as possible up this line was initiated, and during the next few days trains loaded to capacity lifted petrol, food and ammunition to newly created dumps around Hazebrouck. But for this precaution the B.E.F. would have been unable to move or fight and there could have been no salvation through Dunkirk. Plans to land supplies from Britain at the ports in the immediate rear of the B.E.F.—Calais, Boulogne and Dunkirk—were also feverishly devised. For the Allied armies in Flanders were already almost encircled. French reinforcements were marching westwards from the Maginot Line. But they had set off too late. By May 21 the Panzers, keeping the Aisne and the Somme on their left flank, had reached Abbeville and were wheeling north along the coast. The armies in Flanders, isolated and hard-pressed on front and flanks, were now being hemmed in from the rear.

☆

The men of the B.E.F. had been steadily giving ground since the 17th, retiring—for the most part in good order—from one river line to the next, from the Dyle to the Dendre to the Escaut at the southern end of the canalized Scheldt. They were now moving back along the same cobbled poplar-lined highways along which they had advanced only a few days before. The difference was that on their way up to the Dyle smiling Belgians had greeted them as saviours, while now the sullen-faced populace was too concerned with its own plight to bother with British soldiers. The villages through which the British units passed still carried the propaganda posters which had been stuck up earlier: *Nous vainquerons—parce que nous sommes plus forts!* We shall win because we are stronger. But the villages were deserted and the roads leading to the coast were choked with refugees trying to get away from the battle zone. This refugee traffic became progressively more dense as the retreat gathered momentum, and although the B.E.F. lorries moved at night on the crown of the roads when the weary refugees were often trying to snatch a few hours rest at the sides, the presence of these people and their transport added unbelievably to the difficulties of the operation. Even if the B.E.F. had had the freedom of empty roads the retreat would still have been a complicated business because the situation was changing so swiftly that no commander of any unit knew what was

happening anywhere except on his own tiny segment of front.

Louvaine, which had been ravaged in 1914, was among the first Belgian towns to be martyred a second time when the B.E.F. rearguard on the Dyle stood to fight there. (Fortunately most of the inhabitants had been evacuated before the action began—among the last to be taken out in a British army lorry being a party of nuns.) Away from the immediate vicinity of the battle and off the roads the countryside was strangely somnolent. But in the built-up areas the picture was not nearly so peaceful. The weather, sunny and clear and warm, was ideal for air activity and the Luftwaffe had a field day. Wave after wave of German aircraft swept over the British front, dive-bombing the troops in their positions and strafing the roads to make them impassable. Hundreds of refugees were killed and wounded in these attacks,

44

and Captain Bruce, adjutant of the 1st Battalion of The Royal Scots, recorded gruesome effects when a travelling circus was smashed up. 'We have vivid recollections of three wounded elephants charging in terror through the fields,' he wrote. 'They were followed hotly by four white Liberty horses dragging the unconscious figure of a girl rider....'

Estaminets and cafés in the deserted villages and towns had been looted; empty wine bottles lay inside their smashed doors and broken glass littered the doorsteps. The ancient city of Tournai, which had been bombed round the clock for the past thirty-six hours, was burning when the 2nd Battalion of The Durham Light Infantry reached its outskirts on Sunday morning, May 19. Most of the populace had fled and the famous Grande Place was a shambles. Two British officers who had gone ahead to reconnoitre a route through the town centre stopped at one café which still seemed to be open and asked for coffee. 'No service,' snapped the waitress as she wheeled out a bicycle. 'The Boche are right behind you,' she called back as she rode away.

To add to the confusion in Tournai the inmates of the local lunatic asylum had been let loose. The D.L.I. rounded up as many as they could and for their own protection locked them in the Tournai museum. 'First thing we knew that some bright Belgian spark had opened the doors of the asylum,' said one of the D.L.I. officers afterwards, 'was when we came across a chap hanging from a tree—not by his neck of course, but by both arms. Told us he was the repentant thief of the Crucifixion.'

But there was little time to waste on humanitarian tasks. The B.E.F. had to deploy along the Scheldt–Escaut line and a full-scale German attack was imminent.

On the B.E.F's right flank where MacForce was grimly preparing to stem the advance, one of the precious few British anti-tank batteries had been rushed up to St Amand to cover the bridges across the Scarpe. The town itself was full of refugees and to make matters worse the French authorities had made it a 'collecting point' for the demoralized men of their First and Ninth Armies. Between bouts of drinking and looting some of the stragglers tried to persuade the British gunners of the invincibility of the Wehrmacht, recommending that the British should give in now while the going was good, and so not uselessly prolong the war. In the event the gunners chose to ignore their advice—although they were strafed and bombed continuously throughout the next four days; only one of their guns was put out of action, and that by a French general's car which ran into it while careering along the road at great speed.

Away from the immediate vicinity of the battle zone and the roads from it to the coast, people had still to realize that there really was a war going on. At Bouganvilliers behind the La Bassée Canal, officers of the 7th Battalion of The Kings Own were recovering from a regimental dinner night at which they had worn service dress. Further away in Paris most people were equally unaware of the gravity of the situa-

Transports of the B.E.F.
moving up through a Belgian
town.

tion—or unconcerned perhaps. In a broadcast on Saturday night, May 18, M. Reynaud had declared that although 'the situation is grave it is not at all hopeless', and next morning the average Parisien saw no reason to change the habits of a lifetime. In London it was equally 'normal'. The sun was shining, the parks were full, and during the late afternoon people queued outside the cinemas in the Haymarket and Leicester Square. Churchill had 'offered' the nation 'blood, toil, tears and sweat' a few days ago, but the British were in no hurry to partake of this sort of medicine, and they had yet to be inspired by his rhetoric.

Behind the scenes, however, the situation was approaching crisis level. In Paris buses and taxis disappeared from the streets soon after midday and people learned that they had been requisitioned to transport troops and carry refugees from Reims. In the courtyard of the Foreign Ministry on the Quai d'Orsay clerks and sailors were feeding a great bonfire with documents and records which were being hurled from the windows of the government offices. Rumours that the Germans would be in the French capital by the evening now spread like wildfire and the 'normality' of Sunday morning in Paris quickly disappeared. There was panic in the air and those who could look back a quarter of a century were reminded of Paris at the time of the Battle of the Marne.

Although the atmosphere of panic did not cross the Channel, there were plenty of worried men in Whitehall. Churchill was at Chartwell, feeding his sole surviving black swan (the others had been eaten by foxes) and his cherished goldfish, when the telephone rang to inform him—quite erroneously as it turned out—that the French First Army had melted away, leaving a vast gap on the B.E.F's right flank. A police car carried him post haste back to Downing Street where he was told that the report concerning the First Army had been exaggerated but that Pownall, Gort's Chief of Staff, had telephoned to say that Gort was contemplating falling back to the Channel coast. Churchill had himself, two days before, ordered that preparations should be made for such an eventuality and the War Office and Admiralty had begun to discuss the 'possible but unlikely evacuation of a very large force in hazardous circumstances'. The code name 'Dynamo' had been given to the operation, which if it became necessary was to be executed by Vice-Admiral Sir Bertram Ramsay at Dover. On this fateful Sunday, however, the plans for Operation Dynamo seemed to be merely a precaution against a disaster which itself seemed remote.

☆

Guderian's tanks took Amiens on Monday, May 20, and then drove on to Abbeville at the mouth of the Somme. North of them, and behind the million or so French, British and Belgian soldiers who were now completely cut off from the main French armies in the south, a

47

great section of the snowballing mass of refugees which had been moving westwards promptly swung round and surged back east. Realizing that they were heading towards the Panzers, the luckless folk fleeing from the Lille region decided to return to their homes. 'Never was the inhumanity of war so evident,' wrote Sapper-Corporal Jim Anderson, '. . . as when this vast stream of human misery thronged the roads in that lovely weather, and it left an indelible mark on any one of us who witnessed it.'

The men in Whitehall knew nothing of this, of course; the reality of the situation was obscured by the traditional fog of war and little information was filtering back from France. The members of Churchill's War Cabinet firmly believed that the B.E.F.—250,000 strong—was fully capable of dealing with the few German Panzers they had been told were swanning around the Somme. So, on the morning of the 20th, General Ironside, the Chief of the Imperial General Staff, flew from London to Gort's headquarters in Premesques with orders for the B.E.F. to fight its way back to Amiens to take up a new position on the Somme, sweep aside any opposition it met en route, and stop the German infantry divisions marching up from the Meuse from linking up with the Panzers. Gort objected. Such orders, he told Ironside,

But the B.E.F's withdrawal through Belgium was a less happy affair. British Bren-gun carriers wait under the cover of the trees by the Brussels–Louvaine road as refugees from the battle zone stream past.

were quite impracticable. Seven of his nine divisions were deployed on the Scheldt–Escaut line, where a full-scale German attack was imminent. Even supposing his troops could disengage, the Germans would almost certainly cross the Scheldt and follow up. This would mean the B.E.F. fighting a rearguard action while simultaneously doing battle with the Panzers on the Somme and the German infantry marching up from the Meuse—a three-cornered engagement, in fact. Ammunition was limited, food supplies running short, and he had no confidence in the ability of the French breaking through from the south even if the B.E.F. did batter its way back to the Somme. Moreover he had even less confidence in the ability of the Belgians on his left to fall back and safeguard the flank. Nevertheless Gort accepted that some co-operative attempt should be made to join hands with the French, especially as they were supposed to be on the point of launching their counter-attack northwards.

The British Commander-in-Chief was not prepared to commit the whole B.E.F., but he told Ironside that he had already planned a limited offensive with his two reserve divisions—the 5th and 50th, supported by the eighty-three tanks of the Tank Brigade and the ubiquitous but sorely tried 12th Lancers. As both divisions each had one brigade detached for service elsewhere they had only two thirds of their fighting capacity; moreover the tanks whose tracks were designed to give no more than a hundred miles of service had covered 120 miles in the long drive south from Brussels with MacForce. However, as it was hoped that the French would attack northwards in concert with the British operation, Gort believed that all would be well.

Ironside accepted Gort's arguments and went off to confer with Billotte and Blanchard, into whom he did his best to stimulate a spirit of aggression. The outcome of his visit was that the two French generals agreed to co-operate in Gort's offensive and promised that two divisions from General René Altmayer's V Corps would be made available for that purpose.

☆

Major-General Franklyn, G.O.C. of the 5th Division, who had been appointed commander of the composite British force which was to conduct the operation—known henceforth in the jargon fashionable at the time as 'Frankforce'—called a conference that evening at his headquarters in Vimy. He had expected one of General Altmayer's staff officers to attend, but when no French officer turned up Franklyn decided that as speed was the vital factor his attack would have to go in whether or not the French participated. Altmayer had in fact decided that his troops were in no condition to attack on the 21st, but it was not until about an hour before Franklyn's men were due to cross their start line that Gort's headquarters learned of this decision. In the event

49

Right
General Heinz Guderian, 'Father of the Panzers' and a brilliant tactician. If he had been allowed his head, there would have been no 'Dunkirk'.

Below
General Kurt Student, Commander of the Luftwaffe's Fallschirmjäger—Germany's airborne troops—wanted to drop two divisions on south-east England during Operation Dynamo.

Below right
General Von Brauchitch, an officer of the old school, who had little faith in Panzers and new-fangled Blitzkrieg methods.

the only French contribution was a few tanks—which some considered did more harm than good.

The Frankforce attack, spearheaded by sixteen British Mark II heavy tanks and sixty light Mark Is—the sum total of the battleworthy armour—was launched at 2 p.m. on May 21; General 'Q' Martel, the Commander of the 50th Division and a recognized tank expert, directed the assault. He had been told that the aim was to relieve the pressure on Arras where a battalion of Welsh Guards, and 'odds and sods' (as they called themselves) of Petreforce were grimly hanging on in the shambles of shattered brick of the deserted market town after the battering it was still receiving from the Panzers and Luftwaffe. Martel had been told to clear an area about ten miles deep, west and south of the town, and for this purpose a couple of mobile columns of tanks, infantry and artillery were formed; these were to advance along parallel lines a few miles apart into the area constituting the objective.

Although the troops were tired, and for many it was their first action, the operation started reasonably well. Tanks and infantry fought with perseverance, and the left column captured 400 prisoners. But the progress of the right column was upset when the first British tanks hared off without the infantry and then, when the French tanks mistook the British armour for Germans, opened fire on them. Both commanding officers of the British tank battalions were killed in the confused action which followed and by 6 p.m. it was evident that no further advance was possible. The attack had been broken by the 7th Panzer Division, whose commander—a certain Major-General Erwin Rommel—said later that he had been most impressed by the vigour of the Allied assault.

Rommel should also have been impressed by the initiative shown by a little group of infantry—northcountrymen from the 50th Division under the command of a sergeant. Isolated from the rest of Frankforce these men settled down to block a stretch of road in the flat landscape near Arras. Having no anti-tank weapons—not even one of the much-lauded but virtually useless Boys anti-tank rifles—the sergeant realized that his only hope of stopping any German armour coming this way was by subterfuge. So, from a nearby estaminet, he collected a few dozen china plates which he proceeded to lay out in a pattern across the road. An hour later a troop of Panzers came nosing down the road and halted when they saw the unorthodox 'minefield'. When their crews got out and walked cautiously forward to inspect it, the sergeant's men shot them and subsequently set fire to the crewless tanks.

This sort of spirit enabled Frankforce and Petreforce in Arras to hold their ground for the next forty-eight hours. By the end of that time, however, it was becoming clear that they could not hold out much longer. Air raids, day and night, meant little or no sleep, and as the Germans closed in there was a good deal of sniping. The Advanced Air Striking Force had vanished from the scene, and Goering's planes, having broken the French and Belgian will to fight, had been able to concentrate on the British with little interference from the R.A.F. Harassed hourly by dive-bombing Stukas, with much of the town burning and with German infantry attacking at different points all round the perimeter, defence was becoming more and more difficult. When one party of Germans succeeded in penetrating the outer defences and infiltrating as far as the ancient Palais St Vaast where Petre had his headquarters preparations were made for a last stand around the Palais. Fortunately a last-man last-round situation did not materialize. As the troops withdrew to an inner ring a dishevelled and exhausted liaison officer from Gort's headquarters arrived with orders for Frankforce and the garrison to withdraw. In the two hours that remained before daybreak the garrison managed to pull out. Starting down the Douai road, the head of the retreating column found that just outside Arras the bridge over the river Scarpe had been demolished. But what at first was considered to be a misfortune later turned out to be a blessing in disguise, when a reconnaissance party of some twenty men crossed the broken bridge and were captured by a large party of Germans a short way down the road. The Germans had almost closed the ring around the town, but the rest of the troops were switched to the Henin–Lietard road and successfully made their exit down this route.

All the morning vehicles carrying the remnants of Petreforce and Frankforce moved in a packed mass, nose to tail down the narrow road. They were an ideal Luftwaffe target, a bomber's dream. But by some dispensation of Providence not a single German plane was in the air and the whole force reached comparative safety north of Douai without interference and without casualties. Fortunately the Germans did not follow up; had they moved faster they would almost certainly have picked off a large number of stragglers who had lost touch with what was going on. Captain Harry Sell, the Transport Officer of 50 Division's 151 Brigade, has recorded that his 'B' Echelon became separated from the rest of the brigade near Vimy Ridge by a mass of fleeing refugees and French troops. So at 5 a.m. on the morning of May 23 he set off to look for it:

> There was no sign of the enemy on the ridge but I picked up two men of the 9th Battalion who were sleeping peacefully by the side of the road. I then drove forward to the village of Givenchy, which was deserted and in flames, only to find as I entered at one end of the square a German armoured column was entering it at the other! I beat a hasty retreat but on the way back found several 30 cwt lorries parked by the roadside and apparently abandoned. As I passed I blew my horn and to my astonishment a bleary morning face appeared over the tailboard. They were the 8th Battalion's cooks' lorries with the cooks asleep in them. However, the magic words 'Boche tanks' produced instant activity and this merry little convoy competed for international racing honours with the enemy down the Givenchy–Lens road!

As Frankforce failed to achieve its objectives and the most important road junction for the Germans in their advance northwards had to be abandoned, the Arras operation must be counted a failure. Nevertheless the extent of the resistance there undoubtedly gave the Germans a nasty jar, and upset their programme.* Said von Rundstedt later: 'A critical moment in the drive came just as my forces reached the Channel. It was caused by a British counter-stroke southwards from Arras towards Cambrai on May 21. For a short time it was feared that our armoured divisions could be cut off before the infantry divisions could come up to support them. None of the French counter-attacks carried any serious threat such as this one did.'†

Neither Gort nor the French generals to whom he was responsible could know of von Rundstedt's worries; so far as they were concerned all the problems were on the Allied side. With Boulogne and Calais threatened still more British units in the rear area were brigaded into scratch formations—'Polforce', 'Usherforce', 'Woodforce',‡ and deployed along the line of canals running from La Bassée through St Omer to the sea at Gravelines. Soldiers whose normal duties would seldom have brought them anywhere near the firing line joined with engineers, men returning from leave, medical orderlies, P.T. instructors, and men from mobile bath units. There was even, according to General Pownall, a 'posse of Padres' which fought with gallantry in the defence of the bridge at Bergues six miles inland from Dunkirk. In the event these unorthodox units held the ring long enough to enable Gort to redeploy the main body of the B.E.F. and replace them with regular fighting formations. Meanwhile the 30th Infantry Brigade with a battalion of the Royal Tank Regiment hurriedly embarked at Southampton and sailed for Calais, and the 20th Guards Brigade crossed the Channel to reinforce the French 21st Division at Boulogne. The situation was deteriorating rapidly and to conserve supplies the Allied armies in the north were put on half-rations.

It was now that the Germans missed a golden opportunity. Until the troops of the 30th Infantry Brigade reached Calais and were prop-

* By two days—giving time to British troops to be sent from England to garrison Calais and Boulogne, with a corresponding effect on the evacuation of Dunkirk.

† To Sir Basil Liddell Hart.

‡ Polforce, under Major-General H. C. Curtis the commander of 46 Division—originally organized to defend St Pol—was allotted to the protection of the canal line between Aine and Carvin. Brigadier C. M. Usher, a sub-area commander, was put in charge of the right bank of the River Aa, from St Omer to Gravelines. Under him were the 6th Green Howards of 23 Division and five battalions of heavy artillery used as infantry, and some French troops the *Secteur Fortifié des Flandres*. Woodforce was formed to guard Hazebrouck where Gort still had his forward G.H.Q.

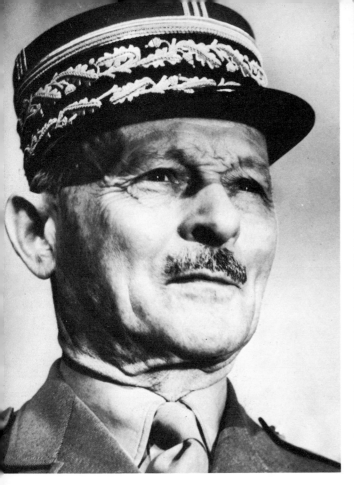

erly positioned the port was virtually undefended; likewise they could have had Boulogne for the asking. Guderian knew this. But von Rundstedt's confidence was waning, as he surveyed the map, read the reports of heavy fighting around Arras and allowed his imagination to dwell on the threat posed by undisclosed French reinforcements being flung across the Somme. As a precaution one of Guderian's three Panzer divisions was pulled back into reserve. Guderian, whose original intention had been to send one division to Dunkirk, one to Calais and the third to Boulogne, now had to revise his plans. Believing as always that speed was the essence, without waiting for permission he despatched the one Panzer division which was ready to move to take Boulogne. On the way it ran into strong resistance by the French, and by British anti-aircraft gunners whose weapons were positioned on the heights above the port and used as anti-tank guns in the same way as the comparable German 88-mm guns.

It took the Germans thirty-six hours to clear Boulogne; and in those thirty-six hours Guderian was given back his other Panzer division and told to seize Calais. But Guderian was not now prepared to give any

Left
General Maxime Weygand, who at the age of seventy-three replaced General Gamelin.

Centre
General Sir John Dill, Commander of the B.E.F's First Corps, and his three divisional commanders— Alexander (1 Div.), Lloyd (2 Div.) and Thorne (48 Div.)—at Douai, during the Phoney War period.

special priority to Calais, although he knew that British troops were arriving there. Calais could be left until later; his aim was to cut the Allied armies off from the coast, forcing them to fight their way through an ever-thickening ring of German armour. To do this the 1st Panzer Division was ordered on the evening of May 25 to advance on Gravelines and Dunkirk—the number one objective being Dunkirk.

Allied resistance in Boulogne ceased on Friday morning, May 24, and elements of the 1st Panzer Division pushed on to cross the Aa Canal—having brushed aside a squadron of the Mk Is of the newly arrived British Tank Battalion which attempted a foray from Calais. By that evening Guderian had 200 of his Panzers within fifteen miles of Dunkirk; two other Panzer divisions and four motorized divisions were roaring up to join him, and—behind them—at least six Wehrmacht infantry divisions were marching up towards Abbeville as fast as their feet would carry them. Dunkirk was ripe for the taking next day. Then came the celebrated order which can now be seen as part and parcel of the 'miracle' of Dunkirk. The Panzers were ordered to halt and stand fast.

55

☆

For a long time to come this famous *Halt Befehl* of May 24, who was responsible for it, and the attendant sequence of events are likely to remain a controversial topic among military historians. It is sufficient to note here that the order originated with von Rundstedt on the evening of the 23rd. Fearing that the attack at Arras might herald an even more serious offensive by both the B.E.F. and the French, he had lost his nerve. According to him the Panzers had suffered heavy casualties, their remaining tanks were in urgent need of servicing, and much of the terrain between the canals and the coast was boggy, wet and difficult for mechanized vehicles. As they would soon be needed to defeat the main French armies and to occupy Paris, it would be folly to waste them in heavy fighting against a desperate foe, short of food and ammunition.

Hitler had also been fretting, and when by pure coincidence Goering suggested to him that the Luftwaffe should be given the honour of finishing the job at Dunkirk the Führer was delighted to find a solution which had the added advantage that it would enable a truly Nazi-orientated organization to seize a larger slice of glory. On the morning of May 24 he visited von Rundstedt, was told of the order to stand fast, and happily confirmed it. 'We were utterly speechless,' Guderian recorded, 'but as we were not told of the reasons for this order it was difficult to argue against it.' Shortly afterwards he learned that it was an order from the Führer, and there could therefore be no question of 'arguing' against it. Hitler had decreed that the Luftwaffe should go in for the kill while the Wehrmacht's infantry maintained the pressure on the ground. So the Panzers stood restively immobile and waited for the Luftwaffe to win a land battle on its own.

On the other side of the Channel, Churchill learned during the afternoon of May 23 that the Germans were in Boulogne, that the attack on Arras had failed and that Gort had put the B.E.F. on half-rations. As it now seemed that the northern group of Allied armies could not join up with the French armies in the south Churchill considered that it was doomed as a fighting force, and that the aim of the B.E.F. must be to disengage and get back to England while there was still time. Telephoning Reynaud, the French Premier, he said that he wondered 'whether it would not be better if the British Army fought in retreat towards the coast'. Reynaud's reply was that Maxime Weygand, the seventy-three-year-old general who had been fetched back from Beirut to replace Gamelin was 'satisfied' things were going well, that the Allied armies were working hand in hand and that 'Weygand's Plan' could turn defeat into victory.

The British War Cabinet was not so sanguine, and that night Churchill expressed his misgivings in a cable to Reynaud. Gort, he said, had wired to say that the activities of the armies of the three different nations on the northern front needed to be co-ordinated,* and that he, Gort, could not do the co-ordinating because the B.E.F. was trying to control fighting on three fronts at once; this was a hard enough task without assuming command of the other armies. How did this, queried Churchill, agree with Weygand's views that the Allied armies under Blanchard were *main dans la main*?

The so-called Weygand Plan can be dismissed in a few words. It was a nebulous conception for a very large-scale Allied counter-offensive, with the French 1st Army, the B.E.F. and the Belgian Cavalry Corps attacking south-west. At least this was the general idea, there were no details. Nothing had been worked out, nothing co-ordinated; in other words it was a plan without substance. In the event it was destined never to take place.

On May 24 Gort ordered the 2nd and 44th Division to reinforce the canal line, and the 48th Division to relieve MacForce which was fighting hard at Cassel; all the northern armies were now enclosed in a pocket about fifty kilometres wide and stretching a hundred kilometres in depth from the sea. With the Germans concentrating for an attack across the canal the outlook was gloomy indeed and Gort told his staff to re-examine the arrangements for a withdrawal to the coast. Suddenly, however, prospects seemed brighter when a message was received from Weygand. The French 7th Army under General Frère was advancing northwards from the Somme, he signalled Gort, and it had already captured Amiens, Albert and Peronne. None of this was accurate, but there was no reason to doubt it at that time and in Gort's headquarters gloom gave way to elation. An intercepted German radio message containing von Rundstedt's order to halt the Panzers appeared to confirm the growing belief that the Germans might well have shot their bolt.

As May 25 was the turning point in the Battle of Flanders a brief review of the general disposition of the B.E.F. on that day seems desirable.†

* Billotte, who had been nominated 'co-ordinator', had been killed in a motor smash on his way back from a meeting with Weygand, King Leopold and General Ironside at Ypres on May 21. Billotte was supposed to be replaced by Blanchard but it was some days before the latter took over, and even after his appointment he did little co-ordinating.

† Only the terrain occupied by troops under Gort's immediate command is considered here, although the B.E.F. also included the 1st Armoured Division, the 51st Division and elements of the 12th and other Divisions—all of which were now irrevocably separated from the main body of the B.E.F.

After a fortnight's hard fighting the area occupied by the B.E.F. stretched across the Pas de Calais like a great cone-shaped bag with its apex at Douai and its mouth opening on to the sea between Dunkirk and Nieuwpoort. The apex was occupied by the French 1st Army; the sides were manned for the most part by British troops. Next to the sea on the western flank were more French troops, and French and Belgian on the eastern. Dunkirk itself was in the French sector and—in accordance with French practice—was controlled by the Admiral du Nord, Admiral Jean-Marie Abrial. Under him the troops in and around Dunkirk were commanded by General Fagalde.

Such was the approximate lay-out on the morning of May 25, when attacks on the canal line led to a further contraction of the defensive bag. Von Bock was concentrating on the sector held by the Belgians and it was plain that under the pressure he was exerting it could only be a matter of time—probably hours—before they caved in. When a dangerous gap opened between the B.E.F. and the Belgians—through which the Germans might soon be pouring to cut off the B.E.F. from

On the outer perimeter at Dunkirk—photographs taken under shellfire by a soldier of the Royal Ulster Rifles from the forward positions occupied by his unit near Furnes.

Dunkirk and their sole remaining line of supply, communications and possible retreat—Gort threw in the last of his reserves—one brigade and a machine-gun battalion.

Every unit in the B.E.F. was now committed, yet in London and Paris it was being criticized for inactivity. From Reynaud a querulous telegram to Churchill complained that the withdrawal of the 5th and 50th Divisions from Arras had jeopardized Weygand's forthcoming operation, just when the troops who had re-captured Amiens and Peronne were making excellent progress, and because of this Weygand had been obliged to stop the advance northwards. So far as both the French High Command and the British War Cabinet were concerned planning for the Allied armies in the north, including the B.E.F., to participate in Weygand's great adventure was supposed to be continuing. On the morning of the 25th General Sir John Dill flew from London to discuss the forthcoming operation with the French, and Blanchard—who had finally been appointed co-ordinator in place of the late lamented Billotte—blithely spoke of contributing two or three French

divisions and 200 tanks. On the basis of this information Dill returned to London to report to the War Cabinet that a five- or six-divisional attack was in prospect. But any enthusiasm for the attack which Gort might once have had was now rapidly waning. Blanchard's estimate of the French forces which could be mustered was a complete mirage, for Gort had learned that the 1st French Army could spare no more than one division for the venture. He had also just learned that some of the 1st Army's Moroccan troops, who had hitherto fought courageously, had broken and bolted from their positions at Carvin, and a couple of battalions from the 50th Division had had to be rushed to the scene to save the day. It was becoming increasingly clear that if the B.E.F. launched a counter-offensive it would in all probability—as at Arras—have to do so without the French. It was also apparent that Gort's resources were inadequate. 'Q' Martel's tank force had dwindled and only two of the Mark IIs and fifteen of the Mark Is were still runners; he would thus be sending infantry with very little armoured support to do battle with the Panzers. Further ominous news from the front, and a report by the Commanding Officer of the 12th Lancers, to the effect that, from his observations, the Belgians were on the point of collapse, gave the British Commander-in-Chief increasing cause for reflection.

Thus it was that at 6.30 p.m. that Thursday, May 25, Gort made the most fateful decision in the campaign. Without asking for advice from London and without consulting the French, he abandoned the idea of participating in any combined Franco-British offensive and ordered the 5th and 50th Division, earmarked for the great Weygand adventure, to move up to fill the gap between the B.E.F. left flank and the fast disintegrating Belgian Army. It was a decision which embittered the French, but one which saved the B.E.F. from death or captivity.

Gort's efforts and those of his staff were then wholly devoted to withdrawing the B.E.F. to Dunkirk and getting as many men as possible back to England. It was natural to suppose that Blanchard would be upset when he was told at 9.30 p.m. that the British had opted out of the Weygand Plan. But overnight he appears to have become reconciled to what some of the French officers were already describing as the latest example of British perfidy, because when Gort went to his headquarters at Attiches on the morning of the 26th he gladly co-operated in drawing up the lines of withdrawal westwards. Gort did not mention the delicate matter of the eventual embarkation as he had been expressly told not to do so. In a telegram to Anthony Eden, Secretary of State for War, Gort had set out the reasons for his decision to cancel the offensive, and Eden who had learned that the advance from the Somme was a figment of French imagination, replied that '... the only course open to you may be to fight your way back to the west, where all beaches and ports east of Gravelines will be used for embarkation. Navy will provide fleet of ships and small boats, and R.A.F. will give full support...' The Prime Minister, Eden continued, would be seeing Reynaud next day and he would clarify the situation, 'including the attitude of the French to the possible move.... In the meantime it is obvious you should not discuss the possibility of the move [i.e. the evacuation] with the French or the Belgians.'

That night Operation Dynamo was set in motion. The Weygand Plan had been ditched and the B.E.F. had been given leave to make its own arrangements for its future—for surrender, evacuation, or resistance *a l'outrance*. Gort himself was pessimistic, and his reply to Anthony Eden's telegrams concluded with an ominous forecast '... I must not conceal from you that a great part of the B.E.F. and its equipment will inevitably be lost even in its best circumstances.' Ironside, who was replaced on May 27, was even more pessimistic: 'Very little chance of the B.E.F. getting off...' he wrote in his diary. '... We shall have lost practically all our trained soldiers by the next few days—*unless a miracle appears to help us....*'

Over the page
Dunkirk under attack. Houses near the docks during an air raid.

4. Dunkirk Bridgehead

May 25 – 27

'On the west British troops defended the narrowing gap to the sea. Day after day the battle continued. At the end of it they had fought themselves to a standstill, but held their ground, and by doing so had enabled the remainder of the Expeditionary Force to get clear. On the east, corps artillery coming into action against the enemy massing for attack inflicted such heavy casualties that the attack never developed.

The stories of individual exploits at this time are legion.... But the triumph is not the triumph of individuals, however gallant. It is the triumph of an army. There is no braver epic in all our annals.'

From a broadcast by Anthony Eden,
2 June 1940

Hitler's Guard unit, the elite SS *Leibstandarte* Regiment—part of the 1st Panzer Division—reached the Aa Canal on the eastern side of the cone-shaped zone into which the Allied armies had been compressed, during the afternoon of May 24. Although the Regiment had had a long tiring march, its 3rd Battalion was ordered to capture the forty-two metre hill, the Wattenberg, lying to the east of the canal, which dominates the otherwise flat countryside. Shortly before the attack was due to go in, however, the standfast command to the Panzers brought an order forbidding any movement across the canal towards Dunkirk. It was an order which the regimental commander, SS Obergruppen-fuhrer Sepp Dietrich, chose to ignore and the attack was launched. Under the cover of a heavy artillery barrage the SS men crossed the canal, smashed their way through the French defences and captured the hill.

Spurred on by Guderian, the *Leibstandarte* continued to push forward until they were halted at Bollezelle by B.E.F. Bren gun carriers and anti-tank guns which had been rushed up to seal off the German break-through at Watten. Meantime Hitler had quite unexpectedly rescinded his order to the Panzers. Why he did so at this particular moment remains a mystery, but Sepp Dietrich had Hitler's ear and it was per-haps because the Nazi SS was now involved that Hitler decided to relax his embargo on the employment of Panzers. In the event, on the morn-ing of May 28 a combined Panzer-infantry force made up of the *Leib-standarte*, the 2nd Panzer Brigade and the 11th (Deutsch) Rifle Brigade, attacked up the Watten-Wormhout road.

Motoring up to co-ordinate the attacks of his battalion, Sepp Dietrich was cut off at Esquelberg. His car, shot up by men of the 5th Bn The Gloucestershire Regiment, caught fire and Dietrich and his adjutant had to hide in a ditch and wait for the *Leibstandarte* men to rescue them. Attacks by two companies of infantry and another supported by armoured vehicles failed to break through to the SS commander, and a full battalion assault had to be mounted before a patrol could bring Dietrich and his adjutant out. Dietrich said afterwards that the British defence of Esquelberg was the most severe opposition that the SS encountered and he and his men thought that they were up against first-class regular troops. The Germans eventually battered their way through Wormhout, repelling a number of British counter-attacks— three of them with the bayonet—in the course of the action and took a number of prisoners. To some of these prisoners Dietrich showed an uncharacteristic old-fashioned courtesy, presenting them with SS badges and flashes as souvenirs. Meanwhile further down the road a patrol of his troops was making sure that a British chaplain, the Rev. Reginald Podmore, whom they had cut down with a burst of machine-gun fire would not live to report that they had shot a non-combatant.*

On all sectors of the B.E.F. front the Panzers were making only slow progress now; they had lost their momentum and the going was hard. Guderian was also having second thoughts about the terrain around Dunkirk and on May 28, in a report to his immediate superior General Paul von Kleist, he wrote that it was '... not desirable to continue operations in this area as it is costing unnecessary sacrifices'. Further-more, he continued, '... a tank attack is pointless in the marshy country which has been soaked by rain ... [and] 18th Army [part of von Bock's Army Group B] is approaching from the east. The infantry forces of this army are more suitable than tanks for fighting in this kind of country, and the task of closing the gap on the coast can therefore be left to them'.† Guderian now feared that the Panzer divisions might be frittered away around Dunkirk.

Judging by the experience of Maurice Few, a young officer of the Royal Sussex, Guderian's worries do not seem to have bothered the Panzertruppen. They were the heroes of the hour and Few, who was captured near Godeswald by troops of Rommel's 7th Panzer Division, writes:

> I found his troops to be correct but courteous and without the arrogance we were to experience later. The entire division seemed to be dressed in brand new British Army battle dress trousers with a Wehrmacht jacket and many wore a gaily coloured silk scarf round their necks and a ten-

* The circumstances of Podmore's death have been described to the author by Mr S. Priest who was serving on the Headquarters staff of the 3rd Corps. Temporary Chap-lain (Class 2) Podmore, an enthusiastic believer in 'muscular Christianity', was caught up in the war when he attempted to collect some kit from the battle zone. In the mining village of Divion-en-Artois his vehicle was stopped by a burst of fire which also severed his legs. The SS men are believed to have refused any medical assistance and the padre, who died on the pavement, is buried in a World War I cemetery in Pernes.

† This report abstracted from Kleist's Corps War Diary is not mentioned in *Panzer Leader*—probably because Guderian did not wish to confirm the view implied in the British Official History that he had not realized how difficult the terrain around Dun-kirk was for tanks until he actually saw it.

dency to long hair. I was told that everyone in the division was under 30 years old but no doubt this did not apply to Rommel and perhaps some of his div staff. Somebody silently presented me with a 'hussif', presumably because my battle dress was in tatters. Someone else—obviously a panzer humorist—held out his clenched fists, one above the other. The upper fist was then vigorously pumped up and down while the lower fist remained stationary to the chant 'Chemblin, Chemblin'. (This was intended to take off Neville Chamberlain raising and lowering his famous umbrella.)

. . . I noted an ingenious money saver. This was a 'mechanized' field cooker which simply comprised a horsedrawn field cooker run up onto the back of a lorry and its wheels lashed to ring bolts. The cook stood on the back of the lorry cooking just as he would have been doing on the line of march when his cooker had been drawn by two heavy draft horses.

Maps throughout Rommel's division appeared to comprise Michelin tourist maps. They were bang up to date but, in so far I can remember after this lapse of time, without grid-co-ordinates. Nevertheless they were vastly preferable to our ordnance survey sheets dated 1924. All vehicles appeared to be fitted with Dunlop tyres and so did some grounded aircraft. . . .

A horse-drawn battery of guns, which I presume did not belong to Rommel's division, had a roadside halt where I happened to be lying on the ground with some other chaps under guard. An officer halted with his horse's feet uncomfortably close to my head. I was able to read a nearly outgrown hoof brand. It was 'INIS'. I remarked, 'This bloody bastard is riding a British Army horse'. The German officer said in English, 'Yes, it was bought in Ashford Market in 1937 and not so much of the "bloody bastard" if you please.' We fell into conversation and he told us that German civilian buyers had gone over to Britain during the 1930s to buy up all that they could find of British Army horses for sale, having been boarded to make way for mechanization. He said all the horses in his battery were ex British Army.

Maurice Few was unlucky: he spent the next five years in a prisoner-of-war camp. But some men who were captured during the early days of the campaign managed to get away in the confusion arising from the rapid pace of the German advance. The adventures of Private Thomas Dabner—a truck driver with the 11th Bn of the Durham Light Infantry—are but one example worthy of record. Dabner's vehicle was ambushed near Beaumetz on May 21, and after disarming him the Germans told him to load his truck with wounded and follow a Panzer returning to an assembly and refuelling point. It was moonlight when the vehicles set off and at a road junction Dabner switched off his lights,

A remarkable picture showing a German column of horse-drawn transport under attack by an R.A.F. Battle. Note the men fleeing across the field.

turned left and stepped on the accelerator as the tank turned right. Driving at speed he eventually succeeded in finding a British Field Ambulance where he was able to drop off his wounded passengers before driving on to rejoin his unit.

☆

Fighting by day and retiring by night, the B.E.F. began to pull back towards the coast during the night of May 26. The plan was to reduce the perimeter of the pocket occupied by the Allied armies in phased moves over a period of these days, finishing on May 29—the aim being to pull back to a bastion covering the evacuation points. In the event the Dunkirk Perimeter as it finally emerged was a shallow salient, about twenty-five kilometres wide and twelve deep at its deepest, extending from a point on the coast midway between Gravelines and Dunkirk to Nieuwpoort in Belgium. There were no quays except at Dunkirk itself, but at intervals along the dunes there were little seaside resorts— Coxyde, La Panne and Malo-les-Bains. The right of the British sector was at Bergues (about ten kilometres inland from Dunkirk), from where the British front stretched in a north-easterly direction, across the frontier and through Furnes to Nieuwpoort. Defensive positions were based on the canals over which the bridges had been destroyed; in some places the locks had been opened and the low-lying terrain flooded.

Apart from the withdrawal to a bridgehead at Dunkirk a scheme had to be organized for the actual evacuation from the embarkation points—beginning with the units which were not required, and leaving the fighting troops to the last. This task Gort delegated to Lt-General (later Sir) Ronald Adam, the commander of the 3rd Corps, and early on the morning of the 27th an Anglo-French conference was held at Cassell at which Adam, Blanchard, Admiral Abrial, General Fagalde, General Prioux (who had succeeded Blanchard as commander of the French 1st Army) and General Koeltz, representing Weygand, were present. It was probably the last time they all saw one another. At this conference the general lay-out of the Dunkirk Perimeter was agreed. The French were to be responsible for the western half, the British for the east. (The Belgians, who were still fighting, were not included in the plan, although the Perimeter could have been extended eastwards to accommodate them.) Everybody at the conference seemed to accept that the only course now open was to pull back into a defensive zone which could be supplied and reinforced by sea. However, in the course of the conference a stirring message arrived for Blanchard, who—as he had no orders from the French High Command concerning the withdrawal—was already in a quandary. Weygand wanted some 'Activité Solidarité and Résolution', and required all concerned to recapture Calais which had fallen the day before— although the zone between the area occupied by the Allied armies and

68

Calais was now occupied by several Panzer and Wehrmacht infantry divisions. Next day the message to Blanchard was followed up by one to Gort calling for the B.E.F's support in the 'forthcoming counter-attack'. Gort rightly concluded that from now on he should be concerned only with orders from Whitehall (although only a few hours had elapsed since Churchill had also suggested that the B.E.F. should send a division to relieve Calais. Where it was to come from and how it would get to Calais is difficult to conceive).

Once the limits of the proposed enclave had been agreed, Adam set Brigadier E. F. Lawson, the C.R.A. of 48 Division, to organizing the defences along the Perimeter. And as a result of superhuman efforts by Lawson and the units he commandeered to man the positions, a defensive ring was created within the next twenty-four hours. Inside the Perimeter Adam was faced with formidable traffic problems. As they pulled back, the troops who had been told what to do disabled their vehicles and abandoned them in assembly areas outside the Perimeter. But it was inevitable that there would be stragglers and units who had received no orders about vehicles. Meantime the pitiful flood of refugees was impeding progress everywhere, and the difficulties which they created on the roads were magnified when the French 60th Division began to arrive from Belgium and the rear echelons of the French mechanized Divisions started to pour in from the south. The transport of the French IIIrd Corps—most of which was horsed—added further to the congestion. (Some of this transport found its way to the beaches, where ultimately the wretched horses, without water or fodder, were cut loose by British soldiers and turned inland.)

During May 27 King Leopold negotiated an armistice and at 11 p.m. that night Gort was told that the Belgians would lay down their arms at midnight. Premonitory messages to this effect had failed to reach him because everything, including his own headquarters, was on the move and communications were difficult. However, as Gort had been expecting the news it came as less of a shock to him than it did to the British and French Governments. But the Belgian capitulation meant that in a bare one hour's time a gap twenty-five kilometres wide would open on the B.E.F. left flank between Ypres and the sea. As the Belgians had been retiring north-eastwards towards Antwerp this gap would have developed anyway, but the event added still greater urgency to the withdrawal within the Dunkirk Perimeter before the Germans could cross the river and attack along the coast.

And difficulties with the French still had to be resolved. Blanchard's instructions did not correspond with those of Gort and when Gort told him on the morning of the 28th that Whitehall had authorized the embarkation of the B.E.F. he was aghast. Blanchard had been told to co-operate in a withdrawal but his understanding was that 'the bridge-head would be held with no thought of retreat'; now the British were proposing to up sticks and sail away. Nor was this all: Gort said that

*Prior to the evacuation, and during 'Dynamo',
Hudsons of the R.A.F's Coastal Command patrolled
the sea-lanes. Smoke rises from burning oil tanks at
Dunkirk, set ablaze by the Luftwaffe.*

owing to the Belgian surrender the Allied armies must speed up their retreat. And when Prioux was told that the First Army would have to fall back that night he jibbed. His men were tired, he said, and unfit for further exertion for at least another twenty-four hours. The move would have to be postponed; meantime he was going to stay where he was, between Béthune and Lille.

Believing that delay would be fatal—that von Bock's troops moving in from the east would seize Nieuwpoort and start to roll up the Perimeter before the B.E.F. were back behind it—Gort told Blanchard that the B.E.F. would pull back anyway. Subsequently appeals to French military pride and prestige led to General La Laurencie's IIIrd Corps and the remnants of the Seventh Army being sent to join the B.E.F. in the bridgehead.

☆

The R.A.F. was back in the fray by this time, and the closer the B.E.F. came to the sea the more support the British airmen were able to give. But as much of the air fighting took place out of sight of Dunkirk, and the men on the ground and the ships taking part in the evacuation were being subjected to heavy and repeated attacks by the *Luftwaffe*

Right
Wing-Commander Basil Embry, whose adventures after his plane was shot down had all the elements of popular escape fiction.

Far right
Lieut-General Sir Alan Brooke (later Viscount Alanbrooke), G.O.C. Second Corps, and two of his divisional commanders—'Monty' (Major-General Bernard Montgomery) and Major-General D. G. Johnson.

anyway, there was a natural tendency to assume that all aircraft were hostile. It was the safe thing to do. (In this connection it is worth noting that even four years later, when the *Luftwaffe* rarely put in an appearance and Allied aircraft painted in large black and white stripes swarmed all over the Normandy beachheads many naval vessels went on shooting with the same gay abandon.) However, even if many of the aircraft the troops thought were German were in fact British, the fact remains that the British fighters were hopelessly outnumbered and the small number of bombers employed were incapable of any really worthwhile contribution. Dowding, with an eye to the coming struggle and determined as ever to conserve the R.A.F's fighters for defence of Britain, refused to reduce Fighter Command's strength below 'the indispensable minimum' of twenty-five squadrons. This meant that Air-Vice-Marshal K. R. (later Sir Keith) Park, A.O.C. of No. 11 Fighter Group, who was responsible for providing an air umbrella over Dunkirk and the English Channel ports during Operation Dynamo, had only sixteen squadrons (approximately 200 aircraft), with which to frustrate the *Luftwaffe*.

At the outset Park's task was complicated by requests from the War Office to provide fighter cover for supply-dropping missions over Calais on the morning of May 27. As the garrison surrendered on the evening

These photographs were taken on the Poperinge – Dunkirk road during the retreat, by Mr R. J. Slack, then a bombardier with 107 Bty R.A. The dead horse and the debris (some of it human anatomy) are the result of a Luftwaffe raid.

of the 26th they were not needed, but the news arrived late, the sorties flew as arranged and packages of food and ammunition were dropped on Calais into alien hands. Meanwhile the Admiralty had been clamouring for continuous air cover over Dunkirk during the hours of daylight. As the beaches and shoreline of the Dunkirk Perimeter were twelve kilometres long and the shipping was liable to be attacked anywhere between Dunkirk and Dover this was a tall order. With only sixteen squadrons it meant a choice between continuity and strength; for continuity it was possible to keep no more than a single squadron over the evacuation zone, since the endurance limits of the Hurricanes and Spitfires allowed only forty minutes of patrolling over the target area. Consequently until Park was able to persuade the Admiralty to relax the demand for continuity in favour of strength the British fighters were almost invariably outnumbered over Dunkirk. On May 27 for example, eleven Spitfires of No. 74 Squadron gave battle to thirty Do 17s and Me 109s, and twenty Hurricanes and Spitfires of Nos. 56 and 610 Squadrons ran into thirty or forty Me 119s. This was one of the two days when the Luftwaffe attacked the bridgehead continuously (the other was June 1) and for the men and the ships below the ordeal was long and terrible. On other days Goering's pilots were hampered either by bad visibility or the R.A.F. fighters, but on May 27 they reduced the town and port of Dunkirk to rubble. Fortunately for the B.E.F. and the crews of the ships in which the troops were to embark the damage to the mole did not stop the evacuation. At least a dozen attacks were made on ships but only two vessels were sunk that day.

The R.A.F. bombers struck at targets beyond the bridgehead. Every day of Operation Dynamo fifty Blenheims attacked the German formations closing in on the B.E.F., and every night an equal number of Wellingtons, Whitleys or Hampdens bombed the roads leading to Dunkirk while others attacked road and railway junctions further inland. The B.E.F. knew nothing of these raids; only when they could actually see the bombers in action were they prepared to recognize that the R.A.F. was in the battle with them.

On other occasions the troops watched the R.A.F. bombers in action against the German artillery bombarding the beaches and the armada of ships in the Channel. But these were the exceptions. Most of the Allied soldiers and sailors at Dunkirk saw nothing and knew nothing of the bombing missions undertaken on their behalf. In any case their grumble was not about the bombers; they wanted to see the fighters in action. (The fact that few of them could distinguish British from German aircraft in 1940 seemed irrelevant and as Spitfires attacked Hurricanes over Dunkirk on more than one occasion this lack of skill in aircraft recognition was not confined to sailors and soldiers!)

While the men on the ground and in the ships may have had cause—based on their own observations—to criticize the lack of R.A.F. presence at Dunkirk, no-one could question its fighting spirit, which may be judged from two examples of the many which could be quoted.* On May 31 Flight Lieutenant R. D. G. Wight of 213 Squadron wrote to his mother:

> Well, another day is gone, and with it a lot of grand blokes. Got another brace of 109's today, but the whole *Luftwaffe* seemed to leap on us—we were hopelessly outnumbered. I was caught napping by a 109 in the middle of a dog fight, and got a couple of holes in the aircraft, one of them filled the office with smoke, but the Jerry overshot and *he's* dead. If anyone says anything to you in the future about the inefficiency of the R.A.F.—I believe the B.E.F. troops were booing the R.A.F. in Dover the other day—tell them from me we only wish we could do more. But without aircraft we can do no more than we have done—that is, our best, and that's fifty times better than the German best, though they are fighting under the most advantageous conditions. So don't worry, we are going to win this war even if we have only one aeroplane and one pilot left— the Boche could produce the whole *Luftwaffe* and you would see the one pilot and the one aeroplane go into combat.

The bomber pilots were cast in the same mould, and although the story of Wing Commander Basil Embry (subsequently Air Chief Marshal Sir Basil Embry and NATO's Commander Allied Air Forces Central Europe) of 107 Squadron is unusual it is in substance typical. Embry's aircraft was shot down on May 27 during an attack on a German column moving towards Dunkirk, but Embry baled out, landed safely and was captured soon afterwards. In the interrogation which followed he not only refused to divulge any information other than the usual number, rank, name but insisted that his interrogator, a German captain, should show respect to a senior officer. With other British prisoners he was set to march to Germany but he broke away from the column, discarded his uniform jacket, took a civilian coat from a scarecrow and was soon making for the Allied lines south of the Somme.

From then on his adventures had all the elements of popular escape fiction. Trapped while raiding a farm for food, he spent thirty-six hours hiding in a pile of straw in a loft with German soldiers sleeping in the barn below. Seized by a German patrol and incarcerated in a farmhouse—and warned that he would be shot if it turned out he was English—he knocked out his jailer with a straight left to the jaw, snatched his rifle, brought it down on the head of another guard outside the door, hit a third German with it in the passage outside and then took refuge in a pile of manure in the farmyard where he remained undetected until nightfall. Later, after operating on his own leg to remove the shrapnel which had lodged there when his plane was shot down, he was picked up again by the Germans. It did not take his fluent

Vice-Admiral Bertram Ramsay, Flag Officer Dover responsible for the overall execution of Operation Dynamo. His headquarters were in the maze of tunnels the chalk cliffs of Dover.

---

* During the nine days of Operation Dynamo R.A.F. fighters flew 2739 sorties over Dunkirk, R.A.F. bombers 651 sorties on operations directly concerned with the withdrawal and evacuation, and R.A.F. reconnaissance aircraft 171 sorties.

76

French-speaking German interrogator long to pierce his pose as a Belgian, and when he did Embry 'confessed' that he was really a southern Irishman 'wanted' for bomb outrages in London. To a demand that he should prove his story by speaking in Gaelic, he responded with a few sentences in Urdu which seemingly satisfied his captor. Then, failing to find either the Allied armies or a boat on the coast, he broke into a garage, built himself a bicycle from spare parts and—although he knew by then that Paris had fallen—made for the French capital with the intention of seeking help as an American. En route a German

soldier commandeered his bicycle but Embry duly arrived in Paris, where having failed to persuade the American Embassy to help him—he acquired another bicycle on which he set off for the south of France. He was challenged many times but he always managed to put across a convincing story. Finally he reached an area still held by the French and after many more vicissitudes he left Perpignan for Gibraltar from where he was taken back by the Royal Navy to England—to disembark at Plymouth ten weeks after being shot down.

Embry's story is in a sense the Dunkirk story in microcosm. According to the laws of probability his chances of surviving all these incidents were negligible. In the same way, on 26 May 1940 nearly 500,000 British and Frenchmen had in theory little or no chance of escaping from Dunkirk—but a large proportion of them did get away. Lady Luck played her part, but Embry owed his freedom to his resourcefulness,* his skill, his toughness, his optimism and his courage. It was these qualities which made Operation Dynamo a 'miracle of deliverance'.

* Another classic example of resourcefulness was displayed by three 'other ranks' of the 51st Highland Division. After the fall of St Valéry these three changed into civilian clothes and tramped the whole length of France to cross the Pyrenees and eventually get home. The crisis in their escape came early in this remarkable trek.

In appearance they were typical Scottish gillies—broad, strong, thick-necked and taciturn. They bore no resemblance to the French peasants, and they spoke not one word of French. At one place they were stopped by a suspicious German officer who asked them who they were, and where they had come from. According to a pre-arranged plan, the three Scots refused to understand and gabbled back in Gaelic. A series of interpreters were called, who tried the highlanders with every known language. Finally, in despair, the German produced a map of the world and indicated by signs that they should point to their country of origin. After careful study one of the Scots slowly and deliberately placed his finger in the middle of Russia.

The German was delighted; the possibility of the three men being Russians had not occurred to him. And, as this was the period of German–Soviet collaboration, the three were released, and allowed to continue their march south.

Over the page
Dunkirk harbour, 26 May 1940—the West mole on the right, the town ablaze in the background.

'The original plan was to lift the B.E.F. off from the mole, which must be known to millions of holiday makers. This entailed ships going alongside, securing bow and stern, and when fully loaded coming out astern turning and making for home. A lengthy manoeuvre, plus the fact that the mole made an ideal aiming point for the droves of JU 87s which came over from dawn to dusk. There were many soldiers who with rescue at their finger tips bought it on that mole; sailors too of course. . . . We hated the mole, to us it was just a question of time before a bomb with our number on it was dropped. Thank heavens we moved over to the beaches, where we remained for the whole of the evacuation, giving what help we could.'

From an account by Mr S. Payne, on board H.M.S. Vega, *29 May 1940*

5. The Most Compelling Hour

7–8 p.m. May 26

Nine months of *Sitzkrieg* had lulled even the best informed, and Britain was not ready for the consequences of the retreat from Dunkirk. Since September 1939 life had gone on much the same as it had in peacetime, and if there were any shortages they were not apparent in Harrods, Fortnum and Masons or even Selfridges. Most people believed that the French Army was invincible, and they had been told that the B.E.F. was the best-equipped and finest fighting force in the world. So if for any reason the French failed against the Germans, the B.E.F. could still take care of itself.

It was not until May 26 that the British public had any real idea of what was happening across the Channel, although a pointer to the possibility of disaster had been given a full twelve days before, during the nine o'clock news on the morning of May 14 when it was announced that:

> The Admiralty have made an order requesting all owners of self-propelled pleasure craft between 30 and 100 feet in length to send all particulars to the Admiralty within 14 days from today, if they have not already been offered or requisitioned.

Such an instruction clearly implied that the need for motor-boats and the like might well arise within the very near future. But as the Government seemed to be issuing so many pettifogging notices few people took much notice. Even the Germans who regularly monitored all B.B.C. broadcasts did not detect any military significance in it.

Brief reference has already been made to discussions on 'the possible but unlikely evacuation of a very large force in hazardous circumstances', in the operation code-named Dynamo. The first of these discussions took place during the morning of May 19 when the possible evacuation of the B.E.F. was discussed in detail. At this meeting it was decided that the ports of Dunkirk, Boulogne, Calais and Ostend would all be available, and that Vice-Admiral Bertram Ramsay, Flag Officer Dover, would control the operation. The first plan envisaged the evacuation being carried out in three phases. Beginning on May 20 2000 men a day would be brought back until all the *bouches inutiles* had been withdrawn and the B.E.F. streamlined to Gort's satisfaction. On top of this the staff of various base units and field hospitals—totalling about 15,000 men—had to be evacuated; these would be embarked on the night of May 22; this was Phase 2. Phase 3 was 'the possible but unlikely': the hazardous evacuation 'of a very large force'.

Thirty-six of what the Royal Navy designated 'personnel vessels' were initially allotted to Ramsay for the operation. These ships, based on Dover and Southampton, included cross-Channel steamers familiar to holiday-makers which were capable of carrying hundreds of passengers and scores of railway coaches, some of the Irish Sea ferries and a few Dutch and Belgian passenger ships. If more ships were needed Ramsay was told that he would have to try and find them in the French ports. He was also told that although the plan envisaged embarkation taking place in an orthodox fashion from quays and piers at night, he should consider the feasibility of embarking troops from other places by means of small craft. Ramsay and his staff did not consider that it would be possible to lift men off the beaches, but when Ramsay expressed this opinion he did not know that Dunkirk would be the only port open to him and that even it would be threatened.

Service planning is a logical process and Ramsay's staff now submitted a formal request to the Admiralty for additional vessels and for naval personnel to man them. Ramsay himself was especially keen to have some of the Dutch motor coasters, known to the Dutch as *schuyts* and to British seafaring men as 'skoots'. These strong wood-built vessels were broad-beamed and of shallow draft, between 200 and 500 tons displacement, with diesel engines and comfortable quarters aft for the master, his wife, family and dog. Skoots, Ramsay reckoned, would be ideal for embarking troops at improvised embarkation points and ferrying them back to England. Some fifty skoots which had escaped from Holland were lying in the Thames and at Poole, and on May 22 the Admiralty allocated eight of them to the War Office for use as supply ships. The Commander-in-Chiefs at the Nore and Plymouth were directed to take over and man the rest and these were the ones that were to be allocated to Ramsay. Forty skoots in all were taken into service by the Royal Navy.

Twenty-two of those lying in the Thames were commissioned between May 25 and May 27 by the C-in-C Nore, and eighteen at Poole were commissioned on May 25 by the C-in-C Portsmouth. The commissioning process was relatively simple for there was no time for ceremonial: crews simply went aboard, loaded stores, fuel and weapons and hoisted the White Ensign. Most of the crews were reservists, called back to service with the colours, and the weapons were obsolescent Lewis guns of World War I vintage whose complicated mechanisms could produce an astounding variety of malfunctions.

Ramsay's headquarters were in the maze of tunnels which had been cut out of the chalk cliffs overlooking the Channel at Dover during

the Napoleonic wars. Some of these tunnels had been extended into barrack-like chambers and the one which served as the operation room for Flag-Officer Dover had been originally intended to house a dynamo (hence the name of operation 'Dynamo'). From his own office adjoining the Dynamo Room a window opening on to a narrow iron-railed balcony permitted Ramsay to view Dover harbour and the Channel beyond. On a clear day an observer from this balcony could see as far as Cap Gris Nez, and on the night of May 24 the flashes of German artillery shelling Boulogne were plainly visible.

Ramsay himself, a highly-strung and volatile individual, had had long experience of Dover and the Channel. As a young commander in World War I he had commanded a monitor which shelled German installations along the Belgian coast. Later he had commanded a flotilla in the Dover Patrol, whose purpose was to keep open the shipping lanes in the North Sea and whose beat was the Channel. He was not a man to suffer fools gladly and between the wars his quick temper, a sharp tongue and an aptitude for upsetting senior officers had slowed his progress in the peace-time navy. In 1938 he had retired but at the outbreak of war had been called back and appointed Flag Officer Dover. During the phoney war he had been mainly concerned with the activities of German U-boats and the control of mine-layers. Now, as the Dunkirk crisis moved towards a climax, Ramsay at the age of fifty-seven faced responsibilities which were to tax his knowledge, his energy, his ingenuity and above all his ability to persuade others that his decisions were the right ones.*

Fortunately he knew how to delegate authority, and he was equally lucky in his choice of subordinates. Rear-Admiral W. F. Wake-Walker was given control of movement across the Channel and around Dunkirk, with the title Rear-Admiral Dover-Straits. Under his authority the loading operations at Dunkirk were to be supervised by Captain W. G. Tennant. At the English ports arrangements for the disembarkation of the troops were assigned to a Principal Sea Transport Officer, Commodore E. G. Jukes-Hughes. Other senior officers at the Channel ports of Ramsgate—Captain W. R. Phillimore—and at Newhaven—Captain A. A. Lovett-Cameron—were also answerable to Ramsay. Commander J. C. Clouston was sent to Dunkirk to act as Piermaster, and he worked there gallantly for six days directing the assembly and embarkation of congested and generally chaotic bodies of troops on the bomb-shattered quay. (Returning from a visit to Dover the motor-torpedo boat in which he was travelling was hit and sunk by a Luftwaffe bomb. Clouston, exhausted by his efforts at Dunkirk, was drowned.)

Ramsay's headquarters staff in Dover was quite small, sixteen men

* Ramsay, who subsequently became the architect of the Royal Navy's part in the Normandy invasion did not survive the war. He was killed in a 'plane crash near Paris on 2 January 1945.

85

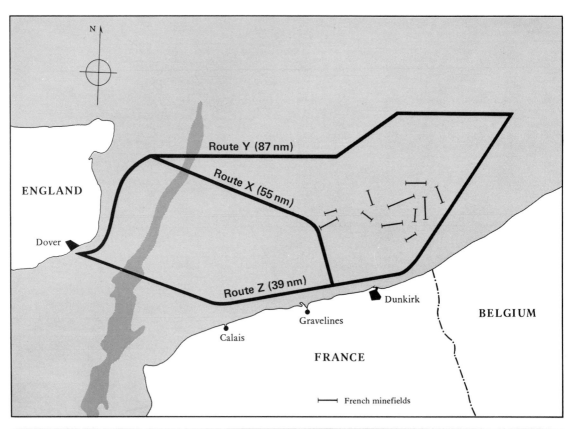

Route Y (87 nm)
Route X (55 nm)
Route Z (39 nm)

N

ENGLAND

Dover

Calais

Gravelines

Dunkirk

FRANCE

BELGIUM

⊢——⊣ French minefields

n-routes between south-east
England and Dunkirk
showing position of the
minefields off the coast.

Troops embarking from the
west mole. Some soldiers who
were on the moles for hours
became hysterical, but for the
most part they waited
patiently to board the ships
for England.

in all. They included a hydrographic officer, Commander A. Day, and it was Day who laid out the three cross-Channel routes used in the evacuation. Route Z, the first and shortest, was thirty-nine sea miles (sixty-five kms) and took only two hours to traverse. Route X, devised later as the Germans closed in around Dunkirk, was a fifty-five sea mile (ninety km) run that crossed the shoals known as Ruytingen Bank and joined the inshore channel about half-way between Dunkirk and Gravelines. Route Y, which became necessary after further German advances, was a series of dog-leg courses totalling 87 sea miles (145 kms) terminating in an eastward inland approach to Dunkirk. Route X went straight through a minefield covering Gravelines and Dunkirk, and Route Y went round another and more extensive minefield north of Dunkirk. But as Luftwaffe planes were scattering magnetic mines all over the Channel, the hazard from these diabolical weapons existed outside the known fields.

Over and above the 230 trawlers and the fleet of small craft which eventually took part in the operation, Ramsay's staff directed the movements of 216 ships of the British merchant fleet, the forty skoots, and 139 naval vessels. At the peak of the evacuation there were among the latter no less than fifty-six destroyers of varying age and condition. Responsibility for supplying the 'little ships' and for providing auxiliary vessels needed to carry stores, water and ammunition and working parties in harbour was that of a department of the Admiralty under command of Vice-Admiral Sir Lionel Preston. It was Preston who saw the need for little ships if it came to a question of the B.E.F. evacuating the Continent, and it was he who was responsible for the B.B.C. broadcast on May 14, requesting owners of self-propelled pleasure craft to report to Whitehall. Thus, when Ramsay concluded on the evening of May 26 that he needed as many little boats as could be found, he turned to Preston. Soon after he had made his requirements known the teleprinter at the Admiralty chattered out what can now be regarded as a historical signal: 'Operation Dynamo will commence.'

It was 7 p.m. when the message reached Ramsay at Dover and the light was fading. In the main harbour which had been rebuilt in the 1890s to accommodate the British Channel Fleet, there was a strange conglomeration of vessels. Some, at the eight berths along Admiralty Pier, were the regular cross-Channel packets which used Dover as their home port. But they had not just returned from their customary trips; gouged and buckled plates on their superstructures and sides were evidence of near-miss bomb blasts, and ragged tears in their decks were the result of machine gun fire by low-flying German fighters. For several days these ships had been evacuating civilians and Allied troops from Boulogne, Calais and Ostend, and the Germans had been doing their best to sink them. Royal Navy destroyers were moored on the western side of the harbour, some of them so damaged as to be barely seaworthy. Tied up near them were skoots and cargo ships which were to be used

*t low tide ladders had to be
sed to climb down from the
ole to the ships' decks.*

as troopships. Closer to the beach in shallower water, lay British, Dutch and Belgian coasters and fishing boats—tiny, shabby vessels but capable of carrying men. By the breakwater entrances were the four powerful tugs based on Dover, the *Simla*, *Gondia*, *Roman* and *Lady Brassey*. It was most important there should be no delay in landing the troops, and passenger ships had to vacate a berth as soon as they had discharged their human freight. Other vessels bringing stores and ammunition for the warships and tankers to refuel the evacuation fleet had to berth at the forty or so buoys in the main harbour. In the never-ceasing surge and swell inside the sheltering arms of the breakwater the tugs were in constant demand. Then there was salvage work to be done in the Channel; all of which meant that the crews of the tugs got precious little sleep in the course of the nine days of the Dunkirk 'deliverance'.

☆

Dunkirk had been badly battered by the Luftwaffe since the middle of May, and on May 23 the British tanker *Spinel*, carrying a full load of oil and berthed in the main basin, was struck repeatedly and set on fire. The facilities in the inner harbour were destroyed in the blaze and the damage was so great that this part of the harbour was abandoned and never used during the evacuation. Three nights later, shortly after the Admiralty teleprinter had relayed the message empowering Ramsay to execute Operation Dynamo, the Dunkirk docks were again aflame. The water mains had been smashed forty-eight hours before so there was no means of controlling the blaze. As the fire spread along the seafront the destroyer H.M.S. *Wolsey* anchored just outside the port, to provide a radio link between Dunkirk and the Admiralty.

The first ship to participate in Operation Dynamo and to make the round trip from England to Dunkirk and back as a troop-carrier was the armed boarding vessel *Mona's Isle*. Leaving Dover soon after 9 p.m. on May 26, she berthed at the Quai Felix Faure during an air raid. There she took aboard 1420 troops, all she could possibly lift—the men standing jammed together on deck, in the cabins, the gangways and even in the galley. Off Gravelines on her way back to Dover, she was shelled by German shore batteries and damaged. By the time she reached Dover about noon on the 27th twenty-three men had been killed and sixty wounded.

May 27, disastrous for both the B.E.F. and the R.A.F. and catastrophic for Dunkirk, was to become known by the survivors as 'Bloody Monday'. Early in the morning the French on the western side of the perimeter were forced back to within five miles of the town, and with German artillery dominating the town and the normal approaches to Dover, Ramsay's ships were forced to approach the port by a round-about route (Route Y) until a central channel (Route X) could be

89

swept clear of mines As Route Y was more than twice the length of the direct passage, Route Z, the number of journeys made by the ships was consequently reduced. Then the Luftwaffe, concentrating its attacks against the town and harbour, created such havoc that the British troops had to be pulled back out of the town, and Captain Tennant—who had only arrived that morning—signalled Ramsay to say that evacuation from then on would have to take place solely from the beaches. The undersea cable which came ashore at La Panne was also severed, adding even further to communication problems. On top of these calamities, of course, came the news that the Belgians had capitulated.

During daylight that day Goering's 2nd and 3rd Air Fleets dropped more than 2000 tons of high explosive bombs, and about 30,000 incendiary bombs on Dunkirk. By nightfall the 115 acres of port installations had been completely flattened and the town had been reduced to rubble. Hotels, shops and other buildings around the main square, *Place Jean Bart*, had been set on fire by the incendiaries; the fifteenth-century Church of St Eloi was a smouldering ruin, and its famous carillon damaged beyond repair; 1000 civilians—men, women and children—were buried beneath the ashes of the town. Only the east and west moles could now be used as embarkation stages. These moles were long wooden gangways spanning concrete plinths, open at the sides to allow the sea to pass through and at high tide in a strong wind it would surge through and over the wooden staging. They had never been intended for use as loading bays; indeed the harbour authorities had always considered that mooring a small vessel alongside one or other of them was tantamount to consigning it to the deep. But they reached 1600 metres out into the open roadstead, and so Tennant decided that the destroyers at least could take a chance and use them as embarkation points. The troops lined up on the moles in columns, three abreast, and for the most part waited patiently hour after hour until their turn came to board ships for England.

The phased plan of evacuation, drawn up in Whitehall almost exactly a week before, had already broken down. Getting the wounded away—French as well as British—was a ghastly problem even before Operation Dynamo was given the go-ahead on May 26. Base hospitals had been overrun by the Germans and the field hospitals and casualty clearing centres that had to take over their work were now threatened. The Southern Railway ship *Canterbury* was one of the cross-Channel ferries whose peace-time avocation was the transport of Golden Arrow passengers to the Continent. Now her stately cabins had been gutted and she had been fitted out as a hospital ship, painted glistening white and handed over to the Admiralty—together with the other S.R. ferries *Maid of Kent*, *Brighton*, *Isle of Thanet*, *Isle of Guernsey*, *Dinard*, *Paris* and *Worthing*, all of which were classified as 'hospital carriers'.

On the afternoon of May 25 *Canterbury* set out for Dunkirk to collect wounded. She was shelled on the way out but arrived at Dunkirk in

H.M.S. Vivacious *takes its turn at the mole, shortly after an air-raid during which the trawler in the foreground received a direct hit.*

Two-stage embarkation— shore to ferry, and ferry to transport—was more complicated and sometimes more hazardous than embarkation from the moles.

the early evening. There she berthed at the *Gare Maritime*, the old peace-time berth of the cross-Channel steamers; it had been bombed but being a substantial stone structure could still be used. She took on board 1246 men and by 9.30 p.m. was back at Newhaven and preparing for her next voyage. (Preparations for another voyage often included the dreadful task of sorting the living from the dead, besides off-loading the casualties and the kit, and refuelling.) Meantime the *Isle of Thanet* and *Paris* had also sailed for Dunkirk and like the *Canterbury* had run the gauntlet of German shore batteries west of Calais. At Dunkirk the two ships moved alongside the *Canterbury* and started loading as soon as *Canterbury* had sailed. The quays were brilliantly lit by fires in the docks and the activity around the *Gare Maritime* was an all-too-clear inducement to the Luftwaffe pilots in the constant air attacks. One stick of bombs fell very close to the *Isle of Thanet* and loading in these conditions took nearly three hours. But 608 casualties were eventually taken on board and she sailed for Newhaven, the *Paris* following, and both reached port unscathed on the morning of the 26th.

That same morning the transport *Maid of Orleans* sailed for Dunkirk carrying water, military stores and a detachment of 250 troops. She got to Dunkirk but the harbour was being shelled and her master decided that he could not get in, so he turned round and returned to Dover. There he was told to go back and try again. This time the *Maid of Orleans* arrived safely and landed the troops, stores and water under cover of a thick pall of smoke from burning oil tanks. Meanwhile the *Canterbury* had returned and berthed on the outside of the *Maid of Orleans*. She arrived at 8.30 p.m., loaded 1340 casualties under almost continuous bombing and it was after midnight before she was away again. Earlier in the day two of the other hospital ships, the *Worthing* and the *Isle of Guernsey* had also appeared. They sailed with one of the S.R. transports, the *Mona's Queen* and as they approached Calais, in ruins and cloaked with smoke, a minor battle developed when two British destroyers opened fire on the shore batteries. The Germans responded and when the two hospital ships and the *Mona's Queen* found themselves in the line of fire they changed course. As they did so a flight of Stukas appeared and attacked them. The bombs fell close but missed and they reached Dunkirk to find a queue of motor ambulances awaiting the arrival of the hospital carriers. Both the *Worthing* and the *Isle of Guernsey* were loaded to capacity; the *Isle of Guernsey* which had beds for only 203 carried 346 by putting stretchers down between the beds, on the decks, in the gangways and anywhere else where it was possible for a man to lie down. There was an air raid during the embarkation, but the volume of anti-aircraft fire put up by the vessels in the harbour and the batteries on shore seems on this occasion to have deterred the Luftwaffe. When at 11 a.m. there was a lull, the two hospital ships pulled out and headed for home. On their way out of the harbour they passed some of the cross-Channel steamers loading civilians being

Taking the wounded aboard the destroyers from launches was invariably a difficult operation. Mercifully the sea were calm.

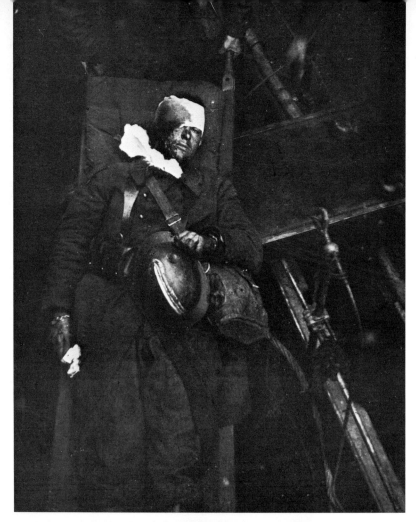

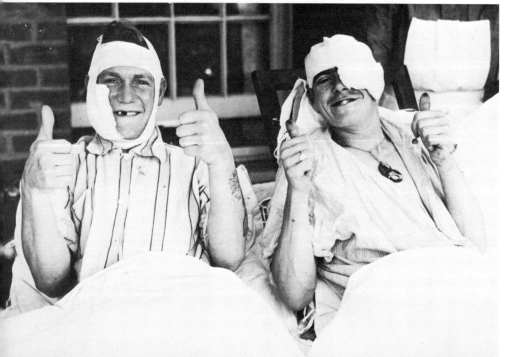

evacuated by the French authorities, and at the head of the pier there was the blackened hulk of the *Jaguar*; near her lay the wreck of another French destroyer, the *Orage*.

During these early days of the evacuation one or other of the Dover-based tugs often had to be sent across to Dunkirk on a rescue mission. H.M.S. *Winchester*, an old destroyer, was bombed on May 19 and could not move under her own power afterwards. So *Lady Brassey* was ordered to haul her back to England. As the stubby little tug approached Dunkirk a flight of Stukas pounced on her, but she was not hit and the damaged destroyer was taken in tow. After that it was merely a matter of steering a course fifty metres from the outer moles where a magnetic mine had been spotted, and keeping a sharp look out for other mines in the Channel. Five miles north-west of Calais the tug's crew reported seeing a bombed and derelict ship; this was the London steamer *Mavis*, one of the B.E.F's supply boats.

Like the *Lady Brassey* the other tugs had their fill of work on the English side of the Channel, in addition to rescue assignments. According to Captain G. D. Lowe, the master of the *Simla*:

> ...The tugs had orders to shift two destroyers from Admiralty Pier on May 24th, in the early hours of the morning to buoys in the harbour, to make room for other ships to berth. They were H.M.S. *Whitshed* and *Vimy*, but the crews of the destroyers were so tired and exhausted from their recent experience of Dunkirk that we let them sleep on, and shifted the destroyers without them. I expect that when they turned out from their much-needed sleep, they were surprised to find their ships in a different position, but were all fresh to go to sea again, and carry on the good work.
>
> During the very dark night of May 24th, the S.S. *Kohistan* (5,884 tons) was outside, waiting to berth at Admiralty Pier. She had about 6,000 troops aboard. The naval people wanted her to berth as soon as possible on account of enemy planes coming over. The job of berthing was not an easy one, for the harbour was full of other ships, no one being allowed to show any light. The tugs *Simla* and *Lady Brassey* decided to do the best they could. It was just like going into thick fog. You could not see the other ships or buoys in the harbour, and it was a great worry trying not to hit other ships. First we would scrape along one destroyer, then just miss another by a few feet. Well, with great care, I for one was pleased to get that ship on her berth without any mishap, and to know that the soldiers got ashore safely.

Veteran tugboat captains like Lowe, accustomed to a fast turn-round in a harbour where time was all important, were horrified by the slowness of the embarkation procedure at Dunkirk. Destroyers took seven hours loading about 1000 men. During this time they were held alongside with only a single turn of the mooring hawsers around the bollards on the mole. Boat hooks were needed to fend the destroyers off as they pitched, yawed and rolled with the surges of water created by exploding

95

bombs. Gangways between moles and ships were narrow planks. But stretcher cases came over them, then the walking wounded and finally the mass of the troops. Some men, who had been on the mole for hours, were 'bomb-happy'—hungry and hysterical.

Whatever their state of mind there can be little doubt that the troops on the beaches had tremendous respect for those they called the 'blue jobs'—the Royal Navy. Even in extreme cases of mutinous anger or fear the Navy held them in check. Captain E. A. R. Lang, a sapper who got away on May 29 writes of the sense of relief when he and his men saw the first British sailors:

> ... They were clean and cheerful with white blancoed leggings and pipe-clayed belts standing with fixed bayonets forming some kind of human chain to guide us down to the beach.
>
> As soon as our Cockney boys met the sailors a verbal battle started and the jokes were cracked in good taste and bad language, some of the following were typical: 'Blimey chum, what about a trip round the light-house?' 'Bye, bye china, where's yer little boat?' Anyhow these sailors were very brave and unperturbed, they were an inspiration and a tonic to us war-weary stragglers. When we arrived at what appeared to be the last sailor in the line down to the beach he told us that he was not doing any more that night as he had a billet and a drink to go to somewhere. . . .

Major C. K. Lewis, then a Staff Sergeant commanding a R.E.M.E. detachment of the 3rd Corps, writes in a similar vein:

> ... There seemed to be a general movement of men towards the south and I followed suit until coming nearer towards what turned out to be a long jetty. There stood a Royal Navy officer, impeccably dressed, and with a megaphone. He shouted that ships were coming alongside the jetty, that they would not tie-up, and that we should come along the jetty slowly, avoiding the large hole in the middle of it by going along the balustrade which was intact. He said that he would blow a whistle for each air attack and then everyone must freeze in a squatting position with their tin hats square on the top of their heads. This happened. The troops were magnificent and completely orderly and in my view this was entirely due to the complete and utter calmness of the naval officer. For at last we had some one who knew what he was doing and was palp-ably in charge. . . .

But some of those who had come to fetch the soldiers were equally impressed by the men who had fought their way down from the Dyle to Dunkirk. Lt-Col. P. B. Longdon, a doctor, whose military training came to an abrupt end when he was sent to the destroyer H.M.S. *Anthony*, to serve as a surgeon during the evacuation, says:

> ... We went straight into the Mole at Dunkirk, which was under shell fire from the Germans. We took off what was left of the Guards. They marched down the Mole in threes and in step. The N.C.O. i/c said

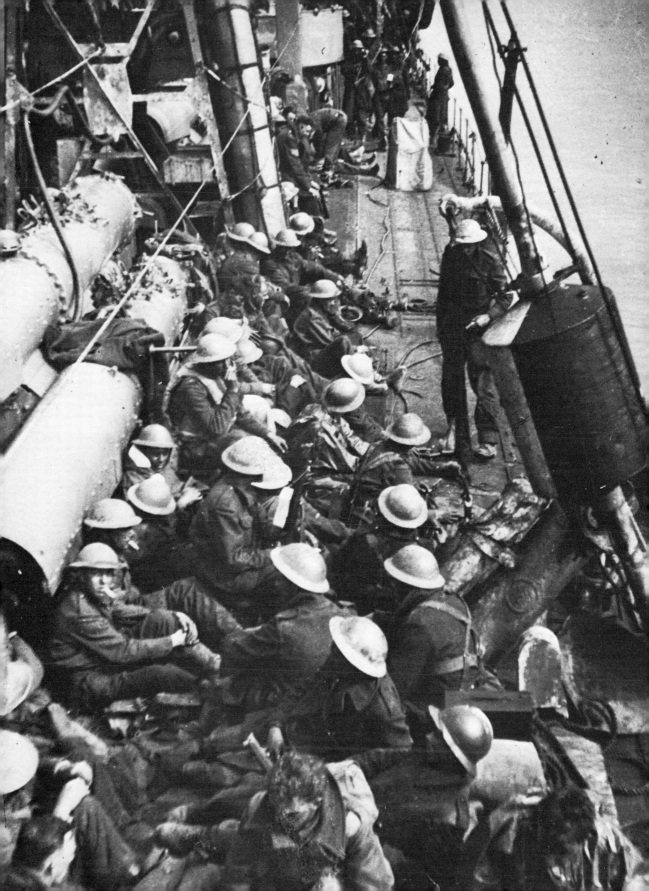

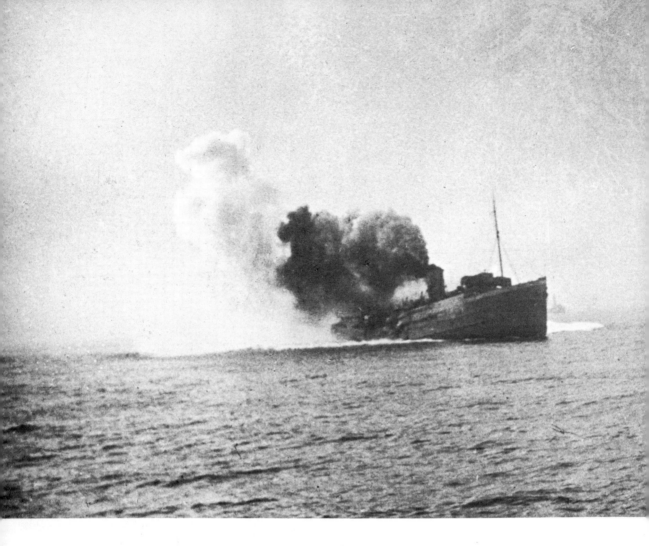

'Guards, 'Alt.' 'Guards, left turn', 'Guards will embark'. I think there was about 1000 of them and they embarked under fire in about 20 mins. (My times and numbers may vary, as it was a long time ago.)

When the ship began to leave, the Bren gunners were divided into two groups. One set up in the bows, and the others in the stern, where they fired at any German aircraft which came near enough. The remainder of the Guards began to clean their weapons and get ready for action. The next day we crawled into Dover as we had had another near miss, and could only move very slowly (approx 5 knots).

I remember it was a superb day and the sky was clear. The R.A.F. had kept German planes away from us during the daylight hours. They (the Germans) got at us at night as they could see the wake of the destroyer.

The Guards paraded on the quay side at Dover and marched to the trains. Unshaven, tired out, very strained indeed with rifles spotless. In my opinion the finest soldiers in the world. . . .

Not all the ships made it. Mona's Queen, the Liverpool and Isle of Man steamer, is seen here after striking a mine off Dunkirk on May 29.

But not all matelots were happy about the way things were going. Mr S. Payne, who was a young signalman on H.M.S. *Vega*, an old World War I destroyer converted to an anti-submarine-cum-anti-aircraft role, has written a vivid account of his recollections:

...The *Vega* was on East Coast convoy duties, ambling up and down the East coast of England from Sheerness to the Firth of Forth. We had been doing this for a year or so and had fallen into a set routine; up and down, up and down; peaceful and serene.

Suddenly the war came alive! We sailed from Sheerness, with utmost despatch and instead of turning north went south to France and trouble. We were sent to Calais but before arriving were diverted to Le Havre. We never got there either, being diverted again. Our radio operators were working overtime, trying to keep pace with streams of signals. ... We were passed by three of our sister ships, steaming at full speed towards the French coast. I think they were the *Viceroy*, *Vimy* and *Vortigen*. An exchange of visual signals told us that they were on the way to land a detachment of Guards direct from the Palace. This is it, I thought, as I read the signal; the Guards will sort it out.

I heard later that the Guards were landed at some little inlet and doubled smartly away to engage the enemy, and the radio operator on *Vimy* swore that he received three signals from them: 'Enemy in sight' ... 'Am engaging' ... 'Am surrendering'.

We intercepted one signal; the three destoyers were asking for fighter assistance; these signals were in the form of a 'Help' message and broadcast in plain language:

'Help. 50 plus JU 87 ... and the ships position ...' (Translated this meant 'Am being attacked by 50 plus Dive Bombers. Send Fighter assistance.')

The reply they received—in equally plain language – was 'Do the Best You Can. No fighters available.' Hell, I thought, the Navy has become expendable. I suppose their Lordships don't think these old destroyers are worth bothering about.

I was soon to learn why there were no fighters available. We were ordered to Dunkirk ... where a pall of black smoke hung in the sky. No need to navigate, all we had to do was to steer for the smoke and watch out for sandbanks. Later, as the pace of evacuation warmed up, one followed the stream of craft of all shapes and sizes plying between Dunkirk and Dover. It reminded me of August bank holiday—trips round the harbour at a bob a time.

My first sight of a sinking ship was the destroyer *Wakefield*, one of our class, with just her forecastle sticking out of the water. We heard later that one of her crew had sworn not to get his feet wet, and had sat on her anchor until a rescue craft came alongside, and he stepped off without wetting his feet.

Shortly after this by the grace of God my own ship escaped a similar fate. Two torpedoes passed directly under us amidships—obviously fired from a sub. I can only assume that they were either set to run too deep or that their depth-setting mechanism was faulty. Be that as it may they missed and we promptly plastered the area with depth charges. However

99

as a direct result of this incident we lost our starboard lookout. He was an old pensioner recalled for the war and he stuttered badly. He saw the tracks of the torpedoes approaching but by the time he could get the report out they were already passed; it must have been the same U-boat who had accounted for *Wakefield*. We claimed a possible sunk or severely damaged, and we must have done something because we had no more trouble from the U-boats.

The original plan was to lift the B.E.F. off from the mole, which must be known to millions of holiday makers. This entailed ships going alongside, securing bow and stern, and when fully loaded coming out astern, turning and making for home. A lengthy manœuvre, plus the fact that the mole made an ideal aiming point for the droves of Ju 87s which came over from dawn to dusk. There were many soldiers who with rescue at their finger tips bought it on that mole; sailors too of course. H.M.S. *Imogen* received a bomb which went straight down her funnel as she was leaving the mole loaded with troops. She literally disintegrated. The few who survived then had to start all over again to find transport, and the sailors who had been transporters now had to look for transport themselves.

We hated the mole, to us it was just a question of time before a bomb with our number on it was dropped. Thank heavens we moved over to the beaches, where we remained for the whole of the evacuation, giving what help we could.

My last impression of Dunkirk: The same pall of smoke hanging in the sky and German tanks popping over the ridge loosing off a couple of rounds and nipping back again. This must be one of the only cases on record of destroyer versus tank....

☆

By the evening of May 27 Captain Tennant at Dunkirk was far from satisfied with the rate of evacuation and shortly before 8 p.m. he sent a long message to Ramsay. Novel and quicker methods must be used, he said. The moles were too restricted; the beaches between Dunkirk and La Panne at the eastern end of the Perimeter must be brought into use. And he concluded with the demand 'Please send every available craft to beaches east of Dunkirk immediately. Evacuation tomorrow is problematical.' Twenty-five minutes later he followed up with another priority signal 'Port continuously bombed all day and on fire. Embarkation possible only from beaches east of harbour.... Send all ships and passenger ships there to anchor.'

The bigger ships would continue to carry the main burden. But a vital part of the evacuation programme was now being allocated to the small craft. They would ferry the men from the beaches and get them to the ships offshore.

rvivors from the stricken
ona's Queen, *pulling*
ngside H.M.S.
nquisher.

Over the page
Goodbye to Dunkirk—some of the rescued troops en route to England at last.

101

6. Hell's Delight

Midnight May 26 – 8 a.m. May 30

'For four or five days an intense struggle raged. Their armoured divisions, or what was left of them, together with great masses of German artillery and infantry, hurled themselves in vain upon the ever-narrowing and contracting appendix upon which the French and British armies fought.

Meanwhile, the Royal Navy, with the willing help of countless merchant seamen and a host of volunteers, strained every nerve to embark the British and Allied troops. . . . They had to operate upon a difficult coast, and often under adverse weather conditions and under an almost ceaseless hail of bombs and increasing concentrations of artillery fire. Nor were the seas themselves free from mines or torpedoes.

It was in conditions such as these that our men carried on with little or no rest for days and nights, making trip after trip across the dangerous waters. The numbers they have brought back are the measure of their devotion and courage.'

From Winston Churchill's statement to the House of Commons,
4 June 1940

Throughout the night of 'Bloody Monday', May 27, naval officers scoured boatyards and backwaters along the rivers and the southern coast of England for craft that might be of use at Dunkirk. Civil servants, slashing red tape and working with unusual and unaccustomed celerity and with the minimum of formality quickly cleared the administrative problems relating to the use of 'civilian' boats. It was agreed that the Ministry of Transport would pay the crews and all travelling expenses, buy whatever stores might be needed to equip the boats, and compensate the owners for any damage or loss.

The first fifty of the craft that were requisitioned for what the Admiralty was calling 'a special requirement' were mustered at Sheerness during the night. But when these boats were inspected most of them were pronounced unsuitable. Meanwhile the search had been extended to the Upper Thames and to East Coast yachting centres like Burnham and Brightlingsea. This yielded forty motor-boats and launches which were sent to Sheerness on the morning of the 28th. Only a few of them managed to get to the Dunkirk beaches by May 29, but they were the fore-runners of the 200 to 300 small boats engaged in the final and exceptionally perilous phases of Operation Dynamo.

A naval officer at Ramsgate was made responsible for the fuelling and marshalling of all the small power-boats. When they were despatched each of them towed rowing boats needed to form what the Navy termed the 'inshore flotilla'. (At this point it is perhaps worth explaining that the current plan was for the troops on the beaches to be rowed out to water deep enough for shallow draft launches to take them in tow. The launches would then tow the boats to bigger ships— transports and the like—at anchor, which in turn would carry the troops to a home port. In the event this system was often short-circuited, and one man with a rowing boat is supposed to have rowed three times back and forth all the way across the Channel carrying a few soldiers. Nor did all the launches bother to transfer their loads to the transport vessels; indeed it was often not expedient to do so.) During the nine days of the evacuation the records show that 170 craft were serviced and minor mechanical defects attended to at the Ramsgate base. These included skoots, tugs, drifters, trawlers and lighters as well as motor-boats and launches ranging from open-decked sixteen footers to large and luxurious diesel yachts.

A number of barges in the Thames were also commandeered and towed to Dunkirk astern some of the more powerful motor-boats. From Sheerness alone 100 motor boats, ten self-propelled lighters, seven skoots, an oil tanker, six paddle-steamers and an unrecorded number of rowing boats were despatched to Dunkirk. From ports all over Britain other vessels of almost every conceivable type were also moving towards the nub of the evacuation scene. Regular mine-sweepers—the famous 'Smoky Joes'—auxiliary paddle-sweepers, herring drifters, trawlers and ships of the deep-sea fishing fleets from Hull and Grimsby and motor torpedo boats (MTBs) were all mobilized for the evacuation.

It was inevitable that the vast number of vessels converging on the Channel ports would create traffic problems. Only a few of what Ramsay proudly called his 'cockleshell navy' were professional sailors. The rest were weekend yachtsmen—lawyers, doctors, retired stockbrokers, Service officers, journalists, clerks etc—and not many of them knew much about navigation. The skippers and crews of the Merchant Navy were a different matter, of course. They had forgotten more about seamanship than many of the young officers aboard some of the naval vessels had ever learned, and there were a few clashes between the old salts and the duration-only sailors of the Royal Navy. Jim Uglow tells of one such clash at this time:

> Captain Bennett was a phlegmatic type when at sea and it took a lot to ruffle him. As the MTB drew near we observed a young officer on the bridge clothed in a peaked cap and vivid striped pyjamas, and with a megaphone to his mouth. After asking the names of our two ships, he ordered us to the Owers lightship until sunrise. This may have been fair enough but he added that gauche remark 'Don't you know there is a war on?" Bennett, who was leaning on his port bridge rail, removed his pipe from his mouth, picked up a megaphone and shouted 'You won't win it in your fucking pyjamas, will you.'

Naval Control at Ramsgate issued about 1000 charts to the various vessels taking part in the evacuation. Approximately 600 of these had the routes inscribed for the skippers of boats who had no means of laying them out; together with the charts 500 sets of detailed instructions were issued. By May 28 it was considered that the direct route Z was impractical in daylight; it was too vulnerable to air attack. Most of the ships were therefore directed to use Route Y until Route X was cleared of mines. Sweeping began at noon on May 27 and this hazardous task was done by the destroyer H.M.S. *Impulsive* with the minesweepers *Skipjack* and *Halcyon* and the Trinity House pilot boat *Patricia*; when they

The ordeal through which these troops have passed is reflected on their faces.

had finished, the Dover–Dunkirk round trip was shortened by sixty-four sea miles.

In the beginning none of the cockleshell craft were armed. Seventy-five of the bigger motor-boats, skoots and tugs were issued with Lewis guns for use in an anti-aircraft role. And as no more were available they were moved around from vessel to vessel during the course of the operation. Twenty-three naval ratings and fourteen men of the Royal Army Service Corps who had been trained in the operation of the Lewis gun (or more especially in the handling of stoppages in the Lewis gun) were sent to man the guns aboard some of the small boats. But troops on the homeward run generally provided their own anti-aircraft defence—using their own Bren guns and rifles.

Finding suitable people to handle the different types of motor boats that were commandeered proved to be difficult. Compounded with this were the problems arising from boats being laid up and their motors not being touched since the spring of 1939. So it was necessary for teams of mechanics to check the boats out before they were handed over to their 'drivers' as the Royal Navy termed the men who were to command the craft. Fresh water, rations, first-aid kits as well as charts also had to be issued before the boats could be away. All the 'drivers' and their crews were volunteers, and many who sailed for Dunkirk arrived straight from their civilian jobs and were lacking the kit—sweaters, rubber-soled shoes, oilskins etc.—generally associated with the boating fraternity, when they went aboard.

A destroyer brings its human cargo back to Dover harbour.

Fortunately during the nine days of the evacuation the weather in the Channel was exceptionally favourable. In the words of Signalman Payne,

> . . . The English Channel is a notorious stretch of water calculated to affect the hardiest of stomachs, yet for days it suddenly remained calmer than a mill pond. During the entire lift off of that multitude not a ripple was seen. This allowed men to stand up to their shoulders in water and boats to operate with a few inches of freeboard, loaded to double and treble their safe carrying capacity. The calm sea was the miracle of Dunkirk.

The calm conditions were primarily due to the prevailing wind around Dunkirk remaining westerly; a north wind which would eventually have been disastrous for boats trying to get to the beaches blew for only part of one day. Wave heights were also less than normal even for May and June, so conditions were such that even the smallest of craft could operate. There were, however, only two and a half days without haze, fog or cloud; and Luftwaffe records repeatedly refer to the lack of 'good bombing conditions', for when the mist descended the German pilots had difficulty in pin-pointing their targets. On the other hand the fog produced problems for the ships, especially at night. In the congested wreckstrewn waters off Dunkirk collisions were all too frequent as the

107

blacked-out vessels shuttled at speed between Dunkirk and the English Channel ports, and some of the volunteer crews of the smaller craft refused to operate in such conditions.

Few of the 'drivers' and their crews had, in fact, any real idea of what they would encounter before they had finished at Dunkirk. They volunteered for what they knew would be a great and grave adventure, but they could not have anticipated the days and the nights of exhausting effort and the conditions under which they would have to work. The carnage, the fear, the noise and the uncertainty were all beyond the margins of imagination, and had no part in their former experiences. Even the Luftwaffe pilots were revolted by the cold-blooded point-blank devastation they were creating. Sensitive, highly-strung Paul Temme, the *Flugzeugfuhrer* of an Me 109, said, 'I hated Dunkirk. It was just unadulterated killing. The beaches were jammed full of soldiers. I went up and down at three hundred feet hose-piping.'

The first of the little ships to be used at Dunkirk went in to the beaches east of the port on May 29. Meanwhile the bigger vessels, designated 'transports' or 'personnel carriers', continued to evacuate large numbers of the B.E.F. On May 26 Ramsay had fifteen of these ships either in Dover or nearby ports. Most of them were the cross-Channel and Irish Sea passenger boats, but there were also seventeen British registered ships and three others under the Belgian or Dutch flag which had been earmarked as troop transports, at Southampton. Additionally six coasters and sixteen barges had been concentrated at Deal, together with most of the flotilla of skoots and fifteen motor torpedo boats. Apart from the cross-Channel ferries the heterogeneous collection of craft at Dover that could be used totalled about fifty, but this included the tugs.

The cross-Channel and Irish Sea ships were manned for the most part by veteran crews, and their officers knew the French coast like the back of their hands and so were capable of handling vessels there in any sort of weather. This was just as well, because the buoys marking the channels through the miles of off-shore shoals had been either destroyed or removed. The Kwinte Buoy, an important turning point for Dunkirk Roads (that expanse of deep water which runs east and west parallel to the coast) was still intact, and so were the lightships marking the desolate reaches of the Goodwin Sands. But the rest of the navigation aids had to be guessed at, and a wrong guess could mean disaster. Fortunately the navigators of the Channel steamers carried a vivid mental picture of the routes and the hazards. Long experience had given them an understanding of the tidal changes and currents in the Dunkirk Roads. (The tides at Dunkirk reach a height of nineteen feet (5·8 metres) and on May 26, six hours before high water the current direction was recorded as 226° with a speed of 2·3 knots; an hour before

Luftwaffe air operations at Dunkirk, May 30. (Note that the German bombers had to travel a considerable distance to their targets, and that a large part of the air effort came from the VIII Air Corps in direct support of the Wehrmacht.)

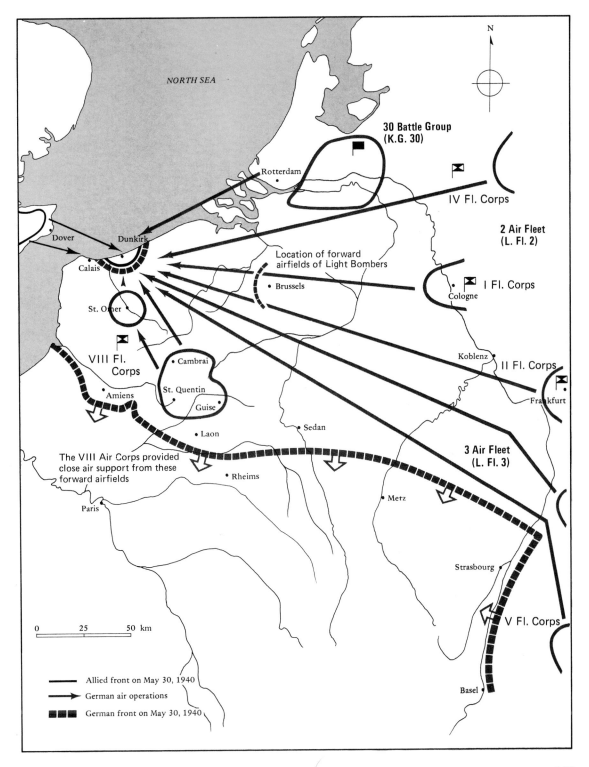

NORTH SEA

30 Battle Group
(K.G. 30)

IV Fl. Corps

2 Air Fleet
(L. Fl. 2)

Rotterdam

Dover

Dunkirk

Calais

Location of forward
airfields of Light Bombers

Brussels

I Fl. Corps

Cologne

St. Omer

Koblenz

II Fl. Corps

VIII Fl.
Corps

Cambrai

Frankfurt

Amiens

St. Quentin

Guise

Laon

Sedan

3 Air Fleet
(L. Fl. 3)

The VIII Air Corps provided
close air support from these
forward airfields

Rheims

Metz

Paris

Strasbourg

0   25   50 km

V Fl. Corps

Basel

Allied front on May 30, 1940

German air operations

German front on May 30, 1940

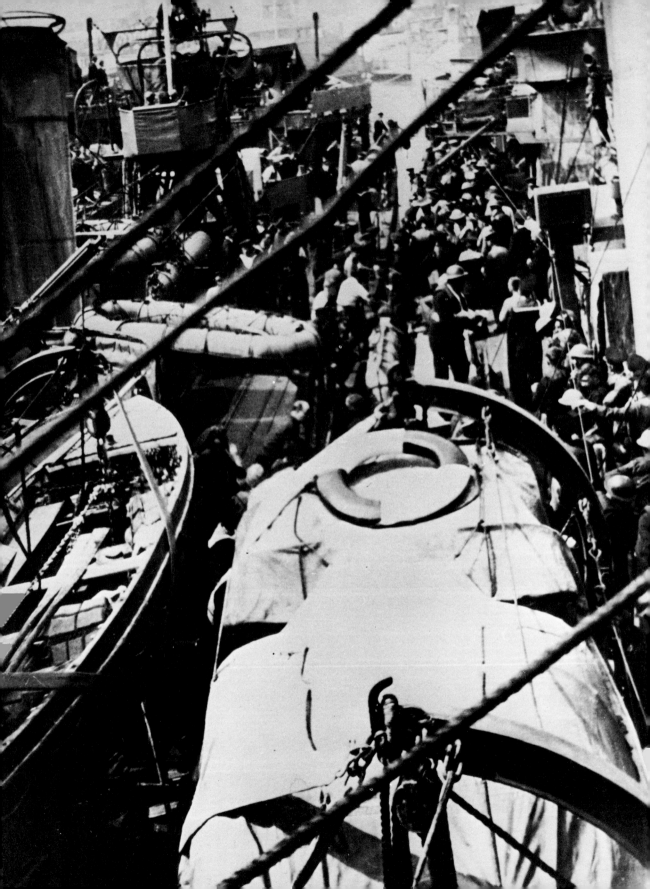

highwater the direction changed to 057° and the speed increased to 2·6 knots.)

With the inception of Dynamo the beaches were measured and designated from west to east: A. B. C. D. But on May 29 the system was simplified and the stretch of beach from one mile east of Dunkirk to one mile east of La Panne was divided into three equal sections known from east to west as La Panne, Bray and St Malo—with a mile gap between sections.

One of the cross-Channel steamers was the first transport to suffer severe damage. On May 27 the *Queen of the Channel* was ordered to Dunkirk. She was a fast motor-ship and had been employed for some months on a daily service to Boulogne carrying B.E.F. men going on leave from France, and back again. This service had stopped at the start of Operation *Sichelschnitt* and her last job had been to take the Irish Guards to Boulogne. Now she sailed on a rescue mission.

The voyage to Dunkirk was virtually devoid of incident and the *Queen*

111

of the Channel berthed about 8 p.m. at the east pier and started to embark troops. However German artillery had found the range of the pier, and before she had more than fifty soldiers aboard her master, Captain O'Dell, was ordered to move. Anchoring about three-quarters of a mile off the beach, and—using four of her boats (not all of them since O'Dell reckoned his ship might be hit and he would need boats for the men already aboard)—proceeded to ferry troops from the shore. About 200 men were ferried aboard but it was a slow business, and by about 11 p.m. when it was really dark O'Dell decided to take his ship back to the pier where it would be quicker. Three boats were collected—nobody knew what happened to the fourth; and back at the east pier again another 700 troops were embarked.

Shortly before 3 a.m. on the morning of May 28 the *Queen of the Channel* sailed from Dunkirk and O'Dell ordered the troops below. Just over an hour later the ship was attacked by a single bomber. Three or four bombs bracketed her and although there was no direct hit the ship was blown out of the water and broke her back. An SOS call was put out on the radio, the boats lowered, and the pumps started. But the *Queen of the Channel* was sinking fast and it was clear that she would have to be abandoned. Yet the boats could not accommodate 950 soldiers and the crew. Luckily, another ship, the *Dorrien Rose* was at hand.

The *Dorrien Rose* was an elderly tramp used to carry supplies to the B.E.F. On the previous morning (the 27th) her master, Captain William Thompson, had been ordered to get across to Dunkirk without delay. Neither Thompson nor anyone else aboard the *Dorrien Rose* had any idea that the situation in Flanders had deteriorated so much or with such rapidity. But ten miles away from Dunkirk they saw Dunkirk in flames. 'We were within ten miles of the port,' Thompson recorded, 'and being almost dark it looked and sounded appalling. So I decided to reverse my course and to proceed until daylight presented a better opportunity of seeing what was happening ashore.'

Dawn revealed a host of ships heading towards Dunkirk and a lot of air activity; then came a 'Mayday' message: *The Queen of the Channel* was sinking. Thompson went to her assistance immediately and the *Dorrien Rose* pulled alongside the stricken *Queen* to facilitate the transfer of her passengers and crew. 'The operation,' wrote Captain Thompson, 'was carried out in thirty-five minutes, despite three attempts by Jerry to intervene; one determined gunner cooled his ardour with tracer bullets.' With over 1000 souls aboard—her normal complement being thirteen—the *Dorrien Rose* then cast off and made for Dover, where she arrived shortly after 2 p.m. after being attacked eight times by enemy aircraft. 'We were now very well armed,' Captain Thompson said, 'as there were numerous machine-gun squads among the army units... and we had the cheering satisfaction of seeing our last attacker baling out, but to whose shot I don't know.' Having discharged the troops at Dover, the *Dorrien Rose* took in water and stores and left for

Dunkirk again the following afternoon. Due to a collision with 'some submerged object' she did not arrive at Dunkirk until next morning, May 30. There 'the prospect was far from pleasing, as the last ten miles to the port were littered with sunken and blazing ships. . . . Bombers were paying us frequent visits. . . . The port lay under a pall of oily smoke and flames. There was no one to look to for instructions, so we poked into the harbour. Someone ashore gestured us alongside a battered wall.' For two hours, in which it seemed there were always bombers overhead, the *Dorrien Rose* remained at the battered wall, loading troops who arrived in small parties. Other troops ran down the quay to catch food thrown to them. During that time her chief engineer was very busy at the back end of the boilers, as he was anxious that her elderly engines should be ready to give their full horsepower and more in getting away. Even at the back of the boilers he could feel the concussion of exploding bombs. With 600 troops aboard, and two bombs just missed, the *Dorrien Rose* left the harbour. 'The Channel was now a navigator's nightmare, with buoys missing, wrecks and wreckage all over the place.' The boatswain found another strangeness. 'That's the first time,' he said, 'that I've ever left Dunkirk without having to round up the crew out of the cafés.'

Having landed her troops at Folkestone, the *Dorrien Rose* had to anchor outside. She could not return to Dunkirk because her old engines had protested against the abnormal high pressure steaming. Her engine-room crew spent the night trying to repair one of the boilers and while the ship lay at anchor the Luftwaffe dropped half a dozen magnetic mines around her. An open-mouthed crew watched minesweepers explode these the following morning. She lay at Folkestone until she was able to limp off to Newhaven on the Saturday. She had been at work for six days and nights with a minimum of rest for everyone and none for her engine-room staff; she had transported some 1600 persons to England; and, but for her engines, she would have fetched more. For their services her master, her mate and her chief engineer each received the Distinguished Service Cross; and her boatswain the Distinguished Service Medal.

Of the forty-five troop transports employed in Operation Dynamo, eight were sunk and six were so badly damaged by bombing or gunfire that they had to be withdrawn; two others were badly damaged in collisions. Furthermore nine of the bigger vessels had already been involved in the operations at Calais, Boulogne and Dieppe even before the evacuation of Dunkirk started, and their officers and crews alike were already feeling the strain.

The *St Seiriol* might be considered as one of the luckier ships, although how she survived was a miracle in itself. She was not new, having served for years as a 'pleasure steamer' on the Irish Sea run from Llandudno to Bangor and back. Most of her crew were middle-aged and her master, Captain R. D. Dobbs, and her chief officer, Mr J.

These French soldiers writing letters home do not appear to have grasped the reality of the situation . . .

. . . although many of them were certainly apprehensive.

McNamee, were both nearly sixty. Nevertheless the *St Seiriol* made seven runs to Dunkirk, carrying an average of 900 troops on each trip. At the end, having had very little rest and under constant strain, the whole crew was in an advanced state of physical and nervous exhaustion.

On May 27 the *St Seiriol* sailed for Dunkirk with the motor-ship *Queen of the Channel* and was first alongside the pier. Of the conditions there John McNamee reported:

> There was an air raid in progress as we arrived alongside. Our guns with others were in action. We landed a man on the pier to hang onto our ropes. About 8 p.m. Lieutenant-Commander Williams, R.N. came on board and told the captain to proceed out of the harbour, lower his boats, and get the men on board from the beach. We got to the anchorage. I lowered the first boat in charge of the second officer and the second boat in charge of Boatswain R. Thomas. The third boat was taken by the crew of a trawler.

It was a dark night and Captain Dobbs was operating in an unfamiliar environment. But burning buildings lit up the beach, the boats were doing great work and Dobbs decided to return to the harbour. 'When I was about to lower the fourth boat,' McNamee reported later,

> we received information that there were a number of troops arriving at the pier. With the remainder of the crew we still had on board we proceeded alongside the pier. We got about 600 men on board; they were arriving in batches; about 11 p.m. we were told there were no more men in the vicinity, so we cut our mooring ropes. On hearing more men running along the pier we got the ship alongside the pier again and got about 80 more men aboard. During our stay alongside the pier we had four air raids. While we were leaving the pier the enemy dropped illuminated parachutes which lit up the whole sea front. Our captain backed the vessel up the harbour under the smoke screen made available to us from the burning town of Dunkirk.
>
> We then proceeded to try and pick up our boats and crew, but were ordered by a destroyer to proceed to Dover via Calais. When off Calais we were attacked by bombs and machine-gun fire, the plane coming down to the level of the navigation bridge, but fortunately for us a destroyer was passing at the time and came into action and the plane was destroyed.

When the *St Seiriol* left for Dover about midnight her lounges and saloons were crammed with troops, and the crew's quarters—including Dobbs's and McNamee's cabins along with those of the other ship's officers—were fully occupied by wounded men.

The *St Seiriol* was back at Dunkirk on May 28 when the trip was uneventful, and again on May 29 when she was under heavy attack. Arriving at Dunkirk during the afternoon she went alongside with the paddle steamer *Fenella*, which was lying next to the modern oil-burning passenger ship *Crested Eagle*. As the Llandudno vessel was not directly connected to the shore she reverted to the ferrying system, using three boats—one commanded by John McNamee, another by the *St Seiriol*'s second officer and the third by her boatswain. Each boat took an average of forty-seven soldiers who waded out from the beaches until they were neck-deep, holding their rifles over their heads. Getting them into the boats was then a problem. Apart from seeing that those who could scramble up did not overturn the boat, many were numb with cold, suffering from shock, lack of food and sleep, and could not pull themselves into the boat. So the *St Seiriol*'s boat crews, grappling soggy collars, equipment straps and—in desperation—men's hair with wet slippery hands, had to drag them aboard. All the time the strafing and bombing continued incessantly.

Meantime the *Fenella* was loading troops and stretcher cases directly from the quay and by about 5 p.m. she had taken between 600 and 700 men on board. It was then that one or other of the planes of the three *Geschwader* of Stukas overhead scored a direct hit on the *Fenella*'s promenade deck, and a few minutes later a huge slab of concrete quay was blown through the ship's side into the engine-room and flooded it. Another bomb, falling between the ship and the jetty, completed the wrecking of the engines.

As the *Fenella* was doomed the troops on board had to disembark, and they transferred to the *Crested Eagle*. Once they were off his ship the master of the *Fenella*, Captain W. Cubbon, reported to the naval Piermaster and suggested that if a tug could be made available, he would tow the *Fenella* away from the quay and so free the berth. There was no tug and no other vessel capable of towing available, he was told; what was more there was no time—Cubbon and his crew should go aboard the *Crested Eagle*. 'Unfortunately,' Cubbon duly reported, 'this ship was herself bombed and set on fire within ten minutes of leaving the jetty, and had to be beached. I regret to say that this caused a number of casualties, among them sixteen of the *Fenella*'s crew, who lost their lives.'

From Cubbon's words it is not possible to get a proper idea of what happened. The *Crested Eagle* was an oil-burning ship, and she became a blazing furnace. Many men were seen to jump overboard, and by the time she was run ashore the ship was a glowing red-hot hulk. John McNamee of the *St Seiriol* took a boat across to help in the rescue work, and he and his crew toiled for over five hours to save men from the flames. Heat prevented the rescuers from getting right up to the stricken *Crested Eagle*, but 150 men were pulled from the water. These were taken aboard the *St Seiriol* and back to England as soon as Captain Dobbs could get under way—two of them dying en route. The remainder were burned to death, drowned, or so badly scalded by the escaping steam that they did not live long. As a result of his efforts in the rescue McNamee also became a casualty. He got back to the *St Seiriol* where

his legs suddenly gave way. He was suffering from temporary paralysis caused by extreme fatigue, said the doctor who examined him at Dover. But McNamee refused to leave his ship; the paralysis would go of its own accord, he told the doctor; moreover he had work to do. And he stayed aboard the *St Seiriol*, regained the use of his legs and kept on with the other runs the ship made to Dunkirk.

The sinking of the *Fenella* and the *Crested Eagle* was only a fraction of the damage inflicted by the Luftwaffe on the crowded shipping that Wednesday afternoon of May 29. One of the new Ju 88s scored an impressive success by sinking the 6900-ton *Clan MacAlister*, laden with landing-craft sent over to assist in the evacuation. She was the largest ship used at Dunkirk and was bombed and set ablaze while embarking troops. A destroyer, H.M.S. *Malcolm*, steamed alongside to take off the soldiers, but boxes of small ammunition stacked on the deck which were exploding in the flames were an additional hazard. When more German aircraft flew in for the kill the *Malcolm* had to cast off, and the *Clan MacAlister* crew had eventually to be taken aboard the minesweeper, H.M.S. *Pangbourne*, and the ship abandoned to her fate.

Meantime, having dealt with the *Fenella* and *Crested Eagle*, the Stukas concentrated on a compact group of five British and three French destroyers which, with the other transports and half-a-dozen trawlers were embarking troops at the Mole. First to go was the destroyer H.M.S. *Grenade*, which was struck by one bomb, turning her slender hull into a charnel house. Blazing fiercely, her mooring lines parted and she drifted away from the jetty. Further explosions ripped through the crippled ship as desperate attempts were made to get her clear of the harbour entrance. She sank eventually just off the harbour mouth and most of her crew were casualties. Blast and fragments of steel destroyed the upperworks of the French destroyer *Mistral* when a bomb

117

freshment arrangements
re provided by the army at
e railway stations serving
ports of disembarkation.

smashed into the quay alongside where she was berthed. Fortunately her two sister ships—close to the *Mistral* and and laden with troops—were undamaged.

H.M.S. *Jaguar*, a smart new destroyer, was also hit and badly damaged but she managed to struggle clear of the harbour, as did the *Verity*, although she too was damaged when grounded outside. Ultimately, when the trawlers *Calvi* and *Polly Johnson* received direct hits and disintegrated, all attempts to embark men from the mole were abandoned, and a message was sent to Ramsay saying that because of this raid the mole was useless for further embarkation. Although this proved to be a false alarm, it led to the bulk of the ships en route to Dunkirk being switched to the beaches—with consequent delay and a slowing down of the loading rate.

Off the beaches other vessels were also badly knocked about that day. One of these was the *Yewdale*, a little tramp which normally carried a crew of eleven, but which had taken some 900 troops aboard during the afternoon. Soldiers had been stowed wherever soldiers could be stowed; some were wounded, some were exhausted. Twenty-seven army officers were packed into the saloon, the mate's cabin and the ship's officers' lavatory. Among them was an R.A.M.C. subaltern who was kept busy throughout the passage back to England, for the *Yewdale* had to run a gauntlet of Stukas. A sergeant of the Durham Light Infantry was credited with some good shooting with one of the *Yewdale*'s Lewis guns and it was claimed that he brought down one of the attackers. But the *Yewdale* was badly hit; the wheelhouse was destroyed, the binnacle smashed, the ship's sides holed in several places and steam pipes fractured. Seven of the soldiers were killed and seventy-seven wounded; the mate received a wound that disabled him permanently and others of the crew were also hit. In spite of this the *Yewdale* limped on to anchor off Deal at 11 p.m. There she had to wait until a lifeboat came out to her with a doctor at 6 a.m. the following morning (May 30). Finally at 8 a.m. she was able to land her troops at Ramsgate. On May 27 and May 30 both the master and mate of the *Yewdale* celebrated their birthdays; Dunkirk was a party they were to remember for the rest of their lives.

☆

By the morning of May 30 Ramsay's staff had learned that the ships could usually take more of a pounding than their crews. Men could go on for just so long, and then they reached a point where nature's defence mechanism came into play. Deck officers' feet swelled so badly that their shoes had to be cut from them; engine-room staff, deafened by the peals of fearful thuds caused by exploding bombs compressing the water against the sides of the hull, were no longer able to cope with signals from the bridge; men were badly scalded when steampipes

119

Civilian organizations, such as the Salvation Army, also helped to provide refreshments.

ruptured; stokers with loaded shovels poised in front of an open furnace, were pitched forward and burned when a ship bucked and gyrated during an air attack; others who were thrown off their feet or lost their balance, got up bruised and sometimes half-crazed. Steersmen forgot the course they were supposed to be following, or looked blankly at a compass whose cardinal points had become for them a vague blur. Gunners fell asleep standing by their guns; old salts, who had been at sea all their working lives—including some who had served in World War I—lost the ability to cope with the effects of disaster. The sight of so many men blown to pieces or drowning, and of mutilated corpses and horrific wounds, was too much for them. Wills were eroded by sight, sound, smell and shock, and after three or four trips to Dunkirk some of the sailors could no longer tie a bowline or run a hawser around a pair of bitts. They cowered when they saw a Stuka peel off into a dive and sometimes screamed when they heard its bombs whistling towards their ship.

But the greatest need for replacements was among the engine-room personnel. They worked in a claustrophobic environment, and there was never any let-up in their work. In the English ports, at sea and at Dunkirk, shafts, pinions and bearings had to be re-aligned or repaired. Violent vibrations due to near-miss bombs caused pumps to seize-up; rivets holding steel plates were shattered and the plates would peel back like banana skins. Bombs and shells pierced great holes in the ships' sides and tarpaulins or mattresses would have to be stuffed into the holes to keep the water out until a more permanent repair could be effected in Dover.

120

At some places civilian assistance was co-ordinated under service direction. Here Kentish villagers prepare meals at a barn next to a railway station.

At the south coast ports officials of the Shipping Federation, working in conjunction with naval officers, met the requisitioned transports returning from Dunkirk and, as Merchant Navy officers and men stumbled ashore, they made a quick estimate of the minimum numbers needed to get the ships back to sea again. Most of the reliefs were recruited in London from engineers with seagoing experience, and sent down to Dover. And, as the railway line from Dover was jammed with trains dispersing the returning troops, urgency dictated they should travel by road. Many of them left their jobs without even going home to say goodbye. Few of them knew or could guess what they were volunteering for until they got out of their buses at Admiralty Pier in Dover, walked through the gate, and saw the ships in which they were to sail, and met some of the dazed individuals they were to replace or serve with.

☆

It is worth pausing briefly at this point to look at the reception in England of the returning troops, and at the heroic efforts made to feed them, tend the wounded and organize transport. For by the time the machinery of Dynamo was brought to a stop on June 4, 338,226 troops had been rescued, 123,095 of whom were French, the rest British. All of them, when they stumbled ashore at Dover and the other southern ports, were hungry, weary, lacking equipment and sometimes even boots. But they were safe, and 225,000 British families had personal as well as patriotic grounds to rejoice. One woman awaiting the birth

121

of her baby in a Manchester hospital learned where her husband was from a newspaper carrying the story of the evacuation; her relief was complete when he telephoned soon afterwards. Another, from Carshalton, remembers a policeman arriving with her address scribbled on the back of a cigarette packet and the message, 'Tell mum I'm OK. Jack.' He arrived in person a little later, wounded but safe.

At the ports the streams of soldiers were packed into trains and dispersed to the barracks, depots and hutted camps which had been hastily prepared for them. And this phase of the operation was itself a miracle—a miracle of railway organization, and a procession of trains that would have brought joy to the heart of any railway lover. All the experience of planning for football crowds and with the rush of commuters at peak hours in peacetime was put to use in an improvised operation characterized by the utmost informality and flexibility. When the troops poured off the boats, British 'Bobbies'—solid and reassuring—directed them towards the familiar green coaches of the Southern Railway waiting at the Dover Marine, Deal, Folkestone, Margate, Ramsgate and Sheerness stations.* Nurses with cool hands and homely voices saw to the wounded, for whom there were priority ambulance trains. As many as 186 trains, each comprising at least ten coaches, had been organized, and as one train full of tired, grimy men— 'with a bun in one hand and an apple in the other'—pulled away, another rolled in to the station to take its place. In nine days these trains made 565 trips—365 of them from Dover alone—to and from destinations in the south and west of England; ambulance trains also made some twenty-one journeys. Between troop trains, other special trains evacuating children from the coast added to the complexities of the operation.

Day and night the trains rolled away from the ports. Control points were set up not only at the ports but at all the main junctions, at Ashford, Faversham, Chatham and Dartford, and of course at the great London terminals—Waterloo, Victoria and London Bridge. The nodal point of the move was Redhill junction through which many lines from the south coast passed. While trains were being marshalled for particular destinations in the south and west their engines were coaled and watered, and by the time the operation ended 300 tons of ashes had accumulated at Redhill. As might be expected one of the main problems was finding train drivers who knew the lines over which they were to operate, and many of those who were brought in from further afield were given only a verbal briefing of the hazards and signals. This was one occasion when there could be no resort to 'working to rule', for there was no paragraph in the railway rule book covering national emergencies of this magnitude.

* Special trains were also provided for the men who were landed at Newhaven and Southampton.

The catering arrangements at the ports were supplemented by improvised snacks at wayside stations. This is Headcorn station at the height of the evacuation.

Emergency feeding arrangements were set up at the points where men of the R.A.S.C., reinforced by civilian helpers, mostly ladies—young, old, plain and pretty—handed out sandwiches, oranges, apples and of course, the serviceman's stand-by, 'char'. Other feeding centres were established at Headcorn and Paddock Wood—tiny Kentish stations staffed by no more than a station master and a couple of porters, who suddenly found themselves faced with the problem of feeding 145,000 troops. At both stations forty R.A.S.C. soldiers and between forty and fifty ladies from the neighbourhood organized into teams, worked in eight-hour shifts handing out tea, sandwiches, buns, hard-boiled eggs, meat-pies and cigarettes. As the whole of Kent could hardly

have produced enough cups for the tea, empty tin cans were used. When a train was about to pull out of Headcorn or Paddock Wood, R.A.S.C. N.C.Os on the platform would shout 'Sling 'em out' and the passing of the train would be signalled by the clanging of the tins on the concrete platform. The tins would then be collected and prepared for the next train.

Many men were too tired to eat; many others could not remember afterwards what they did eat. One Dorchester woman who witnessed the arrival of several train-loads sent to camps around the town wrote, 'They were in a pitiful state. They tumbled out of their trains so weary and tired that they hardly knew what they were doing. Their uniforms were torn and dirty... their boots were cracked and worn out. A few were in stockinged feet. Buses had collected them at the station.... At the barracks they sat down to a meal but they were so sleepy they were asleep before the meal was ended.' But they were safe and back in England—something they had dreamed about. Sydney Porter, of Johannesburg, who was in the Royal Signals, recalled how he had joked about getting home:

> ...we had to silence a couple of Jerry machine guns before we got to the jetty, and suffered a few casualties in the process. During this action I heard one soldier say to his pal, 'Just think of it! Tomorrow morning the old woman will bring you up your breakfast in bed, and say "Do you still take two spoons of sugar in your tea?"' When we finally got going I found he was wounded, having a couple of bullets in the chest.

The French troops who returned with the B.E.F. were sent back to France, to fight in a battle that was already lost.* They travelled first to Bournemouth and from there to Plymouth, where they were re-embarked. At Bournemouth one girl witnessed the arrival of 'thousands of exhausted Frenchmen. I watched them coming along the road from the railway station, dragging their raw blistered feet, trying to arrange themselves into something resembling military order. The crowds lining the road were handing out cigarettes and bars of precious chocolate. Cups of tea appeared from nearby houses and... I saw many in the crowd with tears streaming down their faces....'

A man's regiment and unit decided his individual destination. Units which arrived in formed bodies moved to the transit camps designated as regrouping centres for the battalions, brigades and divisions of the B.E.F.; stragglers were told to report to their regimental depots and the wounded went to hospital. At Waterloo, London Bridge and Charing Cross crowds collected to watch as the troops streamed through the barriers on their way to transit camps in the north and west. Nearly everybody was sent off on forty-eight hours' leave as soon as they had checked in at their barracks and—among other administra-

---

* Some Dutch and Belgian soldiers were also brought back. They stayed.

tive chores—officers were told to compile a list of the personal kit they had lost. The government would replace the losses in kind or compensate them according to the value. Captain Alexander of the 5th Bn East Yorkshire Regiment recollects delegating the compilation of his list to a batman. To his surprise he found that the extensive list that this worthy produced specified uniforms by a Savile Row tailor, and items such as a travelling clock. On pointing out that he had never had a travelling clock, the batman retorted: 'But sir, *every* officer and gentleman has a *travelling* clock.' If Alexander had not deleted these items, the authorities would almost certainly have done so.

Enterprising salesmen now appeared at the barracks and transit camps, hawking shoulder flashes—segments of cloth bearing the embroidered insignia B.E.F. These were snatched up by the men of the lost army, who felt that they had shared a unique experience; they were proud to be 'B.E.F.', they did not feel beaten and they were not averse to a bit of self-advertisement. Out came their 'husifs' and within a very short space of time almost every one of them was wearing the unauthorized flash. But as Churchill said on June 4 when referring 'to the miracle of deliverance' which had just ended, 'wars are not won by evacuations'. In the barracks and regimental depots of the B.E.F. veterans were paraded and told to remove the flashes. 'From the way you're carrying on,' said one sergeant-major, 'anyone would think you'd *won* the bloody war. The sooner you realize you nearly lost it, the better. Now you're going to learn to be proper soldiers....'

The men from Dunkirk knew what he meant, and in their hearts they agreed.

Over the page
Concentrations of troops and equipment were under constant air attack and as the perimeter shrank the Luftwaffe's raids intensified. Here a British soldier and a French poilu are seen running for shelter during a strafe.

7. Within the Perimeter

May 28 – June 1

'From the moment of the collapse of the Belgian Army there was only one course left to the Allied Armies—to hold a line round Dunkirk, the only port that remained, and to embark as many men as possible before their rearguards were overwhelmed. Thanks to the magnificent and untiring co-operation of the Allied Navies and Air Forces we have been able to embark and save more than four-fifths of that B.E.F. which the Germans claimed were surrounded.... The British Expeditionary Force still exists, not as a handful of fugitives, but as a body of seasoned veterans. The vital weapon of any army is its spirit. Ours has been tried and tempered in the furnace. It has not been found wanting. It is this refusal to accept defeat that is the guarantee of final victory.'

From the broadcast by Anthony Eden,
2 June 1940

The men of the B.E.F. did not learn that they were to be evacuated from Dunkirk until the morning of May 28, and forty-eight hours would elapse before the majority reached the Perimeter. Soon after being told about the evacuation came news of the Belgian capitulation; this meant that the B.E.F's left flank had collapsed and that encirclement and destruction was as likely as a return to England.

The B.E.F. was now roughly in three lines, with the 50th Division along the Ypres Canal and the 3rd Division at right angles with it extending to Poperinghe. Behind them on the River Yser and the Yser Canal were the 42nd and 5th Divisions, and behind them were the 48th, in turn behind the 42nd. The 1st, 4th and 46th Divisions were moving back to the Perimeter where they took up positions on May 29 with the western sector held by the French. Far away near Gort's main headquarters at Le Mans, men who still remained at the base and in the reinforcement camps were marshalled into groups and told to find their own way back to England. Meanwhile the fierce mêlée of battle was continuing on the Flanders plain, and the German vanguard—which had pushed through Ostend—was reported already to have reached Dixmude. Fighting a series of stubborn and largely disconnected rear-guard actions the British troops steadily gave ground and fell back from the River Lys to the Yser, and finally to the Perimeter on the Bergues Canal. In the south the French were driven out of Lille and, when the headquarters of the First French Army was over-run near Cassel, General Prioux was captured. Only two of his encircled divisions fought their way out of the trap and struggled north to join the British within the Perimeter.

Because of the traffic and the chaotic state of the roads a shuttle service using vehicles to ferry the troops to the rear was not now feasible; indeed the conditions had deteriorated so much that the movement of any transport backwards and forwards was forbidden. This, of course, meant that the first-line troops, already tired from digging and fighting, had to march. Congestion was particularly bad in the towns, and many units tramped around them—making tedious detours of twenty miles or more to reach the Perimeter by indirect cross-country routes, and passing behind and between German columns en route.

Leaving aside the possibility of a clash with one or other of these columns or merely with a patrol, the mere fact that many officers had no maps of the country near the coast tended to make these circum-ambulatory moves a chancy business.

Closer to Dunkirk, however, conditions changed. The terrain was flatter and duller and the refugees were fewer; somehow they had surged away from the main routes along which the B.E.F. was converging. But there were other difficulties. Air raids became more frequent, and the Luftwaffe had plenty of tempting targets. Trucks which had crashed and been abandoned by the roadside and the plodding horsed transports of the French units caused countless hold-ups. Jim Anderson, who was a corporal in 712 Company Royal Engineers, serving with the 50th Division, recalls that near Hoyville,

> ...There was a long line of abandoned French and British vehicles by the side of the road and a group of French troops opposite the cemetery. Enemy air traffic was heavy at the time and suddenly a Stuka attack swept in. I dived into the roadside ditch next to a small culvert or large drain-pipe, and thought my last moment had come as the Stukas straddled the area with their bombs. One was very close and caused casualties amongst the French troops. Half-buried I struggled out of the loose earth and as I stood up in the smoke and dust a Frenchman popped his head out of the culvert near my feet and shouted: '*A bas, il vient avec la mitrailleuse*'; as I plunged down again I literally 'felt' the bullets passing above my head.
>
> When it was all over there was a neat line of bullet holes along the sides of the vehicles next to where I had been standing. To this day I am very grateful to that unknown Frenchman for his warning, and very glad that I had shown a keen interest in my French lessons at school, as there was no time for sign language on that occasion.

Fortunately the Germans were not pressing their pursuit particularly vigorously. Nevertheless their steel claws were closing around the B.E.F. and the O.K.W. in Berlin was in an ebullient mood. 'Continuing their annihilating attack on the British Expeditionary Force, German troops have taken Ypres and the Kemmel Ridge by storm,' the official communiqué announced on May 29. 'The fate of the French armies in Artois is sealed. Their resistance south of Lille has broken down. The British Army which is pressed together in an area between Dixmude, Armentières, Bailleul and Bergues, west of Dunkirk, is threatened with annihilation by the concentric German attacks.' Next day the O.K.W's theme was the same. The great battle in Flanders and Artois 'was drawing to a close with the annihilation of the British and French armies.... Since yesterday the British Expeditionary Force also is in complete dissolution. The British troops are in headlong flight in the direction of the coast, leaving all their invaluable war material in German hands. Swimming and in small boats, they try to reach the

British ships lying in the roads—ships attacked by the Luftwaffe with devastating results. . . .'

The British troops in the rearguard had no intention of being annihilated if they could possibly help it. Leapfrogging back to the Perimeter, battalions would halt and dig in to cover the withdrawal of the units which had held the line earlier. Probing cautiously forward the Germans would stop in turn, when they came up against the new front line, bring up their artillery, and deploy for an attack. More often than not the British troops would break off and slip back across the next defensive line which had been established behind them before the German attack actually developed. Occasionally, however, they had to stay and fight, and one such defensive action, fought by the 1st Bn Queens' Own Cameron Highlanders at La Bassée, on the B.E.F's right flank at the junction of the British and French armies, was typical of many of the minor battles in the last days of May and first three days of June, although the ferocity of the attackers and tenacity of the Highlanders may be considered exceptional. During the B.E.F's retreat, the Camerons had established defensive lines in half-a-dozen places from the Forest of Soignies to the La Bassée Canal, and they had fought with doggedness and verve in two stubborn battles on two of these lines. At La Bassée they were occupying a position covering the canal crossings: three companies along the canal, one in the village of Violaines. Following a bout of shelling on May 26 the Commanding Officer, Lt-Col. G. D. (Pat) Rose-Miller, noted in his diary:

> . . . We could see the massing of many vehicles behind the German front, and I reported the fact that the Germans appeared to be assembling armoured fighting vehicles behind the railway embankments on the opposite side of the canal. The enemy then shot down our only O.P., which was the church tower. Evidently he thought we might have seen this concentration. That evening the enemy surrounded my Battalion headquarters with the old familiar puffs of smoke, just before dusk. My second-in-command spotted this, and suggested we should move from one end of the village to the other. This was done, and next morning we were very pleased we had moved—as our original headquarters were demolished by shellfire. . . .

Next day the Highlanders learned:

> . . . that the Germans had crossed the canal through the battalion on their right, and 'A' Company, behind a screen of Bren carriers, promptly went to look for them. They were fired on from an unexpected direction, and it was found that the left-hand posts of the neighbouring battalion had disappeared and the enemy was working his way round the Camerons' exposed flank. 'A' Company moved up to cover the gap. It was dark now, but a farmhouse was fiercely burning, and the platoons in turn were exposed by the brightness of the fire. The enemy had been reinforced,

130

and his machine-guns took toll of the Camerons. But the infiltration was stopped, and 'A' Company held the gap till they were relieved from another battalion.

The strength of the company was now only forty-five men, but as the others were closely engaged with the enemy, it was Major Riach, commanding 'A', who was given the task of deleting the German bridgehead. Six French tanks had appeared, and these would lead the attack. The first objective was a wood that grew along the bank of the canal. The tanks advanced, but their drivers' vision was limited, and they took the wrong direction. Company Sergeant-Major Stott, of 'A', ran alongside them under heavy fire, and by hammering their steel sides, brought them on to their proper bearing. He was wounded in the arm and shoulder, but continued to advance with the company.

Casualties were heavy, but the Camerons went on. Then the Germans began to leave their weapon pits, and presently all who survived were floundering through the water in great haste to return to their own side. But fire from the other side of the canal now grew heavier, and field guns, mortars, and machine-guns deluged the wood. One of the French tanks was knocked out, and of the forty-five Camerons, eighteen remained alive, of whom only six were unwounded. They had won the position, but they could not hold it with half a dozen men and five small tanks of indifferent performance. They withdrew to Battalion Headquarters in Violaines.

The gap was open again. The battalion on the right was by now so weakened that it had no hope of holding the enemy, and the Germans, it became evident, were about to make their main attack against it. The Camerons had to form a defensive flank, and hold it until a brigade counter-attack, supported by Army tanks, should come in to seal the gap. They had few troops available for the task. Battalion Headquarters mustered some drivers, signallers, clerks and batmen, there were the remnants of 'A' Company, and by good fortune a machine-gun platoon of the Manchester Regiment was in the vicinity. But that was all.

131

On the beaches troops scattered in search of shelter as the Luftwaffe bombs rained down.

They waited in vain for the promised counter-attack; no counter-attack was made. Instead came news, from 'D' Company and 'B', of German tanks concentrating opposite them on the other side of the canal. 'B' Company put seven out of action, but the concentration continued, and from Battalion Headquarters they were seen to be massing about half a mile away on the right flank, and crossing the canal on the neighbouring battalion front. The Camerons had, all this time, no effectual artillery support, but in the early afternoon their anti-tank platoon of three 25-mm guns arrived from brigade, under 2nd Lieutenant Callander, and reinforced the defensive flank. A wounded gunner officer also appeared and directed his battery against the tanks. But their fire was unavailing.

At half-past two the attack began. To the left of the scene was the road to Estaires, with trucks and lorries running at sudden speed under fire. La Bassée, bombed from the air and shelled from the far side of the canal, was burning under a brown canopy of smoke. Beyond a green copse were the roofs of Violaines, and waiting to attack it were some fifty German tanks, while a mass of German infantry, forming their companies with the deliberation of the parade ground, were preparing to follow the tanks astride the road from Violaines to Givenchy. Givenchy on the right of the scene, was already in flames. Over the canal rose conical slag heaps, and above the battlefield, with the patience of a scavenging kite, circled slowly an old Henschel observation plane. Firing as they came, the tanks advanced on Violaines. They halted about two hundred yards from the village, and the darting tongues of flame from their guns were answered by sudden fountains of dust, smoke, fire, and debris in Violaines. Very soon the whole village was burning hotly.

More tanks, very many of them, moved steadily northwards, then turned eastward to attack La Bassée from the rear, and cut the retreat of the French troops beyond it. The Germans, it appeared, were using a whole Panzer division, and after their tanks, on pontoons, had forced a crossing of the canal, they formed in three large groups for their several tasks: the attack of Violaines, the encirclement of La Bassée, the more remote attack on the French to the left of it.

Some soldiers used their rifles to try to deter low-flying enemy aircraft.

The farmhouse in Violaines, where the Camerons' Battalion Headquarters were situated, was soon ablaze, but steadily firing out of the heat and confusion of the battered village, Callander's anti-tank guns scored hit after hit on the German armour. Some distance in the rear, two troops of a field battery served their guns as well as they could under the direct observation of the Henschel. They kept on firing, and though the drifting smoke from Givenchy obscured their view, they harassed the German infantry and drove them, for a while, over the ridge that rises between that village and Violaines. La Bassée had disappeared in the smoke of burning houses, and the Camerons had lost communication with their forward companies.

Sergeant Morgan and his signallers had most gallantly kept the lines working, repairing them under fire again and again, but now they were cut once more, and Morgan and his linesmen, going forward to look for the break, disappeared in the storm of battle and were not seen again.

Some ammunition had been supplied to the companies by Lance-Corporal Darling, who, laden fantastically with fifty bandoliers and two

Brens, had perilously driven his motor-cycle over fire-swept roads into La Bassée, but nothing more could be done to help them. Now the tanks were within eighty yards of the Battalion's burnt-out headquarters, and lorry-borne infantry had come up behind them.

Colonel Rose-Miller, in wireless communication with brigade, described the situation, and was ordered to withdraw his battalion. It was then a quarter-past five in the afternoon. Though the companies in La Bassée were almost completely surrounded, a despatch rider, Private Ross, succeeded in reaching them, and gave them their orders. But 'C' and 'D' were caught in the trap and none of them got out. The Carrier Platoon, under 2nd Lieutenant Black, carried the wounded and fought their way out. Many of the wounded owed their lives to Lance-Corporal Jackson, who searched for them in burning houses, and under the enemy's fire saved them from the flames. Callander's anti-tank platoon, with a score of twenty-one tanks to its credit, followed the carriers and the remnant of 'A' withdrew across country. All that was left of 'B' Company tried to break out of La Bassée, but its transport was shot to pieces by the German tanks, and they decided to lie quiet till dark. In the blazing village behind them they could hear heavy firing. 'C' and 'D', unable to escape, were fighting still. Shortly before 11 o'clock, Captain Leah, commanding the two surviving platoons, set a cross-country route and began to march. He and the leading platoon were captured while trying to break through the German outpost line at Laventie, but the other party, under Platoon Sergeant-Major Kerr, avoided the enemy and eventually reached Dunkirk.*

One hundred men of the 1st Camerons, who had survived the action at La Bassée, eventually reached Dunkirk, where on May 30 seventy-nine of them embarked for home; the other twenty-one remained as part of the Perimeter defence until the last. They were the only B.E.F. Highlanders to be still wearing the kilt, and as the regiment was the old 79th Foot the number who were taken off Dunkirk mole may seem peculiarly appropriate.

While the Camerons were blocking the German advance at La Bassée a battalion of the British Army's oldest regiment, The Royal Scots, was sitting on the crossings over the River Lys near the village of Merville. The commanding officer, Lt-Col. H. D. K. Money, had been warned that the Germans would try to smash a way through to Merville from the La Bassée Canal, and on Monday, May 27, that is exactly what a column of the Wehrmacht's motorized infantry tried to do.

The Royal Scots had dug in astride the main road near the hamlet of Paradis. The countryside was generally flat and open but Money's battalion had a wide front to cover and on the west side of his position there was a wood in which the men of the 2nd Waffen SS *Totenkopf* Regiment (of 3rd SS Panzer Division) were able to concentrate prior to their attack.

* Précis of the account given in *Historical Records of the Queen's Own Cameron Highlanders*, Blackwood & Sons, Edinburgh, 1952.

134

To speed the evacuation men were organized into long queues which moved forward under the instructions of the naval embarkation staff.

Troops line up to be taken off by boats in front of the Sanatorium at Zuydcoote.

They attacked during the afternoon of May 28, and despite the Scotsmen's fierce resistance the Germans quickly broke through to the farm buildings and little houses of Paradis. One farmhouse in which one of the company commanders had established his headquarters had to be evacuated when it caught fire under the impact of intense artillery and mortar fire. Three trucks containing small arms and mortar ammunition were set alight at the same time and the only line of withdrawal was through the yard where the ammunition was exploding. All the company officers were casualties by this time, but the company sergeant-major, C. G. S. Whittet, rallied the survivors of his company— together with a few stragglers from other companies—at another farm. There, on a little hill, he established a strong-point which was to become the place where the Royal Scots made their last stand.*

Meantime Colonel Money had been wounded and taken via the Regimental Aid Post to the advanced dressing station at La Gorgue. He only just got away in time because shortly after he had left the post the Germans broke into the village from the east and over-ran it. The chaplain, the Rev. Norman MacLean, afterwards described what happened. A German N.C.O., he said, 'wearing white gloves and a white linen collar' (items which seem to have impressed themselves on the padre's memory) appeared and announced that he was proposing to shoot the wounded Scots lying there, because the British had been using dum-dum bullets. However, when the padre remonstrated the N.C.O. changed his mind and no shooting took place, but the medical officer, the battalion interpreter Michel Martel, and some of the others captured at the Regimental Aid Post, were locked up in a barn— from which they escaped through a skylight.

From the post the Germans went on to rush the next building, housing the battalion headquarters and defended by clerks, cooks, drivers and stretcher-bearers. This little force of men whose musketry qualifications were normally of less consequence than their specializations put up a stout resistance. But they had to abandon the building when it went up in flames. As Major Bruce—who had assumed command when Money became a casualty—led the little party along a ditch leading to Whittet's knoll, he was able to look back with grim amusement on his hurried exit from the blazing farmhouse. A driver had come up to him, saluted smartly at the door, and asked: 'Sir, will the C.O. be wanting his car?'

At that moment, Bruce said later, 'I would have gladly swapped all the cars in Flanders for half-a-dozen Bren guns'. However, he managed to get what was left of his headquarters across to the knoll held by C.S.M. Whittet. Meantime the Germans were systematically mopping up the other positions still held by the Royal Scots, and when the posts in the village had been overwhelmed it seems that they decided to by-

* For this action C.S.M. Whittet was subsequently awarded the Distinguished Conduct Medal.

138

pass Whittet's position and dispose of it later. But Bruce, now in command of the strong-point, had no intention of playing a passive role. From the hill his men could command a stretch of the road to Merville, and whenever a convoy of German vehicles appeared his men would shoot it up from a conveniently located cow-shed on the hillside. In the end the fire from the cow-shed was creating such havoc that the Germans sent a small force to deal with it. This was driven off. But the Scotsmen were now running short of ammunition and Bruce decided that they would make a run for it. It was now Wednesday, May 29, and after dark the little party slipped away from the hill, and made for Merville. When they reached the little town they sheltered in some cottages near the airfield, but their presence was revealed to the Germans by a Frenchman and Bruce and his party were captured.

And that was the end of the 1st Bn The Royal Scots, for the only remnants of the battalion to reach Dunkirk were the Quartermaster and his administrative staff and some of the wounded. Among the latter was Colonel Money who was evacuated from the dressing station at La Gorgue. 'Much strafing from the air, no food, water, or dope to dull our pains,' he wrote after he was able to look back with grim humour on the ordeal. During the next move the ambulance was bombed into a ditch, and Money was carried by two Coldstream Guardsmen down to the beach at Dunkirk. His only clothing was a pair of hospital trousers, supplemented by a blanket and a glengarry; and his only personal possessions were bandages and a ticket. 'A long wait on the sand, much machine-gunning from the air, then into a row-boat, which capsized and put me in the water; picked up by a Yarmouth herring-trawler which was mined; in the sea for another hour, then picked up by a naval craft—and so to England.' In Money's own terse words, that was the story of his journey home. He was awarded the Distinguished Service Order.

At the northern end of the Perimeter the 12th Infantry Brigade of Major-General D. G. Johnson's 4th Division arrived in the Nieuwpoort-Dixmude area in the early morning of May 28. From the Lys the three battalions of the brigade—2nd Bn Royal Fusiliers, 1st Bn South Lancashire Regiment, and 6th Bn Black Watch—had had a long weary march via Poperinghe and when they neared Dixmude they found that the Germans coming down the coast road from Ostend had beaten them to it. To make matters worse, although they had not yet captured it, the bridge across the canal there was still intact. Demolition charges had been fixed to the bridge, but the fuse was on the German side. In an effort to capture the bridge while it was still standing the Germans attacked repeatedly, and at one stage they got a foothold on the bridge before they were driven back. Finally the bridge was blown by a gallant sapper who, under cover of a machine-gun barrage, ran across it, fired the fuse and then swam back across the canal.

Shelled and sniped from the far side of the canal, constantly bombed from the air, the brigade held Nieuwpoort for three days. In the middle of the fighting the Mayor of Oostdunkerque presented himself at Brigade headquarters to demand that British troops should come nowhere near his town so that it should be spared damage. When he was told that this was quite out of the question the mayor retired to the beach to dig himself a slit-trench. Finally, orders for the brigade to break off the action, disengage and fall back on the beaches, were received at 2.30 a.m. on Friday, May 31. Positions were thinned out and the men marched the ten miles back to La Panne, to lie down among the sand-dunes awaiting dawn and the chance to get aboard the ships. The shelling was very heavy at this stage, and Lt-Col. D. M. W. Beak, the South Lancashires' commanding officer, told the author later that it was as bad as the Turkish barrage at Helles Beach in Gallipoli where he had won the Victoria Cross. Luckily for the men of 12 Brigade the Germans had registered inaccurately.

Further south the men of the 50th Division were in position along the Bergues Canal by the early morning of May 30—with the 157th Brigade, of three battalions of Durham Light Infantry, deployed in a sector of the Perimeter south of Furnes, and the 150th Brigade in the adjoining sector. To the British the Perimeter was now known as the 'Corunna Line' in memory of the Napoleonic rearguard action which resulted in a British army being safely evacuated under the very nose of the enemy. All the bridges of the Bergues Canal had been blown by the time the 50th Division arrived and the Yser valley had been deliberately flooded. But the watery expanse of flooded fields did not stop the German infantry who had followed up the 50th Division's rearguard so rapidly that the D.L.I. battalions were being shot up before they were properly dug in.

Other than a very few vehicles which were kept in running order within the Perimeter to the very end, the B.E.F. was now bereft of transport and heavy kit. As units approached the Perimeter their vehicles were directed into the marshy fields by the side of the road. Here they were pounced on by squads of Sappers who went to work on the engines and batteries with sledgehammers, before setting them on fire. At night the flames from these great vehicle cemeteries lit the sky. From this point the men had to march, and the problem of supplying them with food and water had to be resolved without vehicles.

John Mannion, who was serving with the 2nd Bn East Yorkshire Regiment (one of the battalions in the 8th Brigade of Major-General Bernard Montgomery's crack 3rd Division), has described what it was like behind the 'Corunna Line':

> We had withdrawn past Nieuwpoort on May 30, and were getting a fair amount of stick from Jerry. We were all young, fit and strong, well trained and well disciplined and confident that we could take on anything that Adolf sent against us. Right until the evacuation we were firmly convinced

Improvised piers, formed from trucks and transports, were useful only at high tide. Right: men of the Royal Ulsters waiting for boats on one such pier at Bray. Below: a second pier on the La Panne beach after the fall of Dunkirk.

that we were drawing the enemy into a trap and that sooner or later we would turn on him and give him such a dose of his own medicine as would settle his hash once and for all.

I was with the drummers of the A.A. Platoon for the protection of Bn HQ at the Coxyde crossroads. Sgt Pip Jacobs told me and old soldiers Thomas and Wilson, both ex-drummers, to make our way to a nearby farmhouse, to establish ourselves on the upper floor and, with a Bren gun I was carrying, endeavour to quieten those Jerries nearest to our position. I had used up my ammunition and, on the way to the farmhouse, I picked up some ammunition and cigarettes which I found lying about. I knocked a hole in the farmhouse roof and thoroughly enjoyed, for a change, blasting away at Jerry, though I must admit he sent a certain amount our way. Years later I was discussing this incident with Pip Jacobs and he said, 'yes, of course, I remember it; you silly twit you were firing tracer and Jerry stonked hell out of us!' Well, at that particular period, beggars couldn't be choosers. That evening Bn HQ pulled out and we had to leave. Thomas and Wilson asked me to hang on for a while as they were going to an adjacent wood to look for Ben Gaulter. As a result we nearly missed a lift on a lorry which was part of the transport taking Bn HQ to La Panne. I was too tired to realize how long we were on the lorry; as we ran out of road I assumed we had reached the beach at La Panne.

We went onto the beaches and we marched and marched; trudged would be a better word, as those who have marched on sand with weapons and equipment will agree. We could see ships of the Royal Navy and sundry other ships standing-to about a mile out. I, and many others, still imagined, indeed fondly hoped that we were to be lifted by boat to get behind Jerry and to cut him off. We marched for an hour or so with little interference when suddenly all hell seemed to be let loose. We hardly knew what hit us. The Guards up ahead of us got it first and our share rapidly followed. La Panne was well alight and shells were exploding all over the place. I flew into the sea, hoping that any shrapnel would be stopped by the water and not by the body beautiful. I came across one youngster who asked me to bandage his head. I did so and have often wondered since whether he managed to get away. We stayed put for that night. Next morning some went on to Dunkirk town which seemed to be completely ablaze. There was no question of re-joining the Battalion; individuals and units were inextricably mixed. In any case, I saw little point marching and decided to take my chance where I was. I glanced out to sea, and through the mist or fog I saw some sort of long boat drifting inshore. Tommy Ramshaw was with me and we made a dash for it, fortunately reaching it as the water reached our necks, I had to go under water to lift Tommy up and over into the boat. He was apparently so relieved to make it that he overlooked the fact that I also needed assistance to get in. Nevertheless there were by now plenty of willing helpers to get me aboard and, eventually, we found ourselves joined by some 90 others. Soon we were picked up by the Minesweeper *Strive* and my adventures for the time being anyway, were over. I was sorry to remember that there were many others who had died, either on the beaches or in the sea and, whilst glad to escape, felt very humble.*

142

While the Luftwaffe expended most of its efforts on bombing and machine-gun sorties it also went in for some leaflet-dropping. On these leaflets was printed a crude map of Dunkirk showing the B.E.F. holding a small area surrounded by a sea of Germans. In bold English lettering were the words THE GAME IS UP, THE INNINGS IS OVER! THERE IS NO ALTERNATIVE BUT SURRENDER. Few of the troops believed the message. Like John Mannion most of them thought that the Germans were being 'drawn, into a trap'. Little did they know that they were being told the truth.

Down on the beaches conditions deteriorated as more and more weary troops flopped down among the sand-dunes and waited their turn to embark. Those not too tired to watch saw the epic of Dunkirk played out before their eyes, as the ships and boats plied to and fro picking up their human cargoes. Every half-hour or so Me 110s or low-flying Stukas came to machine gun and bomb the concentrations of troops. Early on the morning of May 30 La Panne beach also came under fire from German medium and heavy artillery. There was little warning as the shells whistled in on a flat trajectory across the sand to chop down men waiting in the long queues to be taken aboard the boats. Since nothing could be done for the dead the queues simply moved up and closed the gaps. Stretcher-bearers were kept busy with the wounded. And along the columns of men wandered the shell-shocked, the battle-fatigued, the demented, looking for shelter which did not exist. Higher up the beaches men were buried singly or in common graves whose positions were marked by rifle-butts and helmets. But many of the graves were shallow and some of them were disturbed by shell or bomb bursts which disinterred the bodies. To make matters worse packs of terrified dogs ran the beaches from La Panne to the Dunkirk mole—hungry and already vicious, seeking out the corpses. To their clamour and savage foraging was added that of herds of horses which galloped along the dunes after every shell-burst. These were former French or Belgian field artillery and cavalry mounts which had been brought into the Perimeter in defiance of orders. Some had been ridden directly to the beaches and discarded there. One such animal, a white mare, had for many days been used by a French major, who, with a sabre and a fluent command of English, directed troops to the boats. Then he disappeared—perhaps too tired to continue, or shot by some drunken soldier who resented his manner. He was gone, anyhow, and the mare was riderless. There was no fodder for any of the horses. A few soldiers offered wine to the horses. Then, drunk, they mounted the beasts and rode about blindly, shouting and shooting rifles and revolvers, careless of the wounded.

* Mr Mannion revisited Dunkirk on the annual D.V.A. pilgrimage in 1976 and 'returned almost to the self same spot where I had embarked on that former day; La Panne now looked so beautiful and friendly, the beach was as I remembered it, so was the fog and sea-mist—indeed several ships were lying off-shore'.

These men were not alone in creating problems in the beach-head. While Churchill was insisting that the British and French should depart in equal numbers Gort was obliged to telephone the War Office in London to tell Dill (the new C.I.G.S.) that Admiral Abrial was loth to permit fighting troops to be withdrawn. Even when pressure was brought to bear on Abrial by Weygand in Paris, some French officers refused to comply with orders delivered by British officers. One recalcitrant French colonel who refused to take part in the evacuation made such a fuss that a British officer felt obliged to draw his revolver. In the face of this threat the irate colonel obeyed. But he sent a personal telegram to Weygand which read: '*Urgent. Des officiers anglais nous menacent au point de revolver. Situation très pénible.*' Weygand duly informed Reynaud who complained bitterly to General Spears—Churchill's liaison officer in Paris—elevating the aggrieved French colonel to the rank of general in the course of his indignant protestations. There were more important matters to occupy the attention of the generals and admirals at Dunkirk, but the French Government was becoming daily more sensitive to slights from their allies.

In the first phase of the evacuation non-combatant troops were the first to be taken off. But as almost all the British Army's best trained officers and men were with the B.E.F. Gort decided that some of the key men of all ranks and units should be shipped home before it was too late. These men were, as Churchill put it, 'the whole root and core and brain of the British Army', and the reconstitution of a fighting force would depend on them—even if the B.E.F's equipment was lost. So Pownall, Gort's Chief of Staff, was packed off on the 29th, and Brooke—who was told to hand over the command of his Second Corps to Montgomery—followed on the 30th. 'Called in on Monty', Brooke wrote in his diary on the 29th,

> and discussed with him a further retirement that night into the Perimeter defence.... Congestion on roads indescribable, French Army become a rabble and complete loss of discipline. Troops dejected and surly, refusing to clear road and panicking every time a *boche* plane comes over....
>
> On returning to my chateau to pick up some papers I was met by Ciriez, our French Liaison Officer. He was in an infuriated condition and livid with rage. He informed me that a squadron of French cavalry had entered the chateau grounds, had commenced to shoot their horses and to throw their arms into the moat of the chateau. He had dashed out to ask them why they were doing this, and they informed him that the Germans were on the outskirts of the village, and they did not wish to be captured with their arms. He informed them that there were no Germans within twenty miles, that they were a disgrace to the French Army, and a few more very appropriate home truths. He told me that it had the right effect, they mounted again and rode off....

Brooke eventually sailed for Dover in the destroyer H.M.S. *Worcester*, and Lt-Gen. Adam, having completed his task of organizing the Peri-

Collection points and casua[l] clearing centres were for th[e] most part off the beaches. This one was behind the L[a] Panne beach.

The propaganda leaflets dropped by the Luftwaffe planes were eagerly seized [as] souvenirs.

meter, went with him. On arrival at Dover, on Friday morning, May 31, both men drove up to Dover Castle to see Ramsay and give him a full report on conditions at Dunkirk. At that time the evacuation was scheduled to end that night, and they tried to persuade Ramsay to extend the time limit—Brooke saying that he believed that the effort would have to be maintained for several more days. In his memoirs Brooke said of this conversation with Ramsay: 'He was most wonderfully understanding and only too ready to do all that he could, and yet I could see that he had serious doubts as to the possibility.'

Brooke and Adam then left the Admiral in his cliffside headquarters and motored up to London. Of this journey through the lush green countryside of Kent Brooke recorded that:

> Everywhere around us were those spring sights and smells of nature awakening after her winter slumbers. The contrast of this lovely sunlit country and its perfect peacefulness when compared with those Belgian roads crammed with distressed and demoralized humanity, houses shrouded in smoke clouds from burning villages, the continuous rumbling of guns, bombs and aircraft, smashed houses, dead cattle, broken trees and all those scars of war that distort the face of nature. To have moved straight from that inferno into such a paradise within the spell of a few anguished hours made the contrast all the more wonderful.

Gort, meanwhile, had made up his mind that he would stay with his troops to the bitter end. But he had not reckoned on Churchill's reaction nor could he know that as soon as Pownall got to London he would urge the recall of his former Commander-in-Chief. By the evening of May 30, when about 125,000 men of the B.E.F. had been lifted to safety, Gort received a long signal which Churchill had dictated personally. Gort's task was fast approaching completion, for it read . . .

> Continue to defend present perimeter to the utmost, in order to cover maximum evacuation, now proceeding well. . . . If we can still communicate with you we shall send you an order to return to England with such officers as you may choose, at the moment when we deem your command so reduced that it can be handed to a Corps Commander. You should now nominate this commander. If communications are broken, you are to hand over and return, as specified, when your effective fighting force does not exceed equivalent of three divisions. This is in accordance with correct military procedure, and no personal discretion is left to you in the matter. . . . The Corps Commander chosen by you should be ordered to carry on defence and evacuation with French, whether from Dunkirk or beaches. . . .

Gort was distressed because Churchill's orders allowed him no option, but he carried them out without demur or delay.

On May 31 he had a final conference with Admiral Abrial and the senior French commanders in Dunkirk, and then handed over command of what remained of the B.E.F. to Alexander. Finally, early on June 1, he was carried to Dover in a motor torpedo boat—across waters which had remained obligingly calm throughout a week in which rough seas would have been more deadly enemies than the Wehrmacht and the Luftwaffe. General Blanchard followed Gort later. When they left both men fully expected to return to France, for Churchill was working on plans to create a second B.E.F. based on St Nazaire and to build up its strength behind twentieth-century 'Lines of Torres Vedras' on the Brittany Peninsula.

It was not to be. The battle of Flanders was almost over, and the focus of the conflict was about to move from the stricken beaches of Dunkirk to the skies above Britain. For Gort Dunkirk was the end of his career as a fighting general. He had saved not only the men of the B.E.F. but also the leaders—Brooke, Alexander, Montgomery, Horrocks and many others—who were to mastermind the victories of 1943–5. No one deserved greater recognition for the services he had rendered Britain. But Churchill did not favour Gort. 'Wars are not won by evacuations', and Britain's Prime Minister did not consider the erst-while Commander-in-Chief of the B.E.F. was the man to lead or organize the army that would defeat Hitler. In 1942 Gort was made Governor-General of Malta at a time when that island's position seemed hopeless; and here again he displayed his tenacious courage. His career ended as High Commissioner in Palestine and Trans-Jordan in 1945, and he died on 31 March 1946, four months before his sixtieth birthday.

Over the page
A hospital ship takes off the wounded from the Dunkirk mole. Although plainly marked with the red cross, hospital ships still had to run the gauntlet of Luftwaffe raids on Dunkirk harbour.

147

8. Destroyers, Trawlers, and Tugs

May 28 – June 2

'I wish to express my admiration of the outstanding skill and bravery shown by the three Services and the Merchant Navy in the evacuation of the British Expeditionary Force from Northern France. So difficult an operation was only made possible by brilliant leadership and the indomitable spirit among all ranks of the Force.

The measure of its success—greater than we had dared to hope—was due to the unfailing support of the Royal Air Force and, in the final stages, the tireless efforts of naval units of every kind.

While we acclaim this great feat, in which our French Allies, too, have played so important a part, we think with heartfelt sympathy of the loss and sufferings of those brave men whose self-sacrifice has turned disaster into triumph.'

King George VI in a message to the Prime Minister, 3 June 1940

When Admiral Ramsay received Tennant's signal asking for 'every available craft' to be sent to the beaches because the evacuation next day would be 'problematical' he concluded that Operation Dynamo would have to be wound up within the next twenty-four hours. After that German troops would occupy Dunkirk and at least 100,000 men of the B.E.F. would be cut off and taken prisoner.

A flotilla of minesweepers sailed from Deal for La Panne; another flotilla of four shallow-draft paddle-sweepers, the *Sandown*, the *Gracie Fields*, the *Brighton Belle* and the *Medway Queen* sailed from Dover; and a third flotilla consisting of the *Waverley*, *Marmion*, *Duchess of Fife* and *Oriole* from Harwich. The destroyers H.M.S. *Gallant*, H.M.S. *Vivacious*, H.M.S. *Windsor*, H.M.S. *Vimy*, H.M.S. *Impulsive* and H.M.S. *Sabre* were also sent off on troop-lifting duty, together with the cruiser H.M.S. *Calcutta*. (This cruiser, of World War I vintage, had been converted to become a floating anti-aircraft battery equipped with four-inch A.A. guns and multiple Pom-Poms; off Dunkirk she was to become known as 'the flak ship'.) While the destroyers fanned out in front of the beaches at Malo-les-Bains, Zuydcoote and La Panne, the *Calcutta* took up a station directly off Dunkirk.

That night (May 27/28) more ships sailed from Dover. In the van were seventeen drifters—big strong fishing boats that the Royal Navy had been using as flare carriers in the Dover Patrol. Because of their shallow draft they were able to anchor close inshore along the beaches, and they were ordered to stay away from the maelstrom of Dunkirk harbour. When the drifters appeared troops on the beaches threw off their steel helmets, dumped their greatcoats and boots, and began to wade out to them. But the water was cold, a fast current was flowing, the men were tired when they started and the drifters were much further out than it had seemed from the shore. Consequently many of the men were soon in difficulties. In the darkness the drifter crews responded to despairing cries, and some of the little ships, newly arrived from Ramsgate and the Thames, closed in to help.

Those who were there will remember that night as one which passed very slowly. Every ten minutes or so it was punctuated by air-raids over the town and harbour, and then towards morning over the beaches. At his new headquarters in La Panne Gort was told that Dunkirk was now little more than a heap of rubble, with streets blocked by buildings which had collapsed while the harbour was a tangle of wreckage. Civilian telephone lines were down, and as there were no radio sets and very few field telephones in working order, communication with subordinate headquarters and units of the B.E.F. had to be by runner—a slow business and one which created new problems.

A garbled message led to the premature destruction of the B.E.F.'s batteries of 3·7 inch anti-aircraft guns. Having effectively spiked these weapons the B.E.F's A.A. defence now rested solely on the lighter 40-mm Bofors guns supplemented by the brens and rifles of the infantry. Against the Stukas, which struck repeatedly at the ships, and the Me 110s, which ranged up and down the shore-line strafing the troops awaiting their turn for embarkation, these weapons had little effect. On the beaches the wounded were collected together and given priority in the small craft ferrying men to the ships off shore. The dead were left lying in rows, like brown-coloured fish stranded by the tide; as the hours passed the sickly sweet odours of decomposition began to pervade the area.

During the afternoon of May 28 Ramsay appealed to the Admiralty for the services of all Royal Naval destroyers in home waters. If the old destroyers that had been allotted to him could not compete with the situation at Dunkirk, he signalled, modern destroyers should also be used for bringing men off. As a result every available destroyer in the Western Approaches and Portsmouth Commands, including those on patrol and escort duties, was put at his disposal. Ramsay was determined to save what was left of the B.E.F. even if the effort crippled the Royal Navy.

In the event it was the troop carriers, the peacetime Channel and Irish Sea ferries with their ability to carry large numbers of troops in a single voyage, which were to determine the success of the rescue operation—not the destroyers, nor the little ships. The traditional dash displayed by the Royal Navy, and the gallantry of the men who sailed the cockleshell fleet appealed to, captured and held the popular imagination. Soon therefore, a legend centering mainly on the work of the little ships was created, and the troop transports and hospital ships that so many knew and had sailed in were very nearly forgotten. Something of the saga of these ships has been recounted already and a blow-by-blow account of the adventures of them all would make a monotonous story. Nevertheless, the *Tynwald*, one of the Isle of Man Steam Packet Company's 'pleasure' steamers, deserves special mention, because she held the record for the heaviest troop loads—bringing 7500 men out from Dunkirk in five trips. Her average of 1500 men a trip was far in excess of the average loads aboard other ships of her kind.

And it is interesting to compare these figures with the performance of a destroyer, which took something like six hours to load at either of the Dunkirk moles and could carry a maximum of only about 1,000 soldiers—and that with every available bit of space filled. Thus the performance of the troop carriers was substantially better.

The flotilla of minesweeping drifters which took part in the evacuation was headed by H.M.S. *Vernon*, known as 'Vernon's Private Navy', and consisted of five East Coast heavy drifters, the *Lord Cavan, Silver Dawn, Fisher Boy, Jacketa* and *Formidable* (whose name was subsequently changed to *Fidget*, a change which her skipper was said never to have got over!). Each ship was commanded by a Royal Naval Reserve skipper from the Hull or Grimsby fishing fleets, and carried a crew of ten: mate, chief engineer, signalman, cook, four deckhands and two stokers.

When the flotilla was sent over to Dunkirk its orders were that individual ships would act as ferries between the harbour and the bigger ships outside. As soon as they arrived they tied up to the east mole where a long queue of troops awaited embarkation. The drifters took 150 men each and then set out to unload them into whatever bigger ship they encountered. For a while they tried to discharge the troops into a merchant ship and were aggrieved at her apparent lack of interest, until they discovered that she was aground on a sandbank and had been abandoned. Eventually they succeeded in finding other ships and returned to the harbour for a second load.

It was then decided that the *Lord Cavan* should stay at Dunkirk while the rest of the flotilla sailed back to Ramsgate with a load of troops. During the next two days the four drifters continued to do this, sailing from Ramsgate in company, splitting up on the other side to collect men as and how they could, and returning independently as soon as each ship was loaded. Although their skippers had been told to limit loads to a hundred men apiece, they usually took over 200—the record being set by *Silver Dawn*, which on one passage carried 312. Loads of this size would have been unsafe in anything but calm weather but even so a number of soldiers who swam out to the ships had to be refused passage. One of the drifters' officers had described the men who had to swim back to the beach as 'amazingly philosophical': some of course were not.

In common with everybody and everything in and around Dunkirk the drifters were subjected to incessant bombing attacks. However the only one of 'Vernon's Navy' to suffer damage was the *Silver Dawn* which lost a propeller blade on some wreckage in Dunkirk harbour on the third day, but she succeeded in reaching Ramsgate with her troops on board. On their outward passage on the last day the remaining three drifters came up with one of the troop-carriers, the former L.M.S. railway steamer *Scotia*, which had received five direct hits from bombs and was lying on her side burning fiercely. She had been carrying French troops and most of these were in the sea, so the drifter joined the

153

destroyer H.M.S. *Esk* in picking them up.* All in all these four drifters brought back 4085 soldiers. The *Lord Cavan* was sunk by shellfire but her crew got away safely.

Trawlers also did valiant work, although many of their skippers were over fifty years old and most of the junior officers and ratings had seen nothing of war prior to this. Eight trawlers alone brought back 1606 British, French and Belgian troops. But casualties were heavy. One trawler skipper saw a bomb strike a sister ship as he was picking up soldiers from the water. And when the explosion had cleared away there was no sign of her. Another trawler sank near Dunkirk east pier alongside the wreck of the destroyer *Grenade*, whose White Ensign was still flying just above the water when Operation Dynamo was terminated.

The *Cervia*, a 90-foot tug of 157 tons armed with a single Lewis gun, was one of the most active of the ships at Dunkirk. In her log for Saturday, June 1, Captain W. H. Simmons, wrote:

> The great evacuation was on. There were a great number of wrecks about and caution was necessary as few were charted or buoyed. The only means of knowing where they were apart from any wreckage visible above water was the tide rip over them. We passed Dunkirk pierheads where five H.M. destroyers were loading up and we passed two big French destroyers that had been mined and were lying wrecked, up on the beach. We let go our barge off toward the beach at 8.20 a.m.
>
> Soldiers were running down the beach to meet her when an air raid siren began to blow ashore and the soldiers took what cover they could find. We dropped our anchor at 8.30 a.m., all being quiet, when over came about fifteen enemy planes with guns blazing away on shore at them. Two destroyers and a sloop outside us began to open fire as the planes began to bomb them and as the destroyers were twisting and turning at high speed to dodge the bombs I deemed it necessary to keep out of their way so hove up our anchor and paddled in towards shore, our own Lewis gun firing at the planes as they came over us.
>
> At this time our barge's boat was rowing off to us with six soldier stevedores, also the Master and Mate of the *Royalty* which was now beached and at anchor on the shore. Two more barge crews came in one boat and we took them all on board. The destroyer outside of us had a stick of bombs drop in the water alongside of her and they exploded under water as she kept her speed twisting and turning to avoid them. She must have been holed, as she began to take a list and was getting deeper by the head. I began to run off to her, her guns firing all the time at the planes.

* It appears that when the *Scotia* was attacked three of her lifeboats were smashed. When she started to sink the *poilus* rushed to the remaining boats, and order was restored only when a French officer whipped out his revolver and threatened to shoot if the troops did not stand aside and permit the boats to be lowered.

One of the most famous and poignant of all photographs of the Dunkirk evacuation. Troops wade out through the sea to a waiting ship.

On my way I saw a white motor lifeboat with about fifteen soldiers in it. I picked her up, transferring the soldiers to us and towing the lifeboat astern with the other two small boats. Another wave of planes came over and began to bomb the crippled destroyer as I made my way off to her and I was forced to sheer away from her. This destroyer proved to be the *Keith*. I had to keep clear of her as the sloop was circling her at high speed in an attempt to fight off the raiders....

We saw nine bombs leave a plane over us and they dropped alongside the ingoing Channel Steamer, but with her helm hard over she managed to get clear of them and continued on to the harbour. Guns were crashing all around us and a trawler running in let fly with all he had got; 5 bombs were aimed at us from a plane, I could not see them or the plane as our bridge was covered with concrete slabs. The boy F. Wilder of Gravesend was outside the wheelhouse as all who could were jambed inside under the cover, and he told me the direction of the bombs and by sheering off hard to starboard they dropped about 100 feet off our port bow lifting the tug bodily out of the water when they exploded. Fortunately our tow-rope held on. One bomb was aimed at *Persia*, but missed and the spray of its exploding washed down her decks.

But we all got out safely from the Roads and when off the Ruytingen Buoy we were attacked again, but this time we were on our own, the others getting away ahead of us. We now had several Lewis guns and ammo' on board with the troops we had picked up and were able to keep the planes off. Our decks were well packed with troops which we had picked up and we also had on our boat deck a canoe that came alongside with two soldiers in it. When in sight of the English coast several soldiers were overcome and tears were streaming down their faces. I saw a bomb explode between a sloop and a destroyer that he was towing, but we all got out of it safely.

When we arrived in the Downs about 4 p.m. we were ordered by Naval Control tug *Java* to proceed to Ramsgate where we anchored in the Old Cudd Channel. Motor boats disembarked our troops, also took all the wounded out of the *Tollesbury* which could not be taken into the harbour because of the congestion in there. In all about 270 troops were landed from us and from our tow. We were ordered to tow the barge to Gravesend. I enquired as to what had become of a fleet of thirty French and Belgian fishermen who had spoken to me early that morning on my way to Dunkirk, who were sailing with all their families to England. I had given them a course and wished them luck. I was told that they had all arrived safely, well loaded with families and troops after having sailed right over the Goodwin Sands on the high water.

Lady Brassey and her sister tug the *Simla*, were both kept busy on salvage work in the Channel throughout the evacuation. On May 27 these two vessels were ordered to go to the rescue of H.M.S. *Mona's Isle*, a former Isle of Man pleasure steamer converted for service as an armed boarding vessel. Coming out of Dunkirk with a full load of troops and bound for Dover, the *Mona's Isle* had been bombed. Forty soldiers on the upper decks were killed and seventy wounded and the ship herself was badly damaged. But *Lady Brassey* and *Simla* towed her to Dover where the wounded were taken off and moved to hospital by men of the St John Ambulance Brigade. The rest of the troops disembarked when *Lady Brassey* and *Simla* had manœuvred the *Mona's Isle* through the maze of ships in the packed harbour. Then, just as soon as they had been refuelled and taken on fresh water, food and ammunition, the two tugs started back for Dunkirk.

Two nights later, the 29th, the same pair of tugs were sent to help the destroyer H.M.S. *Montrose*, whose bows had been blown apart. Packed with troops she was lying off Calais illuminated by the German-operated searchlights on Cap Gris-Nez. Arriving alongside the *Montrose* about 1 a.m., they towed her back to Dover stern-first—passing through the boom at the harbour mouth at 3 a.m. precisely. Without the help of the two tugs the master of H.M.S. *Montrose*, Commander C. R. L. Barry, said afterwards, his ship would have been lost and all hands with her.

Like the crews of the transports the tugboatmen had to be given a break and following the drama of the *Montrose* the skipper of the *Lady Brassey*, Captain G. W. Blackmore, was relieved by Captain F. J. Hopgood who recorded the *Lady Brassey*'s adventures during the final crucial days of Operation Dynamo:

Dover, May 30, 1940:
Left Dover to assist destroyer *Bideford* off Nieuwpoort, Belgium. Weather fine. Whilst on passage received message to proceed to Dunkirk and stand by the Naval personnel in charge of the evacuation.

During the passage, a German plane came overhead, so we kept our two machine guns firing at it until it sheered off towards France. On approaching Dunkirk Roads through the marked channel across the Sand Banks we sighted a small coaster that had been bombarded and with shell holes through the hull but clear of the water line. We could also see dense black smoke over Dunkirk, and could see vessels of all descriptions lying off the sand dunes, which were crowded with troops being ferried off by the small boats to larger craft in the vicinity.

The troops were being bombed, and the craters made by the bombs were soon full of troops taking shelter there.

We proceeded on, and felt our way past several craft that had been sunk close to the East Pier, and went alongside the west side of the pier. Troops were coming down this pier and embarking on the various craft, destroyers, mailboats and passenger boats. All of these were shallow draft vessels, drawing about thirteen feet and able to cope with the Channel from Dunkirk to England.

During the time we were alongside the pier, shrapnel and fragmentation from the explosive charges fired by demolition squads came over the pier and the tug. A piece of shrapnel slid down inside my raincoat without doing any harm. There was a hospital ship moored close to us that found things too warm whilst she waited for wounded, so she cleared out of Dunkirk.

The evacuation continued whilst we assisted several of the ships leaving the pier. The tide was falling, and these vessels were getting too close to the ground. There were also vessels sunk near the entrance to the pier.

When it became dark, we again assisted vessels off the jetty, and in addition assisted vessels into and alongside the pier, clear of the wrecks. We continued until 12.30 a.m. of 31st May, when I received instructions to return to Dover, but not to take troops aboard in case I was wanted for rescue duty.

Whilst returning, we received a message to go to the assistance of a drifter ashore on the Goodwin Sands. As we approached the northeast end of the sands we could see the drifter on the northeast bank. But the tide was flowing, and she got off without our assistance, and we proceeded on to Dover.

On June 1, the vessels were lined up loaded with troops off the port of Dover, waiting to disembark in turn at the Admiralty Pier railway berths. The people there were hard at it, clearing the troops. Again we received orders to proceed to the Downs and assist the troopship *Prague* which had been mined and severely damaged. We reached her and took her in tow, despite her damage, and kept her from sinking by grounding her on the Sandwich Flats. Temporary repairs were made while she was grounded, then she proceeded to port for permanent work.

On the 2nd of June, I received instructions to proceed to the assistance of the hospital ship *Paris*, sinking off Dunkirk. She had been bombed en route to Dunkirk. We proceeded at full speed through the Downs. It was a dark night, but fine weather, and we set a course for Dunkirk. About 11 p.m. a dark shadow approached. This was a destroyer, steaming full speed and loaded with troops.

She came so close alongside us she sent her swell over the tug. It was a near thing, and if she had hit us, it would have been goodbye *Brassey*. We continued on and searched for the *Paris* and finally located her by the star shells sent up overhead. We could see that the vessel was sinking, and that there was no hope of saving her. But we cruised around her, hailing to find out if by any chance anyone had been left aboard by the craft that had taken off the crew before our arrival. We kept in touch with the ship until she sank at about 4 a.m., and then reported her position, and the fact that her masts were sticking out of the water. We made this report to Dover, to warn other ships of the wreck.

We then returned to Dover.

Captain Hopgood was a veteran of World War I, an old salt who had witnessed many perilous moments at sea in war and peace, but he was shaken by the near destruction of his ship:

It was a pitch-black night and the sea was quite smooth when the destroyer suddenly appeared. Her speed of thirty-one knots piled a bow wave white and mountainous over her fore deck. It drenched the troops who stood there motionless and helpless. It surged around the turret tops and almost reached the navigation bridge, and left in broad, pale gushes over the side.

The destroyer's blowers whined and her engines and her pumps had an intricate, almost musical beat. Her whole structure, plates, beams, rivets, even halyard blocks and wireless antenna had a sound of its own. . . .

But it was the huge coiling stern wash which flailed *Lady Brassey*'s fore and aft decks that worried Hopgood most. As he said, it was a 'near thing' experience.

The loss of the destroyers H.M.S. *Grenade* by air attack (referred to earlier, pp. 117 and 154), H.M.S. *Grafton* and H.M.S. *Wakefield* by the torpedoes of marauding German S-boats, coupled with damage to H.M.S. *Jaguar*, H.M.S. *Gallant*, H.M.S. *Greyhound* and H.M.S. *Intrepid*, led to the immediate withdrawal of all the big modern warships from the evacuation. With six of the Royal Navy's most modern destroyers out of action their Lordships at the Admiralty decided that losses on this scale could not be tolerated. The decision was a severe blow to Ramsay, who was relying on working them through the nights of May 29 and 30. Dunkirk harbour was not actually blocked and he was hoping to get the bulk of the B.E.F. away by the 31st. And if the destroyers had been permitted to continue they could doubtless have lifted large numbers of men.

An account of what happened to H.M.S. *Grenade* has been given by Lieutenant-Commander E. C. Peake, the ship's executive officer:

> The *Grenade* was ordered to Dunkirk early on May 28, her only warning being given the day before when her captain, Commander R. C. Boyle, was told to put her confidential books ashore at her base in Harwich. It was raining heavily as we approached Dunkirk, but the town was visible from a great distance owing to the clouds of smoke above it. We berthed alongside the pier and immediately started embarking troops. We took on board about 1,200, packing them in like sardines. We had them on the ladders, and in the wardroom, and in the galley, even the heads, and everywhere on deck. When we could take no more we sailed for Dover. It was still raining very heavily and the troops on the upper deck had a miserable time.
>
> There was little enemy air activity on this day, possibly due to the weather.
>
> We arrived at Dover on the evening of May 28 and disembarked our troops. Then we refuelled, sailing again on completion.
>
> The morning of May 29 was beautiful, warm, with brilliant sunshine, and a flat, calm sea.
>
> On the way over, there was heavy enemy air activity. And ample evidence of their success. Wreckage, corpses. I shall never forget a red-headed woman who floated face-down. Her handbag was beside her, right on station.
>
> We arrived at Dunkirk during the forenoon and berthed at the land-

ward end of the pier, so that other small ships such as trawlers could berth astern of us.

We expected to load and get back to England as soon as possible. But for some unknown reason whilst other ships filled up with the troops we were kept empty. There was a rumour that the evacuation was to be called off, and that we were being kept to take off the General Staff.

We remained alongside all the afternoon whilst other ships came and went. There was intense air activity the whole time, particularly from dive bombers.

We were unable to use our main armament of 4·7-inch guns as the tide was very low and they would not elevate sufficiently to clear the pier. We were left with two four-barrelled, 50-calibre machine guns and a few Lewis guns.

The general level of noise was incredible—not only from gunfire and explosions but from hundreds of stray dogs which had been driven to the water-front. They were a pathetic sight. All of them were terrified.

We suffered a few casualities on board during the afternoon, but no damage to the ship.

At about 4 p.m. Stukas made a most determined attack on us and we were hit by a stick of four bombs simultaneously. Two hit aft and one went straight down the foremost funnel, not touching the funnel casing, and burst in Number One Boiler. I cannot remember where the fourth hit.

Number One Boiler was directly below the bridge, and its bursting caused havoc on the bridge. Onlookers ashore told me afterwards that we all went up about twelve to fifteen feet. I can assure anyone that being blown up is comparatively painless. It's the coming down that hurts!

As a result of the bombs, the ship was badly on fire and the engines out of action.

I went round the ship to estimate the extent of the damage and reported to the captain that in my opinion, we should abandon and then cut her adrift. There was a strong tide running under the pier, and she would drift away from the pier. He agreed.

Luckily, we had no Army on board. At least I thought so. Actually we had one soldier. But I don't know how he managed to be there, unless he thought we looked a safer bet to get him home than other ships, and so stowed away.

We abandoned ship and cut her adrift and, as I knew she would, she drifted to the other side of the harbour, grounded and eventually blew up.

The berth at the pier was saved for other ships.

Astern of us at the time were four trawlers. I was ordered by the Pier-master to board one of them. I did this, and brought her back to Dover, arriving at about 6 a.m. on May 30.

Altogether, aboard *Grenade*, we had nineteen men killed and an unknown number of wounded.

The R.N.R. Midshipman was standing in a wing of the bridge when the bombs hit, and was blown into the water. Later, after his return to England, the Captain wrote to all officers asking for their stories of this event.

A trawler steams for home her deck crowded with evacuees.

The old Brighton Belle *after receiving a direct hit during one of the Luftwaff raids.*

The Midshipman wrote a most formal letter:

'Dear Sir:

> There was a bloody great bang. I have the honour to be, Sir, your obedient Servant.'

Then he signed himself.

A classic?

A strange codicil to Peake's account of the demise of the *Grenade* has been provided by the stowaway himself, Private W. A. Cordeux, a straggler who, with other men, had become separated from his unit during the retreat. After seventy-two hours on the beach, Cordeux decided he had waited long enough and with some of the others,

> ...ran out to the mole where the ships were. The first ship I boarded was the British destroyer *Grenade*. But Jerry dive-bombed her, and scored a direct hit on depth charges at the stern of the ship. This sank the destroyer, and then I got pulled onto the paddle-wheel ship *Crested Eagle*. Again Jerry scored direct hits and the old paddle ship sank, and it was the minesweepers that picked us up.
>
> And although we were attacked repeatedly we managed to reach Dover. All we had was trousers, undershirts and socks. After being reprimanded for not saluting some minor official we were put on a train for Bulford Camp, in Hampshire.

Many of the men aboard the *Crested Eagle* were not as lucky as Private Cordeux. Their bodies, charred and covered in oil, floated back and forth with the tide. These and hundreds of other corpses constituted a considerable part of the danger met by the crews of the small craft which went inshore to the beaches to pick up the troops. They fouled propellers and oars, and at the high water mark—where they lay four or five deep—they were an obstacle for the stretcher bearers who stumbled over them as they carried the wounded out to the boats.

✡

On Saturday, May 31, rain and fog grounded the Luftwaffe bombers with a resultant lowering of casualties and a change of heart by the Admiralty. The newer destroyers were ordered back into the holocaust and Ramsay sent Rear-Admiral Wake-Walker across to Dunkirk to take charge. He travelled on the destroyer H.M.S. *Keith* during the late afternoon, and has described La Panne beach as he saw it that night:

> Everything was black, ships and boats and shore showed no lights, although arrangements had been made for a light to be shown to seaward to guide boats inshore. Shelling was continuous and seemed to be falling among the ships at anchor. The news was conflicting. Messages from shore said that thousands of men were waiting, but there were no boats, while messages from the ships said that the boats could find no one on the beach.... The ships and the boats were there, and the troops ashore, and one could do no more. I do not know to this day what really took place there.

The new destroyers arrived back off the beaches next morning, June 1, and so did the Stukas. The latter's arrival coincided with a gap of

H.M.S. Wakefield *on it way to Dunkirk on May She was torpedoed soon a this picture was taken.*

The French destroyer Bourrasque, *sinking off Dunkirk—a remarkable photograph that has captu two figures actually fallin off the crowded deck.*

162

three hours between the R.A.F. patrols at 6 a.m. and 9 a.m., and so they were able once more to make undisturbed attacks against the myriad of ships moving to and fro off the beach-head.

The attack started at 7.20 a.m. when the first Ju 87 appeared over the battered town. The warships opened up with their anti-aircraft guns and the ships got under way to take such avoiding action as they could. First to be hit was the minesweeper H.M.S. *Skipjack* with 275 men aboard. She sank like a stone and very few of the troops got away. One of the crew who did survive, Mr. W. J. Webb, has described what happened.

Skipjack made only one trip across the Channel with troops to Ramsgate. First of June, off La Panne, our ship's company was in exhausted condition. Been constantly bombed, and although we were supposed to have shot down thirteen Jerrys—by a very unofficial observer.

Things were getting desperate ashore, the troops coming aboard were getting more exhausted besides being ravenously hungry. Loaves of bread were torn out of my hands also by French troops who had been billeted below-deck in mine-sweeping equipment stores. This was for anti-social reasons on their part. Meantime we had been having plenty of near misses.

Survivors now were getting aboard in their birthday suits. We were

constantly cruising about picking up individual Channel swimmers while our two 4·7-inch guns were still hammering away at the Stukas, manned partly by the Royal Artillery, and also backed up by Bren guns and rifle fire from the soldiers. I heard our steward who was an ammunition carrier shout, 'Ammunition gone!'

It was still early morning when the German planes hit us fore and aft, and she started to turn over slowly.

I remember looking along the messdeck from our starboard side and seeing all the troops sitting about asleep, perhaps dead. We lost 300.

She turned over quite quietly, and like a few more I just had to walk up the side onto the bottom. She had stuck on the sand in a minute.

The Germans had sunk all the big craft, destroyers, etcetera in that area. There was peace and quiet, not a sizable ship in sight. But Jerry was machine-gunning people in the water. I was hiding behind our rudder by this time. Whilst promenading on the ship's bottom, a young French officer came up to me, and in a most polite way in perfect English asked me for my life-jacket. I said, 'No' as I knew I had suffered some material damage, mostly burns and pieces out of my ear.

By this time I was gazing at the more unfortunate shipmates and Army boys, including my captain and engineer officer, who were wallowing in the oil-polluted sea.

Numerous lifeboats had been towed across for the use of the soldiers. There was a large liner-type lifeboat floating some fifty yards away. So I gingerly walked off our gallant ship's bottom and struck out for the boat. I climbed in and was followed by a ship's stoker. We managed to pull the youngest member of our crew aboard, a boy of sixteen. The boat was full in half a minute, mostly by Army types, officers. I could tell by the quality of their jerseys and their bearing.

After the *Skipjack* the destroyer *Keith*, with Wake-Walker aboard, was singled out for attack. She was down to her last thirty rounds of A.A. ammunition and there was little she could do except zig-zag to throw out the bombers aim. The first attack was made while she was under full port helm and no less than nine bombs exploded under her starboard side, throwing the ship right over on her beam ends and severely damaging her hull. Her rudder was jammed and she careered along in a tight circle. Then the Stukas returned to the attack and a bomb went down the *Keith*'s aft funnel to explode in her boiler rooms, enveloping her in great clouds of steam. Near misses damaged her still further and, listing twenty degrees to port with only about a couple of feet of freeboard above the water-line, she came to a stop. A tiny motor torpedo boat scurried up and took off the admiral, who re-hoisted his flag in another vessel. While this was happening another destroyer H.M.S. *Basilisk* was hit aft by a bomb which killed eight men and wounded four. While trying to struggle back to Dover she had to be abandoned and seventy-seven of her survivors were rescued by the French trawler *Jolie Mascotte*. Eleven other sailors of her crew and a midshipman were picked up by the tug *Duke*, and the still floating hulk of the

Basilisk was torpedoed by H.M.S. *Whitehall*. Meantime the Stukas had returned to the attack on H.M.S. *Keith*; hit again, she turned turtle and went down.

Two more destroyers had gone, adding to the losses of the *Grenade*, *Grafton* and *Wakefield*, and others were also being savaged by the dive-bombers. H.M.S. *Ivanhoe* was hit and badly damaged, but was taken in tow by the tug *Persia* and hauled back to Chatham where she was subsequently repaired. H.M.S. *Worcester*, after being damaged by bombs, and involved in a collision with the troop carrier *Maid of Orleans*, just managed to stagger back to Dover. Stukas failed to hit H.M.S. *Whitehall* although she was damaged by several near misses, but the little gunboat H.M.S. *Mosquito* had to be abandoned after receiving a direct hit which set her ablaze.

H.M.S. *Havant*, one of the very latest destroyers sailed straight from the building yard into the cauldron of Dunkirk. On her fourth trip to the beaches she went to the assistance of H.M.S. *Ivanhoe* when the latter was disabled, and some of the Stukas turned their attention to her. Two bombs hit her engine-room and a third bomb landing fifty yards ahead exploded as the *Havant* passed over it. The minesweeper H.M.S. *Saltash* tried to take her in tow but the *Havant* was doomed. After further attacks she rolled over and sank with the loss of thirty-four lives.

More naval vessels went down that afternoon. The French destroyer *Foudroyant* was approaching the mole when she was 'submerged in a cloud of Stukas'. Hit by three bombs and deluged by near misses she capsized and sank. There were alarmingly high losses among the non-combatant ships as well. A 500 lb. bomb landed on the after-deck of the *Brighton Queen*—an old paddle boat converted for mine-sweeping—decimating about half the 700 French troops on board (the *Saltash* took off the remainder before the *Brighton Queen* went down). The London and North Eastern Railway Company's vessel *Prague* was carrying 3000 French soldiers when she was hit and damaged. And of course there was the *Scotia*. At the end of the day the evacuation fleet had lost thirty-one ships sunk and eleven seriously damaged.

Such losses meant that the bulk of the remaining evacuation had to be done by night. The Luftwaffe did not operate after sunset, and although S-Boats and U-Boats were active off the approaches to Dunkirk they were unable to do more than harry the convoys of rescue ships.

Over the page
The little ships go home—a triumphant journey up the Thames past Westminster and the House of Commons.

TO THE SEAMEN

You seamen, I have eaten your hard bread
And drunken from your tin, and known your ways;
I understand the qualities I praise
Though lacking all, with only words instead,

I tell you this, that in the future time
When landsmen mention sailors, such, or such,
Someone will say 'Those fellows were sublime
Who brought the Armies from the Germans' clutch.'

Through the long time the story will be told;
Long centuries of praise on English lips,
Of courage godlike and of hearts of gold
Off Dunquerque beaches in the little ships.

And ships will dip their colours in salute
To you, henceforth, when passing Zuydecoote.

Composed by John Masefield, Poet Laureate, in 1940.

9. Enterprise and Courage

May 30 – June 1

By the evening of May 27 the disappointing total of only 7669 men had embarked at Dunkirk. Next day the little boats started to arrive and with the Luftwaffe hampered by low cloud, rain and drizzle over its airfields, the number of men lifted to safety gradually increased. By midnight on May 30 a total of 126,606 men had been evacuated and the number lifted on the 31st reached a peak of 68,014. Dynamo was now in full swing with every available vessel engaged in the effort; and the great naval bases at Portsmouth and Plymouth and ports along the south and east coast of England were virtually empty. Nevertheless more than 200,000 men still waited at Dunkirk to be taken off. And these were the fighting troops, the men who had covered the retreat and since held the Perimeter.

The crews of the little ships were eager to get to Dunkirk. Nearly all were civilians of every class and calling; quite a few were middle-aged amateur yachtsmen owning the boats they sailed. The only servicemen were aircraftmen manning R.A.F. air–sea rescue launches and a handful of naval officers and petty officers who had been put in command of the ad hoc flotillas into which the armada was organized. All the civilians were volunteers. The Naval Correspondent of *The Times* described how in one small town men were invited to volunteer for a job of which it was only known that it would be dangerous and would not last for more than a few days. In six hours 150 men volunteered. Women volunteers took river boats down to the ports and at least one 'is related to have extorted permission to go to Dunkirk by telephoning to the Admiralty in contralto tones so deep as to be mistaken for a man'. Inevitably, until fantasy was swept aside by the impact of reality, there were many—mature men as well as boys in their teens—who regarded the operation as an adventure. But under fire along the Dunkirk beaches discipline was an important factor and the navy men were there to see that the job was done properly.

The great majority of the small craft of Ramsay's cockleshell navy sailed from Ramsgate at 2.30 p.m. on Friday, May 31. But some little boats had beaten the gun and gone ahead. Among them were the familiar blue-hulled Ramsgate and Margate lifeboats, manned by men of 'riper years' whose ages aggregated 600. Both sailed during the afternoon of May 30, with the Ramsgate boat, the *Prudential*, towing a regular ship's lifeboat and eight wherries. The latter were loaded with tins of drinking water together with coils of rope for hauling small craft from the beaches when they had grounded, or running out kedge anchors. The *Prudential*'s skipper was Coxswain Howard Knight whose report read as follows:

> Proceeded to a given position at Dunkirk; accompanying boats discharged water and rope as instructed, as also did lifeboat, found seas breaking in the shoal water approach to beach; had to lay off on account of the deeper draft of lifeboat; found naval ratings who manned wherries were not skilled at handling small boats under such conditions; members of lifeboat crew took their boats and places, and although an intensely dark night managed by shouting to establish communication with officer in charge of troops on beach; arranged for men to take to the water in batches of eight which was the capacity of the small boats, and each boat conveyed them to the lifeboat, thence to the awaiting craft in attendance. About 800 were safely transported on Thursday night (May 30) and when the last three boatloads were being taken from the water, the officer called, 'I cannot see who you are; are you a naval party?' He was answered, 'No, sir, we are members of the crew of the Ramsgate lifeboat.' He then called, 'Thank you—and thank God for such men as you have this night proved yourselves to be. There is a party of fifty Highlanders coming next.'

Coxswain Knight reckoned that 800 men with their equipment weighed just about 100 tons. So *Prudential*'s crew, working in the dark on a strange beach and often under heavy fire hauled their share that night.

The Margate lifeboat *Lord Southborough* also hauled its share, and Signalman Price, one of the crew, has given a description of the conditions at La Panne at the time:

> That big casino up from the beach had been made into a hospital. The Jerries hit it with salvoes every ten minutes. Then, for ten minutes, they would hit the beach, along the water's edge. This they did straight out. Speak about clockwork.
> We'd come in with the boats from offshore while Jerry was shelling the casino. The lads would run from the shell holes up the beach, get aboard. Then we'd shove off. While Jerry shelled the beach the men stayed still, didn't move. That way, they were quite safe. We got about 500 of them out to a destroyer and a barge.
> But in the morning the wind hauled round nor'west. It made a heavy surf on the beach. The open boats working there were overloaded. Many of them sank, with all hands. And the lads in the water were weary, and still carried their gear. More than a few were knocked down by the surf, too. They drowned.
> We had a six-foot rope ladder out astern. Men started to rush that. Only the lot we could carry got aboard. We had to fight off the others.

Those would have sunk the boat.

Then a destroyer gave an order on her loud-hailer. 'All small boats lay off.' More men were being drowned than saved.

Running low on fuel the *Lord Southborough*'s skipper, Coxswain Edward Parker, was about to turn for Margate when he spotted a whaler in trouble close to the beach. It was a boat which had originally belonged to one of the destroyers, and which was now laboriously making its way through the shallows along the strafing path of low-flying Me 110s.

Parker steered a course that took the *Lord Southborough* alongside the whaler, and found that it was manned by two officers and fifteen ratings of the Royal Navy.

> They had found the whaler on the sands with no gear in it and full of water (said Parker). They got the water out, found enough oars on the beach to get it off the shore far enough for us to pick them up. But as the wind had freshened, blowing right on the shore, they were barely holding their own. They had no rowlocks, but had got the oars lashed to the gunwales, and had been rowing, trying to get to one of the many ships that were in the vicinity from before daylight. They were the remains of a party of 150 that had been working on the sands for four days. They were taken on board the lifeboat and their boat cast adrift. We brought them to Margate and landed them about 3 p.m. I cannot say accurately how many men were able to get aboard the destroyer, H.M.S. *Icarus*, and the barge, but I do not believe it was less than 500. Bombs and shells were falling most of the time.

The *Lord Southborough* was only a few hours in Margate; on June 1 she was ordered back to Dunkirk. During the final trips she brought out French soldiers who had been fighting on the Perimeter and the lifeboat's crew had a high opinion of them. They did not share the belief common among the men of the B.E.F. that the French had failed the Allied cause because they would not fight. And they felt the same about the Belgians. Five Belgian tugs, *Max, Vulcain, Goliath, Elbe* and *Thames* based on Margate since May 25 had been continuously in service since May 25 and on the last day of Dynamo four of them were sunk. The lifeboatmen felt that the Belgians they knew had served Britain well, and they were saddened by what was said of Britain's allies by men in the pubs who had seen nothing of war.

☆

The motor yacht *Constant Nymph*, owned by a London doctor, Basil Smith, was another of the small craft which sailed ahead of the cockleshell armada. Dr Smith had duly registered his yacht following the instructions broadcast over the B.B.C., and shortly after midnight on May 26 a duty officer at the Admiralty telephoned to ask if Smith's boat was ready for sea. At 8.45 a.m. the telephone rang again and the Admiralty

asked me to go to the boat. Having already put a few things in a bag I went to Isleworth on the Thames as soon as possible and arrived there between 10 and 11. It was obvious that some form of permit would be required as my own permit only carried to Middle Blythe Buoy, and my instructions were to take the boat to Sheerness. I found at the boat-house that a naval officer was expected who would issue the permits and was requisitioning boats in the same yard.

He wanted the boats to go down together, but separate permits were issued by the afternoon so that I was then ready to start at any time, and the others did not look like being ready for several hours.

At about 5.30 p.m. I tried to ring up the 'Mate' as I felt sure he would want to be in on the game and might at least be able to help me work the boat down to Sheerness. Luckily he was home early and put such a jerk into things that he got his things together and arrived from Tulse Hill to Isleworth before 7.30 p.m. and we started at 8.30 without waiting for the other boats.

At Sheerness a Royal Navy officer suggested that Dr Smith might like to sign on for a month with the navy:

The opportunity of playing boats for a month with the navy seemed too good to miss in any case, and I had been able to warn my partners that I should be away for a bit. But there was some difficulty in getting signed on and I toured Sheerness Dockyard interviewing numerous people until late in the afternoon, and by about 5 p.m. had formed a pretty accurate idea what the job was and was quite determined not to be put off. So I appealed to the Commodore himself, who was supervising the fuelling and victualling of the motorboats at the basin. Within half an hour I was signed on and back at the basin, and by 6 p.m. was making my way out of the basin with a crew of two young navy ratings, a full tank, and deck cargo of petrol, waterbeaker and enough provisions to last my little gang for about a week, including a large lump of raw beef, and two small sacks of potatoes—raw. The boat seemed very overcrowded.

Constant Nymph and her crew were then held at Ramsgate until May

30 when she finally got her orders to proceed to Dunkirk. Together with some other small boats she was towed to Dunkirk by one of the Dutch skoots, the *Jutland*:

At about 3.30 p.m. (Dr Smith said), we got going ... and were towed to Dunkirk in about six hours (an average of about 12 knots.) This was a very uncomfortable trip. Destroyers kept crossing and passing at high speeds, making a very heavy wash, and we had to try to keep my boat sheered off to port while the cutter and whaler we towed were sheered off to starboard. Sometimes we came together in spite of all effort, but no damage was done.

Constant Nymph and the pulling boats were secured to a curious vessel of Belgian extraction called *Johanna*, and she was on tow to *Jutland* by a wire rope. This wire parted about 4 p.m., but *Jutland* was stopped in time to ease the strain before the last single strand went, thus saving some injuries and possibly lives. *Johanna*'s crew fell on her deck and I crouched behind my cabin trunk as that wire spun and strand after strand parted. *Johanna* was like a heavy old cow and at the rate we were going the wire was like a banjo string and the whip back if the last strand had gone would have been terrific. At 4.50 p.m., a new manila rope had been passed and we got going again.

We arrived at Dunkirk about dusk and turned along the beach eastwards for a few miles before *Jutland* dropped anchor. We cast off tow at once and I took the whaler and cutter in tow myself and set out for the beach. It was slightly misty as well as dark, but it was not really a dark night and visibility was not too bad.

As this point had not been worked before, we did not know whether Jerry was there or our men. Being quite unarmed we had to be canny about hailing until we knew who was there. At first we could find no life on the beach, but after a short time we were hailed by Frenchmen and for a little while found Frenchmen only, and made one or two full journeys back to the ship with them. The procedure was to tow the whaler and cutter to the beach and swing them round and cast off tow in about 3 feet 6 inches—my draft being 2 feet 6 inches. The cutter then dropped her grapnel and went in as close as she dared without grounding the whaler, and troops waded out to board them. As soon as the two boats were full they called for the motorboat and pulled up on the cutter's grapnel. I would come past and take the cutter's rope in passing and swing out towards the ship which had to lie about three quarters of a mile to a mile out.

While the whaler and cutter were loading I patrolled parallel with the beach, keeping as close as I dared without grounding, it being esssential that the motorboat should not take ground as it was the only motorboat in that area and the cutter and whaler had only three men apiece aboard so that they were not in a position to row out to the ship, except at a great loss of time.

While patrolling my job was to pick up any swimmers or waders and any odd craft which had put out from the shore. There were several of these. After the first few loads had been taken to the ship, all Frenchmen, a British officer waded out and was picked up by me and reported that

The London Fire Brigade's fire-float returns in triumph. Manned by a crew of thirteen volunteers it made three trips to Dunkirk, bringing back over 600 men.

a whole division of British were waiting to be taken off a little nearer Dunkirk town than we had been working.

I took him aboard, went back and picked up the full cutter and whaler, and took them all back to the ship, reported to the captain of *Jutland* that the British were further up the beach, and that I was going there. A big fire just inshore was my leading mark as the British were just to the east of this. From then on we worked to this point and the French came down the beach and mingled with the British. *Jutland* was filled roughly half and half British and French.

After we had been going to this point for about three or four trips, a German bomber most inconsiderately dropped a large bomb on our large fire and blew it out like a candle. This did not matter very much, as I had leading marks and the mass of troops had increased so that they were quite visible on the beach.

By about 3 a.m., May 31, *Jutland* was full, and she sailed at once to avoid the dawn bombing. Jerry was trying to bomb the ships as they left loaded. But his efforts through the ten to eleven hours that I worked on the beach were very poorly rewarded.

Dr Smith* had missed the action which had raged during the daylight hours of May 30, and this is described by Mr L. W. Salmons, the skipper of the oyster-dredging smack *Seasalter*. The *Seasalter's* home base was Burnham-on-Crouch in Essex and it was on his way back there from the local oyster beds on Wednesday 29 that Salmons was told that a naval officer wished to see him when he got in to port:

* *Constant Nymph* got back safely and Dr Smith was subsequently awarded the D.S.M. for his work at Dunkirk.

We immediately went ashore and were introduced to Commander Bowles, R.N., who told us the *Seasalter* was required to attempt to help bring back some of the soldiers off the beach at Dunkirk. I volunteered to take the *Seasalter*, and asked for a crew. Dick Cook, the engineer, and Bill Bridge, one of the hands, also volunteered. The Commander said there would be two other boats, one being the oyster-dredging vessel *Vanguard*, whose skipper was Albert Grimwade. *Ma Joie*, a motor yacht, was to be the third boat.

It was 6 p.m. when we spotted the coast and picked up Dunkirk lighthouse right ahead...and by 6.45 p.m. were at the harbour entrance. We asked someone on the breakwall where we should go and were told, 'Get out of the harbour'.

We then approached a destroyer to ask what to do. When we got near the destroyer opened fire at the aircraft, so we sheered off. After this we steamed up towards the east beach. No one spoke to us or took any notice at all. We thought this strange as we had been told there would be hundreds of boats and someone to tell us what to do. Instead of that we were the first three small craft there. By then we didn't need any telling.

The soldiers were coming off the beach clinging to bits of wood and wreckage and anything that would float. As we got close enough we began to pick them up. We saw a rowboat coming off loaded right down with troops. And with this we went to and fro, bringing as many as it would dare hold, and in the meantime we went round picking up as many as we could. When we got a load we would take them off to one of the ships lying off in the deep water. Some were Dutch coasters flying the White Ensign, and the armed yacht *Grive*.

Unfortunately *Ma Joie* had got into difficulties and had to be towed off the beach. We went alongside and were told the rudder was broken and the propeller fouled. It was decided that they should come aboard us as their ship was useless.

All this time the din was deafening, aircraft flying around, A.A. guns banging, and all over the place fountains of water would fling into the air. We went on getting loads and taking them off to the ships. When the two boats came off next time *Ma Joie*'s crew and a soldier took over and these three men rowed back and forth all the rest of the time we were there....

About ten o'clock it began to get dark. The ships got their anchors up and got out of it. We were still getting soldiers aboard and could find no ship to put them on. By 11 there we were with ninety men aboard. We didn't know what to do with them, so we put twenty aboard the *Vanguard*, we gave them some beer we had, and Bill made tea and gave them biscuits and the remainder of our stores. We didn't know whether we were doing right or wrong. Bombs were falling and shells bursting all around, so we decided to make for Ramsgate.

How we got out without seeing or hitting anything I don't know. Any rate we did, and by 12 o'clock we were clear. We then shaped our course for Ramsgate. We hadn't gone far when we met a convoy of small ships going in. They had no lights, as we had no lights, either. Jerry was flying around dropping parachute flares and bombs, but they fell nowhere near us.

We kept going across and all kinds of navy ships came and had a look at us. At nearly 4 a.m. (Friday, May 31) the wind started to freshen and some of the soldiers on deck got a wetting. We heard no more aircraft and steamed into Ramsgate with the *Vanguard* in the rear at 8.30 a.m. The soldiers went ashore. All seemed very happy, if they had been a bit sick. We lay alongside the quay. No one spoke to us until the afternoon when we were told with the other small craft to disperse immediately. We made for Burnham and arrived home at midnight Saturday, dirty and tired but glad to have brought a few chaps across.

In fact, although *Ma Joie* had to be abandoned, the crews of all three Burnham boats got back safely and with no casualties. The crew of the yacht *Grive* which Captain Salmons spoke of was not so lucky.

H.M.S. *Grive* was an old 816-ton steam yacht that had seen service in World War I as H.M. Yacht *Narcissus*. By 1939 most of the Royal Navy steam yachts had been broken up. But the old *Narcissus* was still afloat and she came out of retirement to fly the White Ensign as a Fleet Air Arm tender. To command her a distinguished sixty-seven-year-old officer, Captain the Hon. Lionel Lambart, also came out of retirement. Lambart took H.M.S. *Grive* to Dunkirk on May 27 and during three hectic days and nights rescued 2000 men of the B.E.F. Then the *Grive* was sunk, Lambart and most of her crew of forty-three going down with her (Sub-Lieutenant J. K. B. Miles, R.N.V.R., was one who survived and was later awarded the D.S.C.).

Despite such tragedies the number of men lifted from the beaches was steadily increasing. Thus, on the morning of May 31, Ramsay had good reason to hope that when the main armada of his cockleshell navy arrived at Dunkirk that afternoon the evacuation would go on even faster. He was not to be disappointed: 68,014 men were lifted out that day and another 64,429 on June 1st.

More than a hundred small craft participated in the operation on May 30, and it is impossible to say how many were involved from then on. Boats arrived at the beaches unescorted and under their own power, loaded, sailed back to England where the troops disembarked, took on petrol and water, and returned to Dunkirk for another load.

The armada started to arrive off Dunkirk in the late afternoon of May 31, and it is probably true to say that no other fleet ever put to sea with such a diversity of craft. One big tug *Racia* towed twelve ships' lifeboats across, another tug, *Tanga*, had six; the Thames tugs *Sun IV*, *Sun VIII*, *Sun XIII* and *Sun XV* hauled either ships' lifeboats or barges. With the exception of one which had been left in the Port of London to cope with emergencies there, every single Thames-side tug was now deployed on Dynamo.

The barges that were towed, with names like *Sibyl*, *Savoy*, *Siesta*, *Sunbeam*, *Shamrock*, *Swiftsure* and *Sarah Ann*, were the old spritsail-rigged craft that used to frequent the lower reaches of the Thames estuary. They were cargo-carriers, broad in beam, heavily built and awkward to

Flight-Lieut. 'Sailor' Malan, a South African serving with 74 (Tiger) Sqn, was credited with destroying a number of German aircraft over Dunkirk.

manœuvre, but seaworthy. The column also included Bawley boats and hopper barges—some moving under their own power, others being towed. The unwieldy barges were used in normal times to receive and later dump loads of mud dredged from rivers and estuaries. They were not ideally suited to the rough weather for which the Channel is famed, but they were a means of carrying men and that was what mattered on 31 May, 1940. The Bawley boats (which took their name from Bawley Bay, Gravesend) were the sturdy shallow-draft, cutter-rigged fishing vessels which worked the whitebait, sprat, whelk and shrimp grounds around the Thames and Medway estuaries; their crews were, for the most part, hard-bitten old salts. Some of the Bawley boats trailed the familiar Thames cockle boats astern. These were also shallow-draft sailing craft, deriving their name from their normal work—raking cockles in the Thames estuary.

Among the other craft in the Dunkirk armada were Thames 'whalers'—motor-powered clinker-built boats, about twenty feet long. On their departure from Ramsgate many of them towed smaller rowing craft. These were to prove extremely useful at the beaches, but only when they were manned by crews who knew how to handle them in the surf. The dark blue hulls of Royal National Life-boat Institution

craft were distinctively prominent in the convoy. But only the *Prudential* and the *Lord Southborough* (from Ramsgate and Margate respectively) were manned by their own crews. The coxswains of the seventeen others —from Great Yarmouth, Gorleston, Lowestoft, Aldeburgh, Frinton, Walton-on-the-Naze, Clacton, Southend-on-Sea, Walmer, Hythe, Dungeness, Hastings, Eastbourne, Newhaven, Shoreham, Poole and Cadgwith—had told the naval authorities that they did not believe their boats were suited to picking troops up from Dunkirk's beaches. So the lifeboats had been requisitioned and naval crews sent aboard. Ramsay's staff at Dover reckoned that the lifeboats could carry 100 or more soldiers, and if there was risk, then that was war.

Intermixed with the Bawley boats, the hopper barges, the cocklers, the sailing barges, the tugs with their strings of whalers and rowing boats, and the trim blue R.N.L.I. lifeboats were the yachts and power boats. Some were the tall-masted sailing craft more usually associated with Cowes regattas than this sort of venture. Now they used their motors or were towed.

Then there were the cabin cruisers, mostly between sixteen and twenty-five feet, with names like *Dinky*, *Dumpling*, *Miranda*, *Peggy*, *Polly*, *Sarah* and *Emily*, and *Sundowner*. Neither the boats nor their motors were new. Having been laid up since the summer of 1939 paint was cracking and varnish needed scraping, sanding and renewals. Pumps did not work very well and as the heads had not been connected the crews urinated over the side. (Not all the men in this section of the armada had anything to do with the ownership of the boats in which they sailed. They were volunteers and had simply been assigned on an ad hoc basis to vessels in the Small Vessels Pool.)

Just what the volunteers had let themselves in for soon became apparent. Vessels returning from Dunkirk bore the evidence of battle— hulls holed by machine-gun bullets, blood and bodies on their decks. There was no waving, no exchange of banter; no curiosity was shown. Most of the men bound for Dunkirk averted their eyes; some were quietly sick. Then, as they got closer to their destination, they heard the drone of aircraft engines followed by the scream of diving Stukas and the whistle of falling bombs, coupled with the dull thud of artillery and bursting bombs overlaid with the constant rattle of small-arms fire.

A few miles from the beaches the fleet dispersed and individual boats headed through the channel, steering between the wrecks for the shore. Now the crews were able to see the full extent of the disaster which had brought them to Dunkirk—the blazing oil tanks, the pall of smoke over the town, the wrecked destroyers, the beached and burnt-out ships, and the mole where men were still waiting, five abreast, until their turn came to embark. All the buildings on the waterfront, including the *Gare Maritime*, the Dunkirk Casino and the hotels and boarding houses along the whole length of beach to La Panne appeared to be under fire. But this part of the story is best told by the men who were there.

179

Robert Harling, an amateur yachtsman from London who volunteered with most of the others in the navigation class being run by Captain O. M. Watts,* wrote an account of his service in the May 31 phase of the evacuation. Harling and the others reported initially at the Port of London Authority on Tower Hill. From there they were sent to Tilbury:

...We eventually joined the 2.30 convoy. With eleven other boats in charge of Thames tug *Sun IV* we moved off down river, a strange cortège, nestling in the wake of the fussing tug with its two small white stern lights. Midnight donged on one of the riverside churches. The river and the night were wholly merged.

In the first ten minutes the tug was stopped twice for adjustment to towing ropes; two of the boats had swung round, broadside on to the tug, and had almost capsized. There were shrill calls and curses in the darkness from huddled shapes at the tillers. The throb of the tug's engines died; ropes were moved to more precise positions; 'O.K.,' shouted somebody through the night, and the procession moved into life.

We divided ourselves into watches; one hour on, three hours off.

All through the afternoon of the next day we passed our own ships returning with men. British and French destroyers, sloops, trawlers, drifters and motorboats were on their way back. They were packed tight with masses of khaki figures lining the decks, crowded to the ropes of the bulwarks. The destroyers slit the calm seas as if this were a journey against time and 'the quicker back to Dover, the quicker back to Dunkirk written all over 'em', someone said.

In the middle of one of the discussions which started from time to time, our starboard companion-boat swung round, crashed into us at what seemed terrific speed, forcing us far over, so that we lay dangerously upon our beam. The other boat buried her port side completely under water. Three ratings were hurled into the sea. The fourth yelled and hung onto a thwart. I saw two go clean under our boat; the other was caught as he was swept past a boat astern. I looked to port; two white faces were carried astern very swiftly.

One still wore a tin helmet, and the other yelled fearfully. I think he yelled, 'I can't swim', but he went down once and was gone. Voices cried frantically to the tug. She swung round quickly to port; as skilful and as swift a turn as a London taxi driver's. Engines were slowed for the search. One was picked up. The other had gone. The tug cruised around for about ten minutes, but it was a vain search and we turned once again to our course.

An hour later we were nearing the French coast. Subtly the feeling in the boat changed. There was a nervous tenseness amongst us; we no longer talked, but stared ahead as if looking for a reef. We were moving up the coast with a stranger miscellany of craft than was ever seen in the most hybrid amateur regatta: destroyers, sloops, trawlers, motorboats, fishing boats, tugs, Dutch schuits. Under the splendid sun they seemed like craft of peace journeying upon a gay occasion, but suddenly

* Still a well-known name in the sailing world.

180

we knew we were there, for someone said, 'There they are, the bastards!' My eyes followed the line of his pointing arm, but I could see nothing; but not for long this blindness.

There were over fifty German planes. I counted them swiftly, surprised to find how easy it was to count them. We did not get as many at a time in the Norwegian campaign. I imagined that they were bombers with fighter escorts, but my silhouettes were never very sound. They were like slow-flying gnats in a vast sky, seeming to move deliberately and with a simple purpose towards us, flying very high.

I got a heavy sick feeling right down in the stomach. The bombs dropped out of the cloudless sky. We watched them fall as the planes directed their principal attack upon two destroyers. The destroyers seemed to sit back on their buttocks and spit flames; the harsh cracks of their ack-ack guns were heartening. Then we got the kick from the bombs as their ricochet came up through the sea. Our little boat rocked and lifted high out of the water. One, two, three, four.... We waited, counting them and held tight to the gunwale.

The bombers seemed to be dispersing. Our own fighters suddenly appeared. It was quite true, I thought, all that I had read in the newspapers: our pilots really did put the other chaps to flight. Far above us the German formations broke. Some came down in steep dives. From the 15,000 or 20,000 feet we had computed they were down to 2,000 or 3,000.

One came low, machine-gunning a tug and its towed lifeboats. Then came another. We knew it was coming our way. It was crazy to sit there, goggle-eyed and helpless, just waiting for it, but there seemed singularly little else to do. The seconds were hours. 'Wait for it and duck!' shouted someone above the roar of the engines. 'Now! And bale like bloody hell if he hits the boat.' We ducked.

The cockleshell fleet had been timed to arrive just after dark. By then the chaotic conditions that had existed on the beaches earlier had been sorted out; there was now some sort of system. Under cover of darkness Harling's boat and the other lifeboats cast off from the tugs, went in through the shoals, took on a load of troops and were met by motorboats which waited for them further out. The motorboats then towed the lifeboats to the troop-carriers, the destroyers, the minesweepers and the skoots waiting at anchor still further out. And when these were fully loaded and had sailed the men being ferried from the beaches were off-loaded into the tugs until they too were fully loaded and sailed for England.

Things seemed to be going well, when dawn broke on the morning of June 1. Goering's Air Fleets had managed to sink only one vessel the previous day, although no less than six destroyers had been damaged in collisions; artillery fire against one end of the town and the eastern

181

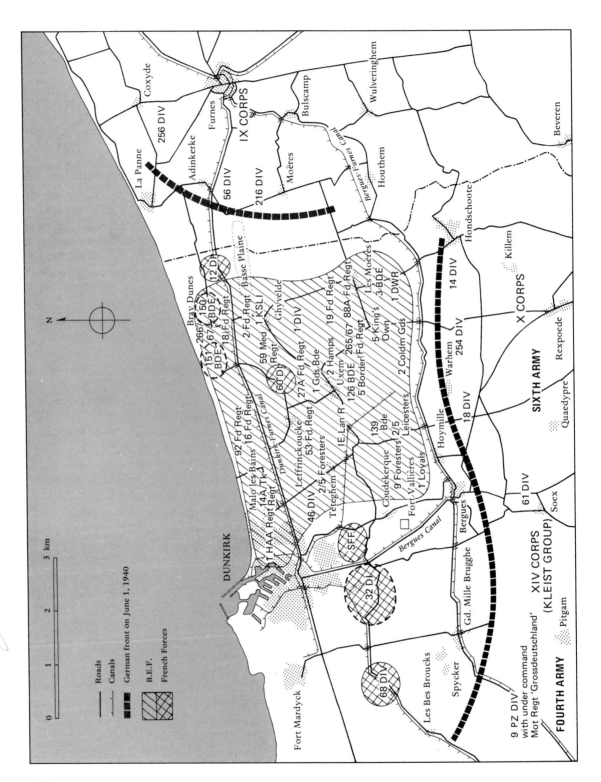

beaches was also an ever-increasing menace. But things were not as bad as had been feared. Nevertheless even more strenuous efforts were now needed, for the French had decided to share in the withdrawal and Churchill had decreed that henceforth the evacuation should proceed on equal terms between British and French—'bras dessus bras dessous' as he put it. The new destroyers were on their way back to help, but the end of the evacuation—which Ramsay believed was in sight at dusk on May 31—was now receding.

June 1 turned out to be a splendid summer's day, and as the sun rose the mist and low cloud which had hung over Dunkirk rapidly dispersed. And never was the cool splendour of a summer's morning less appreciated by the men on the beaches. There had been one or two air raids during the night, but they had been relatively ineffective. Now, however, the real thing began. Bombed to hell, the soldiers and sailors began asking the same old question: 'Where is the R.A.F.?' Heavily outnumbered—thanks to the Treasury's parsimony in the past, and the inability of unimaginative politicians and dessicated Civil Servants

Casualty sustained in an air raid being hoisted aboard one of the rescue ships.

to speed up production in the months of the Phoney War—the R.A.F. was in fact doing its best. Some of Dowding's treasured Spitfire squadrons earmarked for the defence of Britain had been drawn into the battle. Pilots of the Hurricanes, Spitfires, the new Boulton-Paul Defiants,* and a few Fleet Air Arm Gladiators flew as many as four sorties a day, fighting battles miles above or away from the beaches: '... the whole Metropolitan air force, our last sacred reserve was used. ... Hour after hour they bit into the German fighters and bomber squadrons, taking a heavy toll,' wrote Winston Churchill. This was not true; Dowding continued to hold some of his squadrons in reserve and although the R.A.F. claimed to have destroyed seventy-six German aircraft on June 1, the Luftwaffe actually lost only twenty-nine machines all told—of which ships' gunfire accounted for a dozen. Thus, as the R.A.F. lost thirty-one planes that day, Churchill's claim that Britain had scored a 'victory within a deliverance' may be seen as a gross exaggeration.

Yet this does not detract from the magnificent courage and astonishing skill displayed by individual R.A.F. pilots, who were in their own words 'just doing their job'. Alan Deere, for example, flying a Spitfire, was shot down by a Dornier 17 and landed on the beach fifteen miles from Dunkirk. After stealing a bicycle he joined the refugee traffic towards Bray Dunes and when the road became choked with refugees he continued on foot into Dunkirk. 'The sight on arrival at the beach,' he said, 'I shall never forget. ... Discipline and control despite the obvious exhaustion and desperation of thousands of troops ... snake-like columns stretched from the sand-dunes to the water's edge.' Deere made his way towards the mole where men were boarding destroyers. As he reached the end of the causeway three Ju 88s streaked across. 'There was a mad scramble for cover ... mostly the troops just dived into the water, re-emerging at neck level to fire their rifles in desperation and defiance ... A crescendo of bombs ... machine-gun fire descended on the beach. In a few seconds it was all over. A number of British soldiers would not be requiring transport back to England. ...'

As he ran towards the destroyer Deere was stopped by a 'brown job'—a B.E.F. major. 'I'm an R.A.F. officer,' Deere explained, 'I'm trying to get back to my squadron.' 'I don't give a damn who you are,' the major retorted. 'For all the good you chaps seem to be doing, you might as well stay on the ground.' Deere told him to go to hell, and eventually he was allowed to board a destroyer. Below in the ward room he was greeted in stony silence by a crowd of other army officers. 'Why so friendly?' he asked. 'What have the R.A.F. done?' 'That's just it,' someone said, 'What have they done?'

While the B.E.F. did not believe the R.A.F. was 'doing its job', the

* In appearance the Defiant was not unlike the Hurricane except for its power-driven gun turret. But the heavy turret and the fact that it carried a crew of two degraded its performance, and against the Me109 it was hopeless.

184

Luftwaffe crews thought differently. 'From the British fighters we met heavy and spirited resistance,' said Rudolf Braun, a Stuka pilot. Men like Braun had been trained at the Stuka school at Graz, where they had learned to put a bomb in a 120-foot diameter circle. At Dunkirk, where they were attacking ships for the first time, they picked the target and waited until they were at 1500 feet before releasing the bombs. The recommended height was 2000 feet and the usual good luck cry exchanged between Stuka pilots before take-off was the droll Berlin greeting 'Hals- und Beinbruch'. Breaking necks and legs did not appeal to the Messerschmidt and Heinkel pilots who provided the umbrella under which the Stukas operated. They thought that the slow-flying Ju 87s flew much too low and stayed in the target area far too long.

Targets were designated before the Geschwader took off, and every Stuka carried either 250 kg. or 500 kg. delayed-action bombs. Because of their low speed they were vulnerable to Spitfires and Hurricanes for the greater part of their missions. However, once individual targets had been located and pilots were screaming down towards them with dive-brakes off, they were momentarily fairly safe from fighters. Their next hazard derived from the blast of the exploding bombs—oil tanks were the worst because they went up in a colossal explosion which would take the Stuka with it if the pilot had pulled out too low. Meanwhile the pilot would be wrestling with the controls, trying to put the plane into a climb and away from the sea. (Never, if possible, did the Stuka pilots at Dunkirk fly out to sea; the Royal Navy's A.A. was too hot.) With their speed so reduced that they seemed almost to hang in the air, this was the Stukas' moment of greatest vulnerability. Pilots were fully occupied—resetting dive-brakes and bomb-release switches, reopening radiator shutters, and adjusting elevation trim, while simultaneously re-positioning the planes in a tight tactical defensive formation.

Braun's opinion of R.A.F. effectiveness has been echoed by other Luftwaffe sources. The Dornier 17 which shot Deere out of the sky was one of a formation which set Dunkirk's oil tanks ablaze before it was jumped by Deere's Spitfire squadron. Six of the Dorniers were shot down or forced to make crash landings, and Major Werner Kreipe reported, 'The enemy fighters pounced on our tightly knit formation with maniacal fury.' That night the Daily Situation Report of Goering's Air Fleet 2 stated that it had been a 'bad day'... 'With sixty-four air crew missing, seven wounded and twenty-three aircraft gone, today's losses exceed combined total of at least ten days.'

But the B.E.F. knew nothing of this, and the point has been made already: for them it was the R.A.F's apparent shortcomings which counted, not its achievements.

Over the page
The return trip, across a Channel now crowded with rescuing vessels.

'The Board of Admiralty congratulates all concerned in the successful evacuation of the B.E.F. and the soldiers of the Allied armies from the Dunkirk area.

Their lordships appreciate the splendid endurance with which all ships and personnel faced the continuous attack of enemy aircraft and the physical strain imposed by long hours of arduous work in narrow waters over many days.

Their lordships also realize that success was only rendered possible by the great effort made by all shore establishments, and in particular by the Dover Command, who were responsible for the organization and direction of this difficult operation.'

The Board of Admiralty in a signal,
4 June 1940

10. Final Phase

June 1 – 2.30 p.m. June 4

Throughout the morning of Saturday, June 1, the evacuation continued. But the Luftwaffe was making its most determined effort to ruin the lifting, and until the clouds mercifully rolled over and blanketed the scene the shipping off-shore was under constant attack. Men who had been there on the Thursday, May 30, thought things were bad enough; now they were much worse, for the ships had to face an extra hazard. As the Perimeter shrank the Germans had moved their artillery forward and their guns now covered the central route (X) to Dunkirk as well as the direct (Z) and eastern (Y) approaches. By noon ten vessels—including three destroyers—had been sunk; several others had been seriously damaged, and four troop transports and a couple of hospital ships had had to lie off the harbour entrance because of the bombing and shelling.

Meantime daylight had revealed about 6000 men of the 4th Division on the exposed beaches or among the sand-dunes at La Panne. A mile off-shore, and even more exposed, several ships lay at anchor. But there was no means of reaching them, nor did it seem likely that boats would become available. So General Johnson, the division commander, decided that his men should march along the coast by way of Bray Dunes to Dunkirk where they would embark from the mole.

At Bray Dunes the situation was, if anything, more chaotic than at La Panne. Fifteen thousand men who had gathered on the beach had formed up into columns stretching back across the debris-strewn dunes. They stood or sat three abreast, with the columns separated lengthwise at ten-man intervals. Thirty men was the average boat-load, and the organization was intended to simplify loading procedure. Here as at La Panne, however, the problem was a shortage of boats, many of which had been lost or cast adrift when their load of soldiers had boarded the bigger vessels off-shore. Unmanned, these boats now bobbed about beyond the reach of all except the strongest and most daring swimmers. Some bridging pontoons—blunt-nosed, double-ended, shallow-draft craft—were pressed into use—the men loaded into them paddling with their rifle butts and bailing with their helmets. Along the ten-kilometre stretch of beach only one motor-boat remained to tow smaller craft off-shore. She belonged to one of the destroyers which, under direct enemy attack, had been compelled to abandon her. Not until dawn on June 2 did other motor-boats arrive to help in the ferrying. And when they did arrive they became almost instantly a target for the Luftwaffe.

Early on May 30 one of the beach-control naval officers, Commander H. N. A. Richardson, had suggested to Captain Tennant that emergency embarkation piers would speed up the loading procedure. Hundreds of the B.E.F's three-ton trucks, hurriedly diverted from the vehicular knacker's yards, were driven into the sea and planks laid across them to make a pier. When the tide rose—and there were boats to put in to them—the troops would embark from these jetties. But at low water the improvised piers were as fatuous as they looked, more so because for sixteen hours there were no boats to use them.

When they trudged down from La Panne, men of the 6th Bn The Black Watch attempted to devise their own methods of getting to the ships off-shore. Capturing a couple of the loose horses some optimists tried to swim them out to the ships, but the horses refused. There was no way without boats. So in an attempt to overcome the impasse orders were signalled from the ships instructing the 4th Division to split up into parties of forty, and to walk the eight miles to Dunkirk.

By this time the beach-head had been reduced to a small area, with the Perimeter being held by what was left of the B.E.F's 46th Division in the centre and the French 68th and 12th Divisions on the right and left flanks. Most of the 50th Division was on the beaches, but when in the course of the morning the Germans broke into the Perimeter two columns were created from the remnants of the 151st Durham Light Infantry Brigade, one mobile and one marching. Their task was to break out from Dunkirk and to attack the Germans so as to cover the embarkation of what was left of the B.E.F. The survivors were then to fight their way back to Dunkirk where they would be taken off if it was not too late. To the relief of those concerned this particular suicidal operation was never carried out. It never, in fact, became necessary. By 2.30 p.m. it was cancelled and the D.L.I. columns moved to Dunkirk where they embarked—carrying their weapons and a few extraneous items they had 'liberated' during the retreat. (Sergeant Joseph Malone of the 8th Bn D.L.I., for example, carried a Lewis gun he had picked up and which he preferred as 'something solid rather than them new-fangled Brens'; while Lance-Corporal Wilson of the same battalion is said to have embarked with an alarm clock round his neck and carrying a sandbag of French currency.)

With other first-line fighting troops the pattern was much the same. Most of the battalions went home in little groups whose history has not been recorded. Lt-Col. Garry Carthew-Yorstoun, Commanding Officer of the 6th Bn The Black Watch, for instance, travelled in two destroyers both of which were sunk, and—having been wounded aboard the second when the destroyer was strafed by an Me 110—

would have drowned if an elderly, cheerful seaman had not insisted on the colonel wearing his own life-jacket. And one very young second-lieutenant of the same battalion is said to have marched his platoon, in threes and in step, along the mole of Dunkirk to the ship in which his men were to embark, with every man singing an old song that has been sung by generations of Black Watch soldiers.

A few pets, smuggled aboard the ships during the first few days of the evacuation—and even a few of the shell-shocked dogs from the beaches of La Panne—got back to England. Most of them dodged the quarantine, for the R.S.P.C.A. and customs authorities at the disembarkation ports would not have been able to cope with this type of mass influx from the Continent even if they had wished to do so. As some of the terrified animals jumped ship and slipped away, it is quite possible that quite a few of today's dogs in and around Dover, Margate and Ramsgate could lay claim to having true French poodles in their lineage.

French and Belgian ships joined the British rescue armada on Friday, May 30, and Saturday, June 1. Belgian trawlers, which had gathered at Brixham in Devon, sailed on the Friday—the same day that the French destroyer *Léopard* left the Downs Anchorage for Dunkirk escorting two French trawlers, three motor fishing boats, and ten Belgian trawlers. Pilote Malet was in charge of the Belgian vessels; Lieutenant Drogon of the French Navy was responsible for the rest. The French cargo ships *Ingénieur Cachin* and *Margaux*, the French trawlers *Pierre et Marie*, *Emma* and *Duperre*, the patrol vessel *Diligente*, together with the Belgian trawlers *Lydia Suzanne* and *Yvonne*, the drifters *Gérard-Léon*, *Anne-Marie* and *Thérèse Compas*, sailed about the same time. Because of their draft the French fishing vessels were restricted to working within the confines of Dunkirk harbour or the narrow roadstead off the beaches. Their manœuvrability was limited and as they had nothing in the way of anti-aircraft armament they were ideal targets for the Stukas. Nevertheless these ships were to lift hundreds of men to safety.

Ensign Le Coniat of the French Navy came relatively late to the beaches. On the morning of May 25 he was called to the Maritime Préfecture at Cherbourg and told to go to Saint Vaast la Hougue and pick out a number of vessels capable of going to Dunkirk from the motor-powered Belgian coasters there. Le Coniat selected six seaworthy boats and forty-eight hours later crews for these vessels reported to him—eighteen inexperienced sailors under the command of a quartermaster-signalman who was a journalist in civilian life and who had not been to sea for fifteen years. Having taken on fuel and stores Le Coniat got under way on the night of May 28, and sailed first to Le Havre. He himself travelled in the *Pharailde* together with a Belgian—the sole

190

remaining member of the original crew—a French Navy cook, one of the inexperienced French sailors, and the quartermaster-signalman-journalist. After an anxious twenty-four hours' wait in Le Havre, he was ordered to proceed to Dover—a twenty-hour run for low-powered coasters like those in this convoy—but during the voyage the *Pharailde's* motor seized up. So Le Coniat transferred to another vessel and at 4 p.m. on May 31 he led a convoy of seventeen craft out of Dover harbour. Six of these vessels were Zeebrugge coasters; the others were French boats, with names like *Jolie Rose Effeuillée*, *Ciel de France*, *Jolie Mascotte* and *Ave Maria Gratia Plena*, which had come from Grandcamp or Port-en-Bessin.

Le Coniat's convoy, sailing in single file, followed Route X to Dunkirk. Because of the vast concourse of shipping moving in both directions the steersmen needed steady nerves. Derelict craft were a constant menace, while destroyers and cross-channel ferries threw up waves capable of swamping smaller vessels or driving them off course into collision with larger vessels. *Jolie Mascotte* was the only boat to drop out of the column, when she went to the aid of H.M.S. *Basilisk*—rescuing seventy officers and men from the sinking destroyer. Meantime Le Coniat's sixteen other boats continued to Dunkirk, through the welter of wreckage in the harbour, to tie up at the inner Felix Faure quay. There they took aboard nearly 1000 men of General Prioux's First Army, and carried them across to Ramsgate where they disembarked around noon (on June 1).

That afternoon Le Coniat sailed again from Ramsgate to Dover for further orders. By this time only twelve of his convoy were able to make the run, as the motors of the others had given out under the strain and overheating of the first trip. At Dover Le Coniat was told curtly to head back across the Channel and 'continue the good work'.

As the convoy neared Dunkirk at 4 a.m. on June 2 it was subjected to intense artillery fire. Le Coniat took his boats close enough inshore for his shouts to be heard. There were thousands of French troops at the inner end of the mole, but none of them appeared anxious to splash out to Le Coniat's craft. Those who answered Le Coniat yelled that the boats were too small to get them safely to England. Little did they know what had happened to some of the bigger French ships. Since Operation Dynamo had begun, three destroyers of the French Navy had been lost. *La Bourrasque* had struck a mine on May 30 while carrying a full load of troops, 150 of whom were drowned. *Le Siroco*, also fully loaded and heading for England, had been sunk by a German S-boat; and *Le Foudroyant* had been sunk by Luftwaffe bombs only the day before, June 1, in sight of the beaches while still in Dunkirk roadstead.*

Frustrated by the troops' hesitation and furious at having to hang around under shellfire, Le Coniat explained in brief but unmistakable terms and language precisely why the reluctant Frenchmen should come aboard—and quickly. With equal eloquence and profanity some of his men in the other boats pressed Le Coniat's argument. Slowly the troops started to move. Most of them were clinging to their rifles; many wore their greatcoats and steel helmets and were festooned with equipment and rolled blankets. Some were further encumbered with sacks full of loot—silver, bottles of wine or brandy and baubles. To support themselves in the water a few of the more heavily laden were clutching inner tubes taken from the tyres of vehicles. The crews, cursing, dragged the soldiers over the sides, kicking rifles over the side and dumping sacks of loot. Some of the troops who refused to get rid of their sacks were pushed back into the water. The shelling was getting worse and there was no time to argue: men who were unwilling to cooperate were left behind.

The convoy sailed for Ramsgate with 800 men, off-loaded them there and returned via Dover—arriving off Malo-les-Bains beach about 2.30 a.m. on June 2. Le Coniat had expected to find troops there, but as there were none in sight, he ordered his boats to move westwards nearer the port. The area was illuminated by flashes of exploding shells and as his ship approached the harbour Le Coniat was able to see through

* During the Phoney War *Le Siroco* sank three U-boats. But her crew's skill in anti-submarine warfare was of no avail against the marauding S-boats. The two British destroyers H.M.S. *Wakefield* and H.M.S. *Grafton* were also sent to the bottom by these craft. (One of them was sunk by S-boat, S-25, commanded by Kptlt. Siegfried Wuppermann, who was to become one of the best known 'ace' commanders in the Mediterranean.)

his binoculars a black swarm of men on the east mole. Operating separately the boats went in and took approximately another 800 aboard. During the run back to Ramsgate German batteries at Gravelines shelled the convoy and several shells bracketed some of the boats. Otherwise the voyage was interrupted only by one other incident. Halfway across the Channel look-outs aboard the convoy spotted a drifting boat. When he closed on it Le Coniat found to his surprise that it held twenty-six Spanish sailors. As none of them appeared to speak French and Le Coniat knew only a few words of Spanish he took their boat in tow and handed the Spaniards over to the Royal Navy when he got to Ramsgate.

Le Coniat's quartermaster-signalman-journalist had not accompanied him on this trip. He had been left behind in Dover to organize the repair of a motor in one of the boats which had been immobilized after the first voyage. When he saw it would be some time before this boat would be seaworthy, he collected a crew of French-speaking sailors, boarded the French patrol vessel *Diligente* and shoved off on June 3 for Dunkirk. Night had fallen by the time he arrived, and Dunkirk was eerily silent as he sailed past the sunken ships to bring the *Diligente* to the beach.* Volunteers from his crew slipped over the side and waded through the shallows; on shore they made contact with French troops, more than a hundred of whom were ferried out to the *Diligente* and carried to Ramsgate.

Enseigne de Vaisseau (Sub-Lieutenant) Philippe Duval was another French naval officer who commanded a flotilla of small vessels like that of Le Coniat. On May 30 he was at Lorient naval base, when he was ordered to take a detachment of twenty-seven French petty officers and ratings to Caen. There he would be told where to pick up some fishing boats which had been commandeered for service at Dunkirk. At Caen Duval learned that the boats were at Ouistreham (on the coast ten kilometres from Caen, at the mouth of the River Orne); seven were French, two were Belgian and half the civilian crews had deserted.

Duval took over the boats and sailed them in convoy to Le Havre. En route the motor of one of them spluttered and died, and as it looked as if it would take considerable time to repair it Duval decided to abandon this boat at Le Havre. Meantime the owner of the *Charles Léon* reported that his motor was out of commission and that he proposed to stay with the *Charles Léon* in Le Havre harbour.

Duval sailed for Dover with the remaining seven vessels on Saturday June 1; chugging along at a maximum speed of five knots he made Dover twenty-four hours later. Two of his flotilla had to be towed in but as soon as they arrived engineers from the *Diligente* went to work on their motors.

---

* An Admiralty message had ended Operation Dynamo at 2.23 p.m. but the crews of many ships still at sea were unaware of this. The last ship to pick up stragglers was probably the *Princess Maud* which left Dunkirk at 1.50 a.m. on June 4.

Owing to the confusion surrounding the decision as to when Operation Dynamo would cease it was the afternoon of June 3 before Duval cleared Dover harbour and set a course for Dunkirk. He sailed aboard the coaster *Belgica*, in a convoy of twenty-eight vessels. The ships were bombarded as they approached the outer harbour; Duval had expected to be shot at but not by a man with a revolver standing on the east mole. This individual, Duval learned a little later, was the second mate of a sunken merchant ship, demented by the fear that he might be left behind at Dunkirk.

Duval ran the *Belgica* close in to the battered concrete mole and the gun-happy second mate and thirty other men leaped aboard. Docking in the inner harbour, Duval started to take troops aboard from the French 405th Infantry Regiment—a rearguard unit which had just pulled out of the Perimeter, whose discipline was good and morale unaccountably high. They kept their ranks and boarded the ship only when ordered to do so. Shells were bursting on the quay as they moved up and there were casualties. But the column closed up and the loading continued.

194

ft
e last soldiers of the
lant French rearguard
ve the doomed port.

ght
scene of one corner of the
olation, just before
nkirk capitulated.

By about 11 p.m. *Belgica* was loaded to capacity and Duval had the tricky task of backing her out through the wrecks. Bursting shells provided a certain amount of illumination in the outer harbour and one salvo straddled the ship as she moved through the harbour entrance. Fog descended soon afterwards and when Duval had set a course along Route X he reduced speed; floating mines were his greatest hazard at this stage. With dawn and good visibility however the *Belgica* put on speed and by 9 a.m. on June 4 she was alongside the quay at Ramsgate and had started to discharge her human cargo.

The *Madeleine Camille*, one of the boats in Duval's flotilla, arrived soon afterwards carrying 118 men. From her crew Duval learned that the *Jacqueline* had had engine trouble but had hoisted a sail and completed the trip to Dunkirk and back to Shoeburyness on the north side of the Thames estuary—although the crew, who spoke very little English, had not learned the name of the place before they sailed on to Ramsgate. The *Sainte de Padoue*, which together with *Agneau de Dieu* also belonged to the flotilla, towed the latter after she had broken down off the North Goodwin buoy. Between them the two vessels had brought

195

ninety-four soldiers out of Dunkirk making a grand total of 451 for the six small boats of Duval's original flotilla.

Another flotilla sent on June 1 by the French Navy to assist in the evacuation included the Belgian coasters *Prins Boodwin, Rockall, Frieda, Joseph Marcel*, and the French coasters *Notre Dame des Miracles, Irma Marie, Pierre* and *Sainte Isabelle*. The three French boats were under command of *Enseigne* Aguttes of the French Navy, and when Aguttes reported to the Dynamo Headquarters in Dover he was ordered to load ammunition and take it to Dunkirk.

Aguttes's vessels duly loaded up with cases of small arms ammunition and chugged across to Dunkirk, arriving in the early hours of June 3 and in the middle of an air raid. All three of Aguttes's ships managed to get into the harbour and to tie up at the east mole. It was the last day of the evacuation and the mole was crowded with tired, wet and hungry French and British troops who had been standing there for hours. In these circumstances finding one of Tennant's pier-masters among the crush was something of an achievement in itself. But Aguttes could hardly have considered his efforts to be worthwhile when his request for permission to unload the ammunition was brusquely refused. He and his ammunition were a menace, the Royal Navy's representative said. Aguttes must take his boats out of the harbour immediately. Then, if they were hit, nobody—apart from Aguttes's crews—would be likely to get hurt.*

While Aguttes was away his boats had taken off some of the men, together with a number of Dunkirk women and children. And when he returned and ordered the ships to cast off and get clear of the harbour these people remained on board. Outside the harbour the French coaster *Bernadette* passed close by Aguttes's ammunition carriers, and in a shouted exchange about their predicament the *Bernadette*'s skipper suggested Aguttes should go back and report not to the British but to the French Headquarters. So Aguttes sailed back and his vessels tied up at the mole immediately astern of a big French oil tanker, the *Salomé*. Scrambling ashore he set off in search of the French Headquarters, and when he found it, explained his problems to one of Admiral Abrial's staff.

A lorry and squad of men were detailed to help him and Aguttes returned with them to the mole. But it was now the middle of the morning and in broad daylight the Germany artillery observation officers were extremely efficient. While the *Pierre* was unloading, a salvo of shells fell around her setting fire to several cases of ammunition on the mole.

---

* It might have been some consolation if Aguttes had known that he was not the first French officer bringing ammunition to Dunkirk to be told to take it away. On May 31 *Enseigne* Royer reported to the R.N. piermaster that he was in charge of a convoy of seven trawlers carrying artillery ammunition. Nobody in Dunkirk wanted the ammunition and nobody was prepared to unload it, so Royer took it back to Ramsgate.

The *Irma Marie*, moored alongside, promptly cast off and moved away to safeguard her own cargo. And the *Pierre* followed—after the men, women and children she was carrying had been sent off up the mole; for these wretched people the bombing of the *Pierre* probably meant an end to their chances of getting to England.

Finally the French cross-Channel passenger ferries *Rouen*, *Côte d'Argent* and *Newhaven*, which are estimated to have carried 11,347 men out of Dunkirk, deserve special mention. Although these vessels operated under Ramsay's control and took orders from his staff, their crews were French. When they were not employed in their normal role a host of submarine-chasers, mine-sweepers, patrol craft and miscellaneous French Navy vessels also made troop-carrying trips across the Channel, or to Cherbourg and Le Havre—ports still under French control. When Dynamo was over the French Navy authorities estimated that approximately 150 vessels under their control had participated in the evacuation—about one third of them being Belgian, the remainder French. Some other French and Belgian small craft also participated 'unofficially', but there is no record of their activities. The Franco-Belgian fleet was only about a sixth of the size of the British evacuation armada, but it carried over 20,000 French soldiers to England, and about 4000 more to Cherbourg and Le Havre.

☆

Shortly before midnight on June 2 Tennant in Dunkirk sent the signal for which Ramsay in Dover was waiting. It was a terse but very welcome message: 'B.E.F. evacuated.'

It had been a Sunday to remember. More than 40,000 men—16,000 of them French—were lifted to safety, bringing the total evacuated so far to over 285,000. But the French were still waiting in their thousands and, as has been described, the heroic work of rescue continued for two more nights. On Monday, June 3, as on the Sunday, the embarkation virtually ceased at dawn and began again in the evening. H.M.S. *Express* and H.M.S. *Shikari* were the last ships to attempt to operate in daylight, and they were bombed; luckily the mist made the aim poor. These ships took off the last of the British naval pier-staff and about 1000 soldiers. After that the evacuation ceased until nightfall.

During the morning the R.A.F. had sent strong fighter patrols over the Dunkirk area. But a good deal of haze hung over the city and the Luftwaffe stayed on the ground; Goering's bombers were preparing for a massive raid on Paris. Round about 7.30 a.m. a squadron of Hurricanes encountered some Ju 87s which made off as the weather closed in. Meanwhile R.A.F. bombers were looking for German troops concentrating around Dunkirk. But the roads were deserted and when no suitable targets were forthcoming the bombers flew on to attack the batteries at Bergues and Gravelines on the flanks of the Perimeter. The Germans were within a mile and a quarter of the sea, held back by a courageous French rearguard on the outskirts of the town with another 30,000 or so of their comrades around the harbour still hoping to escape.

It was these 30,000 that Ramsay proposed to save, when at 10.25 a.m. on June 3, he signalled all Royal Navy vessels engaged in Dynamo:

> The final evacuation is staged for tonight, and the Nation looks to the Royal Navy to see this through.
>   I want every ship to report as soon as possible whether she is fit to meet the call which has been made on our courage and endurance.

The plan for the final phase was for the bigger ships to attempt yet again the hazardous manœuvring necessary to get them into the harbour. The largest vessels—the destroyers and troop transports— would try to take troops off the east mole; smaller vessels such as corvettes, sloops and the cumbersome paddle-wheel minesweepers, would go alongside the west mole; while the smallest craft—tugs, trawlers, drifters, motor-boats and anything else with a reasonable chance of survival—would try to use the inner harbour. H.M.S. *Locust*, a cruiser, was ordered to anchor just outside the harbour where she would receive troops from boats working inshore. Tugs were sent out with strings of lifeboats in tow for this purpose.

When the time came to execute Ramsay's plan the French troops behaved in an orderly and dignified fashion. (Some would say that their behaviour was typically French; it certainly bore no comparison with that of the demoralized regiments which Guderian had routed at Sedan.) But they were first-class soldiers, hard disciplined fighting men.

198

Behind them they were leaving a once great and busy seaport which was now just a filthy, black, smouldering heap of ruins. They were sad, but glad to go, although they refused to embark unless a complete unit—a platoon, or a company, was intact. When one of the French generals came down the mole with his staff, he was seen to halt ten metres from a column that had been patiently waiting for some hours to board one of the ships. Drawing himself up he solemnly saluted the men of the column. The general was not a very big man, but in his high-crowned kepi, flared tunic, breeches and polished boots, he seemed—against the flickering background of the burning town and oil tanks—a truly martial figure.

Most of the stragglers were also glad to get out of Dunkirk. A boat from the tug *Tanga*, looking for stragglers on the beaches off the west mole, was challenged: '*Etes-vous Allemands ou Français?*' On being assured that the boat was British he was happy to go aboard. But occasionally men would demur, and the *Tanga*'s crew encountered a solitary French officer, standing at the water's edge, who flatly refused. In good English he explained that he had just eaten and so was not ready for a sea voyage. In the event the *Tanga* collected only thirty-four French soldiers before she was ordered to leave, but on the way back to Ramsgate she came across a disabled French fishing boat with a load of troops aboard and took it in tow.

At the west mole H.M.S. *Whitshed*, a destroyer which had barely survived a collision at Dover, had difficulty tying up. Then her crew had to wait for what seemed to be an excruciatingly long time as interpreters argued with French troops who were reluctant to go aboard. Nearly all of these men came from the interior of France, and they had concluded that the sea might well be as great a source of danger as the Germans. However some 800 of them were eventually talked into crossing the precarious gang planks on to the destroyer's deck and the *Whitshed* sailed.

Other British destroyers loaded and departed. Around them French and Belgian trawlers were also taking troops. Their loading rate was slow and by using the west mole these smaller ships prevented the bigger ones getting in. The *Lady of Mann*, one of the troop transports, had to wait a couple of hours before she could find a berthing space. *Côte d'Argent*, *King George V*, *Tynwald*, *Royal Sovereign* and *Princess Maud* all lifted about 1000 men apiece, and when *Princess Maud* was ready to sail about 1.40 a.m. there were only a few stragglers left on the mole. Somehow or other a number of dogs found their way aboard—though how they did remains a mystery, since no gangways were used.

The Germans were right in Dunkirk by this time; some had actually infiltrated to within a few hundred yards of the harbour, and the rattle

British P.O.Ws file dejectedly into captivity. For most of them the war was now over.

of their Spandaus and Schmeissers could be heard in the streets leading to the harbour. A semi-circle of French defences still held, although the troops defending Rosendael, a suburb on the eastern outskirts of Dunkirk, had run out of ammunition. Yet it seems that the Germans were slow to realize they could push on without opposition, and this slowness allowed several thousand French troops to withdraw after nightfall, move through the town, and board the last ships leaving the port.

The forts of the massive defensive system known as the Eastern Works—which had been designed and built by Napoleon's famous engineer, Auban—were abandoned one by one after dark. At the nub of this system Bastion 32, the great steel, stone and concrete redoubt where Admiral Abrial had his headquarters, was one of the last to be evacuated.

During the morning of June 3—to the accompaniment of walls shaking from the effect of German shells bursting outside, and the crash of heavy French guns firing from inside the bastion—a mass was celebrated in the subterranean dining hall. A French Navy ensign, taken from the destroyer *Jaguar* just before she sank, covered the improvised altar and the service was conducted by a Benedictine monk, Dom de Morant, who had been serving with the 32nd Infantry Division. Some of the wounded from the hospital within the fort were among those who received the sacrament; the rest of the casualties were in a sorry state for there was very little morphine or drugs, and the supply of bandages was exhausted. Nor was there any fresh water, for the local wells were polluted.

Abrial and his deputy, Rear-Admiral Charles Platon, *Amiral-Gouverneur* of Dunkirk, left the Bastion soon after the service. Both were taken to England—Abrial travelling on the French motor-torpedo boat VTB-25. Leaving the harbour, the VTB-25 struck a sunken wreck, losing a propeller and starting a leak. On Abrial's instructions the young sub-lieutenant in command of the boat steered for the North Goodwin lightship. At dawn, as the VTB neared the lightship, men were seen clinging to some wreckage. They were the survivors of a collision between the Belgian coaster *Maréchal Foch* and the British trawler *Leda*. The VTB picked up these men but the now overladen boat damaged her second propeller in the process and, unable to make way, she lay pitching and rolling in the North Sea swell. Fortunately help was not long forthcoming. Lookouts from the destroyer H.M.S. *Malcolm* spotted the VTB-25, closed on her and took everyone on board. Abrial himself was set down at about 6 a.m. on Admiralty Pier in Dover, from where he was sent up to Dynamo Headquarters to have breakfast with Ramsay.

Back at Dunkirk the French continued to resist until the early hours of June 4. North-east of the town a battalion of the 137th Infantry Regiment was reduced to a mere fifty men, but they had been ordered to hold their positions at all costs, to cover the evacuation of other French units. At the Bourbourg Canal, near the Petite Synthe works, there was heavy fighting—with a battery of the famous 75-mm guns of World War I continuing in action until ammunition was exhausted and every one of the guns over-run. Lieutenant Menesson, one of the officers of this battery of the 89th Artillery Regiment, reported seeing 'the Blacks' approaching. (Whether he was referring to the black uniforms of the Panzer troops, or to black shoulder straps on the uniforms of the infantry is not clear. It is unlikely that the élite Panzer troops would be operating without their tanks.)

> They were right across the canal from us (Menesson wrote). Firing started, and as the Germans crossed the canal and came close, our range was down to 100 metres.
>   Among eight officers in the battery, five were killed, and two seriously wounded.
>   That evening, when there were no more shells in the ammunition cases, and none at the rear, Captain Fabre and Lieutenant Durand destroyed the guns. The mission was finished.

In the streets of the town Civil Defence workers continued to collect dead and wounded from the debris-strewn streets until nightfall on June 3, and lists of the casualties were compiled. They made sorry reading:

> Unknown infant, sex male, age about two years, dressed in a white shawl, a blue and white vest, two white woollen vests, a red sweater, and wrapped in a black woollen shawl.

> Unknown infant, undetermined sex, about ten years of age, dressed in a blue jacket belonging to a sailor costume with white buttons.

> Unknown man, one metre 75 centimetres tall, strongly built, bandage on left foot and thigh, wrapped in a sheet.

> Unknown woman, in a state of pregnancy (five to six months).

> Unknown, undetermined sex, aged between sixteen and eighteen years...

In the dock area there were problems of a different sort. Apart from the mass of French troops awaiting evacuation there were sinister groups of deserters and miscellaneous rogues. Most of them were armed; many were drunk, and some had teamed up with sleazy trollops who 'worked' the dockside in happier times from rooms and basements in Place Jean Bart. These groups, intent on making the most of the opportunities which now presented themselves, were looting and mugging.

Meanwhile the Germans were making steady progress, and the Daily Intelligence Report of the 18th Infantry Division for June 3 makes interesting reading—especially as whoever compiled it wrote in rather a less crisp and concise fashion than the general run of German staff officers:

Situation at Dunkirk on the night of June 3. In this first phase the front was held entirely by French troops.

French prisoners, including North African troops.

202

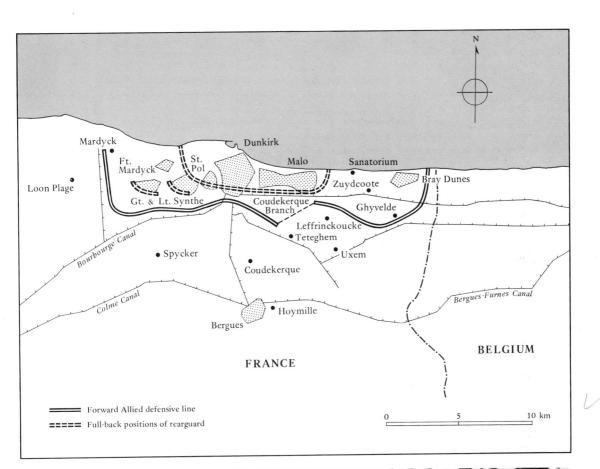

Mardyck

Ft.
Mardyck

St.
Pol

Dunkirk

Malo

Sanatorium

Loon Plage

Zuydcoote

Bray Dunes

Gt. & Lt. Synthe

Coudekerque
Branch

Ghyvelde

Leffrinckoucke

Bourbourg Canal

Teteghem

Uxem

Spycker

Coudekerque

Colme Canal

Bergues-Furnes Canal

Hoymille

BELGIUM

Bergues

FRANCE

━━━━ Forward Allied defensive line

═════ Full-back positions of rearguard

0   5   10 km

N

By taking Bergues, we had the key to Dunkirk.

The Recknagel infantry regiment continued its advance during the night and reached Boomkens although the flanking regiment did not follow.

The Army Corps ordered the attack renewed at 11.00 a.m. on the 3rd, but since dawn the regiment had been forced to defend itself against several enemy attacks supported by armour. In spite of our anti-tank guns, and the infantry which fought with courage, our defence might have fallen without help from the 3rd Artillery Group which fired at sight range from positions right behind the front line. The enemy lost a dozen tanks, and a number of men killed or wounded.

During the afternoon, two regiments of the division, met on three sides by the enemy, still took the suburb southeast of Dunkirk and Fort Louis.

Exposed to violent artillery fire coming mainly from the northeast, the division rested in an exposed corner, suffering severe losses.

Until the morning of June 4, the enemy showed by fierce artillery fire that he would resist at any cost. Then, very suddenly, his firing stopped. In our lines, too, before the historic moment, there was a strange calm. Our men slept in their holes in the earth after their great efforts.

British and French soldiers marching into captivity along the Dunkirk quayside.

Major Chrobek was the first to understand what had happened. With dawn, the tired soldiers were loaded into trucks. Dunkirk lay lifeless. The streets were filled with burned automobiles and abandoned armoured cars. Buildings on all sides were demolished. We asked ourselves, 'Did the enemy save himself during the night?'

Then our hearts leaped. Here was the sea—the sea!

Ships and boats continued to lift men from the harbour through the night and the morning of June 4. Indeed, the records show that more than 25,000 men were carried to safety between midnight on June 3 and 2.30 p.m. on the 4th. But by then the time had come to halt. Twenty or thirty thousand French troops still remained in and around Dunkirk but they had expended their ammunition and—as the 18th Division's report suggested—the Germans were in a position to reach the sea along the whole front. After the morning embarkation the French commandant of Dunkirk acknowledged that further resistance was useless, and it was decided that the machinery of Dynamo should be brought to a stop. Thus, at 2.30 p.m. on June 4, the Admiralty announced 'Operation Dynamo is now completed.'

The rescue work did not, however, come to an abrupt end even then. R.A.F. aircraft continued to fly regular reconnaissance missions over the evacuation routes until nightfall on June 5, and R.A.F. air–sea rescue launches searched an area between Goodwin Sands and Boulogne where the planes reported sighting a ship on its side and a barge with troops aboard. The launches returned with thirty-three French troops and two British seamen; and during June 5 various other patrol craft picked up more French soldiers and landed them at Dover, Margate and Ramsgate. French troops also arrived in these ports aboard French and Belgian trawlers, and when the numbers were totted up it was reckoned that 1,096 more men had been saved.

☆

Now, as the bodies and wreckage floated backwards and forwards up and down the Channel and in the North Sea, only the final scene in the epic of Dunkirk remained to be enacted.

Over the page
Abandoned trucks and stranded ships litter the Dunkirk beaches after 'the great escape'. Stretching out into the sea on the left is a line of trucks which formed one of the improvised piers for taking off the troops.

11. Aftermath

June 4 – July 6

'Soldiers of the West front!
    Dunkirk has fallen... with it has ended the
greatest battle in world history.
Soldiers! My confidence in you knew no bounds.
You have not disappointed me.'

Adolf Hitler, Order of the Day, 5 June 1940

With their Schmeissers cocked and ready, German foot patrols moved cautiously through Dunkirk's empty streets soon after first light on June 4. They encountered no resistance; the town and harbour were completely open to them.

There were between 30,000 and 35,000 French troops on the beaches and in the harbour area, but few of them now had any stomach for fighting even if the ammunition had been available. Some were already disposing of their weapons, flinging rifles into the sea or burying their bolts in the sand. Battalion and regimental colours were burned to prevent them falling into German hands and finding their way to Berlin's museums. After the racket and roar of the last week Dunkirk was strangely silent. There was no sign of the Luftwaffe, and no ships were to be seen offshore. But the odd shot now and then, the filthy mess in the streets, the litter amid the ruins, the stricken ships in the harbour and the dead men floating in the sea served to remind those who were left in Dunkirk that they were witnessing the end of a chapter in its history.

A detachment of German Marines under an *Oberleutnant zur See* arrived at Bastion 32 about 8 a.m. The medical officers, orderlies and clerks of Abrial's headquarters staff who had stayed behind were collected together and questioned. 'Where are the admirals?' asked the *Oberleutnant*. 'And where are the *Engländer*?'

Soon after dawn General Beaufrère, the senior French officer in Dunkirk, had gone to the Town Hall in the middle of Dunkirk. There he discarded the steel helmet and donned his gold-leafed képi to make the surrender ceremony as formal as possible. At 8.20 a.m. a French car with a Wehrmacht driver pulled up in front of the Town Hall and a German colonel got out. He told the French sentry at the door that he wanted to see the senior French officer. When Beaufrère went out to meet him, the colonel, speaking in impeccable French, congratulated him on the stubborn defence the French troops had put up. 'Are any *Engländer* still here?' the Colonel asked. 'None,' replied Beaufrère, and went on to say that his men urgently needed food and drinking water. 'You shall have them straight away. We German soldiers respect the courage of your soldiers; we shall do whatever we can for them,' the Oberst said—adding less grandiloquently: 'But you must wait for our general.'

About two hours later a German staff car drew up outside the Town Hall. From it, in field service uniform, stepped the bemedalled commander of the Wehrmacht divisions encircling Dunkirk. After expressing his admiration for the conduct of the French troops, he too asked where the British were. 'Not here,' said Beaufrère. 'They are all back in England.'* Then he spoke again of the need for food and water for his men. 'As soon as they have been collected and counted,' said the German, 'all that is necessary will be done.' Standing stiffly erect he saluted, and Beaufrère returned the salute. It was a final gesture. Beaufrère was taken away to a prison camp and the German drove off to tour the desolate town and to find a vantage point from which he could observe the harbour and the empty Channel beyond.

At midnight on the day Dunkirk fell Hitler decreed that bells should be tolled throughout the Reich for three days, to celebrate the end of the 'greatest battle in world history'. An hour later, on June 5, an O.K.W. communique announced: 'The second great offensive is being launched today.'

In the six days since they had been pulled out of the battle on the northern front the Panzers had been rested, reorganized and redeployed. Along a 360-kilometre front, stretching from the sea to the Meuse, ten Panzer and ninety-four infantry divisions had been waiting for the order to advance and take Paris. Against these, the French could muster only forty-three infantry divisions, three weak armoured divisions and three cavalry divisions,† plus the British 51st (Highland) and 1st Armoured Divisions. (Two more divisions, one of them Canadian—the only two trained and equipped formations remaining in the British Isles—were on their way.) In the air there was the same disparity as on the ground and Weygand, the French Commander-in-Chief, reckoned the combined French Air Forces and R.A.F. were 'ridiculously weak'.

---

* This was not strictly true. There was still a sizeable number of B.E.F. stragglers and a few deserters in Dunkirk or on the beaches. They were assembled with the French troops and became prisoners of war.

† The armoured and cavalry divisions were at no more than half strength. According to Weygand French losses up to the fall of Dunkirk amounted to the equivalent of thirty divisions. The British 1st Armoured Division was only at one third strength and most of its tanks were lightly clad cruisers. The Germans had also had heavy casualties especially in the élite formations—although they were comparatively light by World War I standards. Many of the Panzers which were knocked out in the fighting were put back on the road during the six days' 'rest' period.

The new French front rested on the 'Weygand Line' behind the Somme and the Aisne. Weygand had abandoned the 'continuous front' philosophy and his 'Line' was actually a chequer-board of 'hedgehogs'. Each hedgehog was intended to be a self-contained unit based on a natural obstacle such as a wood, and relying on 75-mm field artillery pieces—many of them World War I weapons fetched out of retirement—as anti-tank weapons. These were to be pointed 'like revolvers' at the Panzers. In theory the hedgehogs would hold out at all costs, allowing attacks to 'wash' around them. Behind them battle groups, constituted from what remained of the Allied tank formations, would deal with the attackers who penetrated past the hedgehogs. If they failed to do so, however, there were no more lines on which to fall back. Once the Weygand Line was broken it was all over, for Weygand himself believed that one last battle should be fought 'for the honour of France'; after that the government should sue for peace.

The fact is the French Army had died at Dunkirk and, although some of the French troops fought with a determination and a spirit of sacrifice that had not been seen on the Meuse, the battle for France was lost even before the Germans penetrated the Weygand Line. Within two days of the start of the offensive, the Panzers had mastered the chequer-board system. All they had to do was to drive across country, by-passing the hedgehogs and leaving them to be dealt with by the infantry following on behind. The Panzers suffered heavy casualties, but Guderian has recorded that on June 11 his units were progressing 'as though this were a manœuvre'.

With the fall of Rouen in the west and the crossing of the Marne in the east, Paris was threatened, and for the third time in seventy years it began to resemble a city under siege. The restaurants and small hotels on the Champs Elysées and the Place de La Concorde were empty; the Government had already moved to Tours 'for imperative military reasons', and a steadily growing stream of refugees poured out of the city. Nevertheless, right until the night of June 11, when Weygand declared the capital 'an open city' the French Government repeatedly declared that Paris would be defended to the last. (That Paris should have capitulated without a struggle when Warsaw, London, Leningrad and Moscow were prepared to risk devastation has been a bone of contention ever since.) Psychologically the fact that it was abandoned struck a grievous blow to what remained of French morale, although there would have been little military advantage in fighting for the city. But France deprived of Paris became in the words of André Maurois 'a body without a head. The war had been lost.'

On the morning of June 14 troops of the German 87th Infantry Division made a bloodless and orderly entry into the French capital. That same day the Government of the Third Republic departed for Bordeaux, and Reynaud appealed to President Roosevelt asking the United States to declare war on Germany. If she did not do so 'in the

German officers arrive in Dunkirk in style.

The German rank-and-file cycle through the Dunkirk streets. Discarded French helmets lie beside the hous

Footsore German infantry relax. The wine had probably been 'liberated' too.

It took the Germans a long time to clean up the mess left behind. The apparent calmness prevailing is in marked contrast to the chaos and carnage of a few days before.

An abandoned gun on the beach—and a few hundred yards from the shore the burnt-out corpse of a ship.

very near future', he said, 'France would capitulate'. When Roosevelt said 'No' Reynaud was at the end of his tether. Exhausted physically and mentally, he tendered his resignation to President Lebrun and suggested that the only man to save France now was the eighty-four-year-old Marshal Pétain.

Meanwhile General Charles de Gaulle, Reynaud's Under-Secretary of State for National Defence since June 10, had flown to London to ask Churchill for ships to transport French troops to Africa and persuade the British Prime Minister that some 'dramatic move' was needed if France was to stay in the war. In Churchill's words, de Gaulle 'suggested that a proclamation of the indissoluble union of the French and British peoples would serve the purpose'. So, on the afternoon of Sunday, June 16, a 'Declaration of Union' of staggering historical importance was duly approved by the British Cabinet. But the Declaration could have no immediate effect on the military situation, and at least one of the French ministers suspected Britain's motives. The ambitious and silver-tongued M. Camille Chautemps, Minister without Portfolio, voiced his suspicions when he declared that he 'did not want France to become a Dominion'.

So, by way of the Spanish Ambassador, Senor de Lequerica, Pétain asked the Germans for an armistice, and the news that he had done so was received by the majority of the French people with feelings of relief. In Paris on June 17 the *Grossdeutschland Regiment* paraded in triumph through the city, to hold a thanksgiving service in Notre Dame, and next day William Shirer, the C.B.S. Berlin correspondent, observed that there was already 'open fraternizing between German troops and Parisians'. A week later a German war correspondent lunching at a restaurant in Lyons was astonished to see a bourgeois French family at the next table going through the ritual of a French Sunday lunch as if nothing in the world had happened. They spent approximately half an hour: '...bent over the menu, discussing the food, and then at length and with great seriousness discussed city gossip. It seemed remarkable to me that their thoughts should not be concerned with other matters, but the meal was something very important for them.' Three days after that, following the armistice,* Ilya Ehrenburg, the *Pravda* correspondent, watched Paris coming back to life and noted: '...The Germans bought souvenirs, smutty postcards, pocket dictionaries in the little shops. Notices appeared in restaurants "*Wir sprechen deutsch*". Prostitutes lisped, "*Mein Süsser.*"'

---

* The armistice was signed on Saturday, June 22, in the historic wagon-lit where the armistice ending World War I was signed in November 1918. (The wagon-lit was then moved to Berlin and subsequently destroyed in an air-raid.) However, the shooting did not end officially until 35 minutes past midnight on the 25th.

☆

While the *Grossdeutschland* was forming up outside Notre Dame cathedral the news that Marshal Pétain had asked for an armistice was announced in the B.B.C.'s 1 p.m. bulletin. The British had barely absorbed the shock of Dunkirk and the fall of France made a deep impression. One woman teacher at a school near Peterborough recalled that she had welcomed her husband home on unexpected leave that morning, and he had been pressed into giving a talk to her class. The subject was 'Our Allies' and she had written on the blackboard a list of the Allied countries. When her husband came to the school in the afternoon, having heard the news, he promptly wiped the name of France from the list. A North London woman, working in the office of a munitions factory, remembers one hysterical typist shrieking as the news came through, 'Whatever will we do now?' 'Do,? Do?' snarled her boss, a grumpy, middle-aged character, 'We'll bloody well get on with it ourselves.' At Accrington in Lancashire, one panic-stricken business man turned up at his bank and announced that he wanted to draw his money out. 'What shall we do when the Germans get here?' he moaned. With a sample of what has come to be known as the 'Dunkirk spirit' the bank's deputy manager answered: 'Do? I'll tell you what we'll do. We'll get a gun and shoot the buggers!'

Next day Churchill broadcast the famous speech which ended with the quotation:

> Let us brave ourselves to our duties, and so bear ourselves that, if the British Empire and its Commonwealth last for a thousand years, men will still say 'This was their finest hour'.

Because of such leadership this was not a gloomy time in England, and when it became apparent that Hitler was not going to follow up Dunkirk with an invasion of England the shock of defeat turned into a kind of relief that, somehow, life had at least become simpler. King George VI spoke for many when he wrote to his mother: 'Personally, I feel happier that we have no allies to be polite to and to pamper.'

For a time, however, an invasion was expected hourly and countermeasures—especially road-blocks and pill-boxes—began to mushroom all over England. Across parks, fields and other open spaces sprouted obstacles to prevent enemy aircraft from landing. On May 31 the Government had ordered that 'any sign which furnishes an indication of the name of...or the direction of...or the distance to any place' must be taken down. Signposts were removed first, and then followed a wholesale uprooting of milestones, the defacing of the names of towns on war memorials and the painting over of shop and other signs identifying the town or village. All this was very inconvenient for the ordinary civilian, and it was not until October 1942 that signposts could again

Inside the harbour lay th[e] tangled wreckage of a gr[eat] many small ships.

One of the many graveya[rds] of B.E.F. equipment.

214

But for the wreck this could almost have been a holiday snap.

More French prisoners are rounded up.

be displayed in towns, May 1943 before villages became identifiable, and October 1944 before all the restrictions were removed.

At the same time as the Order to take down the signposts was issued, the ringing of church bells was banned, except to announce invasion, and there was a wholesale round-up of aliens—mostly German and Italian male adults. Four hundred British citizens of known fascist sympathies were also interned. The Government also distributed to every home a leaflet 'If the Invader Comes: What to Do—and How to Do it: Hitler's invasion of Poland, Holland and Belgium were greatly helped by the fact that the civilian population was taken by surprise. They did not know what to do when the moment came. *You must not be taken by surprise.*' Everyone was urged 'to stay put' to avoid blocking the roads if the Germans did attack. Calmness was also requested.

By this time many civilians were actively involved in the war as part-time soldiers. On Tuesday, May 14, the recently appointed Secretary of State for War, Anthony Eden, had broadcast an appeal for men to join a new force of 'Local Defence Volunteers'—the L.D.V., soon to be nicknamed the 'Look, Duck and Vanish' Brigade. The response was immediate and overwhelming. In Kent, the most threatened area, men were signing on even while Eden was still speaking, and at some places eager volunteers were still queuing up to join at midnight. The official age limits were seventeen to sixty-five, but the first batch of recruits included men in their eighties as well as fifteen and sixteen-year-olds. Within twenty-four hours 250,000 men had enrolled; by mid-July the total had risen to more than a million.

In effect none of the anti-invasion preparations were ever to be needed, for the Wehrmacht had arrived at the Channel coast without any plan of what to do next. Hitler and those who had created *Sichelschnitt* failed to consider how one got to England. An invasion plan was scrambled together in the ensuing months, but it proved to be an exercise in leisurely futility. The Germans had missed the bus, as Chamberlain would have said.

Although it has been suggested that Hitler never intended or simply did not wish to invade Britain, it is more likely that it was his 1914–18 mentality which decided the issue. There had been no plan for the evacuation of Dunkirk until the B.E.F. was falling back on the coast. Yet 338,226 men had been shipped over the Channel. Under the circumstances, therefore, it does not seem unreasonable to suppose that the Germans, in the full tide of victory, were fully capable of doing a Dunkirk in reverse and putting an army across the Channel onto a virtually undefended and helpless shore. Only a handful of fighting units existed in the country; the returning B.E.F. was a disorganized rabble and most of its weapons had been abandoned in Flanders. The 'Look, Duck and Vanish' Brigade could be written off as a raggle-taggle of old men and boys; only the opposition of the R.A.F. and the Royal Navy was worth considering. And if at the end of May and beginning of June Hitler had seized the opportunity to commandeer every available vessel afloat in western and northern Europe, and then hurl an invasion force across the Channel, the Germans might well have succeeded. The Admiralty would have thrown in every ship they had, of course, and the Germans would have suffered very heavy losses; they would also have faced monumental logistical problems. On the other hand, the U-boats would have wreaked havoc in the narrow Channel against a fleet deployed in a defensive role. Hitler would have been staking everything on one throw. But in the hindsight of history this was the best course open to him. So long as Britain remained inviolate, it was inevitable that sooner or later the immense power of the United States would be brought in too.

In the event Hitler faltered, and his professional generals were not prepared to argue with their amateur Führer. The one general to whom he might have listened had been seriously wounded in Rotterdam. This was Kurt Student, the founder of Germany's airborne forces. Student, looking ahead, had worked out a plan for an airborne assault on Britain even before his *Fallschirmjäger* were involved in the invasion of the Low Countries. Paratroops and glider-borne commandos would be dropped near the ports in Kent, prior to a full-blown sea-borne invasion. Three weeks' preparations was all that was considered necessary, and Student had already earmarked some of the Wehrmacht's best infantry regiments to be flown in to reinforce the paratroops as soon as the latter had captured one or more airfields.

The *Kriegsmarine* had also roughed out a plan, for landings on Britain's east coast 'on a grand scale'; its architects said that their seaborne assault appeared 'to be a possible expedient for forcing the enemy to sue for peace'. The draft of this plan was passed both to the Wehrmacht, who showed little enthusiasm, and to the Luftwaffe, which was equally sceptical, and it then got bogged down somewhere in the files. Hitler knew nothing of this plan until Admiral Raeder told him about it. When he did it was at a time that the Führer was preoccupied with thoughts of a honeymoon with victory. For in the first summer days after the armistice—while German troops clambered up the Eiffel Tower, gazed down at Napoleon's tomb in Paris, and paddled in the warm water off the wreckage-strewn Channel beaches—Hitler was driving round on a sight-seeing tour. With two World War I cronies he was touring the battlefield where, as a company runner in the 16th Bavarian Reserve Infantry Regiment, he had won two Iron Crosses and a corporal's stripes. Meantime at O.K.W. headquarters in Berlin military affairs stagnated.

The Führer's return to Berlin on July 6 had all the trappings of a triumph. Flowers strewed the streets and when Hitler appeared on the Chancery balcony a massed choir of the *Bund Deutscher Mädchen* sang *Wir fahren gegen Engelland*. But the Führer was not prepared to give the order to 'sail away to conquer Eng-el-land'. Invasion, he told Raeder,

would be tried 'only as a last resort if Britain cannot be made to sue for peace any other way'. When there were no signs of any response to German peace-feelers, Hitler made a 'peace offer' speech in the Reichstag suggesting that Britain should allow him to keep his conquests. A few weeks before Dunkirk some people, at least, might have welcomed such an offer; now it was contemptuously dismissed. (When German aircraft dropped copies of the speech, entitled *A Last Appeal to Reason*, on Britain, copies were auctioned for local Red Cross and Spitfire funds and a newsreel showed a grinning Londoner tearing one into squares for what were euphemistically described as 'shaving papers'.)

Meantime, while Hitler hesitated, the O.K.W's planning staff were perfecting the details of *Operation Sea Lion*. Student's parachutists of the 7th *Flieger* Division and another *Luftlande* (Air Landing) division were

to be set down near Folkestone to secure bridgeheads for the nine sea-borne divisions scheduled to land in the first wave of the invasion. (The 7th *Flieger* Division's objectives were the high ground north and north-west of Folkestone; from here it would go on to capture crossings over the Royal Military Canal, and block the Canterbury–Folkestone road. Other airborne troops were to be dropped on the downs behind Brighton.) Giant cargo-gliders—capable of transporting a fifteen-ton PzKpfw III tank or an eight-ton 88-mm gun—were specifically developed for the operation and barges were collected and assembled in ports along the French coast. The latter became a regular target for R.A.F. raids.

From hospital Student complained that it was already a good six weeks too late to take advantage of Britain's weakness. The British had already recovered, he said. 'Had we launched an airborne operation to occupy the ports where the B.E.F. was disembarking England's fate would have been sealed. . . . Of course, I had only one airborne division immediately available . . . because I had not been able to persuade the Wehrmacht to raise the four others I wanted. And this was something which rebounded with a vengeance when it came to dealing with Britain at the time of Dunkirk. . . .'

In the event although the first heavy German air attacks on London on 7 September 1940 triggered the invasion alarm, *Operation Sea Lion* was never attempted. In September when rumour had it that Hitler 'seriously expected' an outbreak of revolution in England it was post-poned. Finally the idea was abandoned although the German forces earmarked for the invasion were not officially released from their role until February 1942 and in Britain precautions continued to be taken until the Allies had returned to the Continent in June 1944. Invasion, throughout the summer of 1940 a dagger pointed at Britain's heart, became for a few months thereafter merely another of Hitler's empty threats; for already he had an attack on Russia in mind.

☆

The British public had barely had time to decide whether the success of Operation Dynamo meant that a great victory had been won or that something very terrible had happened before news that the 51st (Highland) Division had capitulated at St Valérie-en-Caux. A few days later, of course, when the fall of France was announced, doubts were resolved and the remaining feeling of elation about Dunkirk was quickly dis-pelled.

Churchill, obdurately pursuing his plan to keep the French armies intact and maintain a front on the Continent, ordered a second B.E.F. to be formed. The command was given to Lt-General Sir Alan Brooke who disembarked at Cherbourg on June 12, the day after being knighted for his efforts at Dunkirk. Guderian's tanks had crossed the

Marne that morning, Weygand's armies were disintegrating, and the 51st (Highland) Division—one of the three divisions which were to be the nucleus of Brooke's new B.E.F.—was penned in the Havre peninsula with its back against the sea. The division fought well but after an unsuccessful attempt by the Royal Navy to rescue what remained of it, it had no option but to surrender.

☆

The British returned to Dunkirk five years later—a year after the Normandy landings. On D Day, 6 June 1944, Admiral Ramsay commanded the Allied naval forces, and he carried the same telescope through which he had watched the comings and goings of the Dynamo fleet in Dover harbour. Montgomery, a B.E.F. divisional commander— and in the final days of the evacuation an acting corps commander— now a Field Marshal commanding the British 21st Army Group, directed the British assault into Belgium along the same roads down which the B.E.F. had retreated. En route he cleared the Channel ports from Le Havre to Calais. But Dunkirk, stubbornly defended by a German garrison under command of Admiral Frisius, *Kriegsmarine* commander of the Pas de Calais sector, proved a tough nut to crack. As in 1940 the canal locks had been destroyed to flood the low-lying terrain around the town, and a wide shallow lake covered an area embraced by the Bourbourg Canal, Bergues, Hondschoote and the Belgian frontier. Behind this lake, secure within Dunkirk's fortifications, 10,000 well-protected German soldiers and sailors fought to the end. Montgomery was not prepared to sacrifice time, effort or men in winkling them out, so the First Canadian Army simply by-passed the Dunkirk enclave and for seven months it was contained by a force of mainly Czech troops. It was to the latter that Frisius surrendered on 11 May 1945 following Germany's unconditional surrender. In five years of German occupation the face of Dunkirk had changed considerably. Dragon teeth anti-tank obstacles and the massive walls of Hitler's Atlantic Wall ran along the beaches. Great new lock gates protected by bomb-proof bunkers had been built at the entrances to the Ecluse Watier, which was the centre of the evacuation area, and the old timber moles had been replaced by concrete structures.

Since 1945 more building to repair the devastation has obscured many of the landmarks that the B.E.F. once knew, although wrecks are still uncovered at low tide at Malo-les-Bains. The evacuation beaches are clear now and on a summer's day they are crowded with French—and sometimes British, and sometimes German—holidaymakers. Few of the holidaymakers know or care about Operation Dynamo; their concern is for sun, sand, a swim and food. Only on May 23, when a dwindling band of Dunkirk veterans make an annual pilgrimage to the beaches, is the great escape truly remembered.

Epilogue

'What the future course of the war would have been if we had succeeded at the time in taking the British Expeditionary Force prisoners at Dunkirk, it is now impossible to guess.'

General Heinz Guderian

The Cost

In terms of blood and bones, it is comparatively easy to cost the epic of Dunkirk. Up to the fall of France, i.e. including the casualties incurred by the 51st (Highland) Division and other British troops remaining in France after the evacuation, total British casualties came to 68,111, Belgian 23,350, and Dutch 9,779. French losses are put at somewhere in the region of 90,000 dead, 200,000 wounded and 1,900,000 prisoners and missing (no accurate figures have ever been published). German casualties amounted to 27,074 killed, 111,034 wounded and 18,384 captured and missing. Thus the overall total of German casualties was approximately 150,000 compared with 390,000 Allied casualties—of whom only just over 68,000 were British.

In the course of the evacuation Britain also lost stores and equipment for about 500,000 men, about 100 tanks, 2000 other vehicles, 600 guns, and large stocks of ammunition and supplies of all kinds. In addition the equivalent of six squadrons of fighter aircraft were destroyed, six destroyers were sunk, and five severely damaged. A sloop, a hospital ship, five minesweepers, eight transport vessels and seventeen trawlers—together with 188 smaller vessels—were sunk, and an equal number were damaged—some beyond repair. The final statistic must of course be the 338,226 soldiers who were lifted to safety.

The Effects

The effects are less easy to assess because they are still reverberating round the world. Dunkirk was followed directly by the collapse of France, although it did not precipitate it. And for four grim years France disappeared from the forefront of the battle. This was the most immediate consequence of Operation Dynamo.

224

Of no less importance was the fact that the evacuation of Dunkirk left deep scars in the Entente Cordiale relationship, which may still be discerned. After 1940 disillusionment and distrust at the French performance led to Britain's determination never again to rely on other nations for her security. In 1949 she agreed to contribute to the collective security of NATO, but she was developing her own nuclear weapons to ensure Britain's 'independence'. Meanwhile although it was the Germans who had driven Britain out of Europe in June 1940 it was the French who for years kept her waiting on the doorstep when the Common Market of the Six was formed. Moreover it was the man who had suggested that there should be an 'indissoluble union of the French and British peoples' who was largely responsible. Yet this was not just General de Gaulle's resentment of the patronizing British whose attitude for so long has been that 'those fellows on the Continent will never be able to get along without us'. In France the consequences of Dunkirk do not cease to engender suspicions that if the going ever gets tough in Europe—militarily or economically—the British will always be tempted to pull out as they did in 1940. In retrospect perhaps by saving the B.E.F. and thus winning the war, Britain lost the peace for herself.

The Imponderables
The 'ifs' of history are invariably fascinating, and those associated with the evacuation of Dunkirk particularly awesome. *If*, for example, Operation Dynamo had not been successful, or *if* General Student had not been wounded at Rotterdam and had been able to talk the Führer into airborne assult on Britain's south coast—followed perhaps by a full-blown seaborne invasion—how might the situation have developed?

To begin with there can be no doubt that if the Germans *had* put a small force—even a couple of divisions—across the Channel in that 'very dark hour'* early in June they might well have established a foothold. And if their assault were compounded with a slowing down of the evacuation programme—due to lack of initiative on Ramsay's part perhaps, or an irrevocable decision to withdraw the destroyers— it would have stood a very good chance of success. For two or three weeks after the last of the B.E.F. was lifted out of Dunkirk the physical means of repelling the invaders simply did not exist. The B.E.F., tired, disorganized, and without artillery or transport, was no longer a coherent force. Some units, much depleted, could have gone into action, but brigade and divisional formations existed as such only on paper. A few half-trained and ill-equipped formations which had not been in a fit state to send to France could have been moved—by rail— to meet the invaders. But that was all; certainly the L.D.V. volunteers

* Churchill's words two months later.

would not have been of much use for they were still in the armband, shotgun and pike stage. More important, the people of Britain, though outwardly defiant, had not yet captured the 'spirit' of Dunkirk; they were still dazed by the turn of events. Thus if either the B.E.F. had not got back home, or Hitler had launched an invasion at the beginning of June it seems likely that the Germans would have conquered the British Isles by the autumn of 1940. The consequences would have been world-shattering, and it would have been the Soviet Union that would have suffered most.

The Royal Navy, or what was left of it, would in all probability have sailed across the Atlantic to Canada, and the only British forces still in contact with the Axis forces would have been Wavell's army in the Middle East. In the circumstances even Wavell would surely have hesitated to have launched his Western Desert offensive in December 1940. The Italian armies opposing him were numerically far superior, and although he might still have been able to count on reinforcements from India and Australia, his troops—and more especially his tiny air force— were wholly dependent on Britain for their equipment. Hitler would therefore not have needed to send Rommel and the Afrika Korps to rescue Mussolini's North African empire.

Nor would Hitler have had to direct troops earmarked for the invasion of Russia to the Balkans, because there would have been no British intervention in Greece and hence no threat to Italy or the Rumanian oilfields. Had Hitler not felt himself compelled to forestall the British in Greece, D-Day for the attack on Russia, Operation Barbarossa, need not have been postponed from May 15 to 22 June 1941. And, if the attack on Russia had been launched when it was originally intended that it should be launched, it is highly probable that the Germans would have taken Moscow before the weather baulked them. The capture of Moscow would not of itself have meant the collapse of Soviet resistance or even the eventual conquest of Russia, but it would certainly have gravely weakened the Soviet will to resist.

Moreover, with Britain out of the war, German strategy would not have been hobbled by the need to build the Atlantic Wall and turn occupied Europe into a fortress; nor would the Germans have had to withstand the drain which the need to maintain a force in North Africa imposed on them. The occupied territory would probably have spawned resistance movements, but these would not have been supplied with arms from Britain and their diversionary effects would have been smaller than they undoubtedly were.

The effects on the Far East should also be considered. Following the squalid precedent set by Italy when she declared war on France, Japan could be expected to seize the opportunity to grab Britain's Far East possessions with even greater alacrity and far less effort than actually was the case. The extra resources released by the swift—and probably bloodless—creation of the Great East Asia Co-Prosperity Sphere would then have been deployed against India and Australia. In the circumstances the treacherous attack on Pearl Harbour in December 1941 may not have been necessary—partly because the United States would have taken extra precautions and partly because Japan would have had her hands full. (This is not to say that Japan would have abandoned her aggressive designs on America but she would have had cogent reasons for not embarking on them prematurely.) If Britain had been knocked out of the war in 1940 the three Axis powers would have been in a position of overwhelming strength by the end of the following year. With the Germans in Moscow; with Italy mistress of the Mediterranean and an empire stretching along the shores of North Africa, through Egypt and down past Ethiopia into Kenya and beyond; and with Japan consolidating bloodless conquests all over Asia, the free world would have been presented with a daunting *fait accompli*.

No doubt the U.S. defence programme would have got into stride by the end of 1941. But the bulk of her newly raised forces would have been only partially trained and completely devoid of combat experience. Their primary task would have been to defend U.S. territory, and until the threat of a Japanese invasion on America's Pacific coast could have been discounted, it is difficult to imagine circumstances in which any U.S. Government would have felt justified in sending an expeditionary force overseas. The Americans would have had little interest in war in Europe, and all their efforts would have been directed to fighting the Japanese.

But enough has been said about how great the benefits would have been to Germany and her Axis associates if the evacuation of Dunkirk had not been successful. No one can say for certain that Hitler *would* have won the war if the B.E.F. had been crushed in France. But its escape left in the hands of his enemies the tools with which they laid the foundations of his ruin and that of the Third Reich. In sum, without 'Dunkirk' Britain had no hope of winning the war even if she had been left to stew in her own juice. At best this would have meant a return to the Phoney War, but the odds are that the Germans would have occupied Britain sooner or later and this book—presenting a somewhat different theme perhaps—might well have been written in German. The only other alternative, equally horrendous, rests on the premise that the Soviet Union was capable of defeating Germany unaided. If so the whole of Western Europe would now be screened by the Iron Curtain, and Russian—not German—would be the lingua franca.

The Spirit of Dunkirk
Finally there is the question of the 'Dunkirk spirit' to which, in recent years the British nation has constantly been exhorted to rally. In effect this so-called 'spirit' was a sequel to the evacuation and not part of it, for peoples' attitudes then were motivated by much the same avidity

as they are at any other time. Most of the men on the beaches and in the rescue craft behaved as the British are expected to behave in such circumstances, but there were some servicemen at Dunkirk—and quite a few civilians in the U.K.—whose prime concern was their own skins or their own selfish interests.

What the events terminating in the evacuation of Dunkirk did was to stimulate a new interest in the war. To the British people the outcome of the war now seemed for the first time to present a clear choice between better and worse, if not between good and evil. Few considered the question of survival; they simply accepted that they had to stand alone because someone had to beat the Nazis, and in June 1940 Britain was the only candidate for the job. It was perhaps typically British to assume that even foreigners would eventually come to realize that their lives and interests were also at stake and that when this was apparent they would come in on Britain's side.

Churchill's leadership and the spell of his eloquence was unquestionably part and parcel of the 'spirit'. On June 17 when France was seeking an armistice, Churchill broadcast: 'What has happened in France makes no difference to our actions and purpose. We have become the sole champion now in arms to defend the world cause. We shall do our best to be worthy of this high honour. We are sure that in the end all will come right.' The next day in an address to Parliament he said: 'Hitler knows that he will have to break us in this island or lose the war. . . . If we fail, then the whole world, including the United States, including all that we have known and cared for, will sink into the abyss of a new Dark Age, more sinister, and perhaps more protracted by the lights of perverted science.'

Both speeches contrasted strangely with the attitude of the French at that time, and with the mood in the United States—where people were stunned by the defeat of France and thought that Churchill was bluffing. Years later, musing over the events of June 1940, Churchill wrote: 'Foreigners who do not understand the temper of the British race all over the globe when its blood is up might suppose that they [Churchill's speeches] were only a bold front, set up as a good prelude for peace negotiations. . . .' Hitler was among the foreigners who did not understand the temper of the British race and the stimulus which Dunkirk had provided.

Under the threat of invasion in the months that followed, the British people were brought closer and made stronger. Dunkirk had been a memorable event and the mood it engendered was equally memorable. With the Royal Navy overstretched, the Army lacking equipment and the R.A.F. sadly under strength, the British began at long last to organize themselves for total war. 'This is the War of the Unknown Warriors,' Churchill told Britain in the summer of 1940. 'The whole of the warring nations are engaged, not only the soldiers but the entire population, men women and children. The fronts are everywhere. The trenches are dug in the towns and streets. Every village is fortified. Every road is barred. The front lines run through the factories. The workmen are soldiers with different weapons but the same courage.'

It was typical of Churchill to dwell in this fashion on the realities brought about by the Dunkirk epic. It has been the aim of this book, too, to remember and re-live those realities, as well as the legend which still attaches to it.

'I have myself full confidence that if all do their duty and nothing is neglected and if the best arrangements are made, as they are being made, we shall prove ourselves once again able to defend our island home, ride out the storms of war, and outlive the menace of tyranny if necessary for years, if necessary alone. At any rate, that is what we are trying to do. That is the resolve of the Government, every man of them. It is the will of Parliament and of the nation.

The British Empire with the French Republic, linked together in their cause and in their need, will defend to the death their native soil, aiding each other like good comrades to the utmost of their strength, even though large tracts of Europe and many old and famous States have fallen or may fall into the grip of the Gestapo and all the odious apparatus of Nazi rule.

We cannot flag or fail. We shall go on to the end. We shall fight in France, we shall fight on the seas and oceans, we shall fight with growing confidence and growing strength in the air. We shall defend our island whatever the cost may be. We shall fight on the beaches, we shall fight on the landing-grounds, in the fields, in the streets, and in the hills.

We shall never surrender, and even if, which I do not for a moment believe, this island or a large part of it were subjugated and starving, then our Empire beyond the seas, armed and guarded by the British Fleet, will carry on the struggle until in God's good time the New World, with all its power and might, sets forth to the liberation and rescue of the Old.'

Winston Churchill, the House of Commons, 4 June 1940

Appendix 1

Composition of the British Expeditionary Force in France 1939–40

Commander-in-Chief: General Lord Gort, V.C.
C.G.S: Lt-General H. R. Pownall

FIRST CORPS (Lt-General M. G. H. Barker)

1st DIVISION (Major-General Hon. H. R. L. G. Alexander)
1st Guards Brigade
3rd Bn Grenadier Guards
2nd Bn Coldstream Guards
2nd Bn Hampshire Regiment
2nd Infantry Brigade
1st Bn Loyal Regiment
2nd Bn North Staffordshire Regiment
6th Bn Gordon Highlanders
3rd Infantry Brigade
1st Bn Duke of Wellington's Regiment
2nd Bn Sherwood Foresters
1st Bn King's Shropshire Light Infantry
2nd DIVISION (Major-General H. C. Lloyd)
4th Infantry Brigade
1st Bn Royal Scots
2nd Bn Royal Norfolk Regiment
1/8th Bn Lancashire Fusiliers
5th Infantry Brigade
1st Bn Queen's Own Cameron Highlanders
2nd Bn Dorsetshire Regiment
7th Bn Worcestershire Regiment
6th Infantry Brigade
1st Bn Royal Welsh Fusiliers
1st Bn Royal Berkshire Regiment
2nd Bn Durham Light Infantry
48TH DIVISION (Major-General A. F. A. N. Thorne)
143rd Infantry Brigade
1st Bn Oxford & Buckinghamshire Light Infantry
5th Bn Royal Warwick's
1/7 Bn Royal Warwick's
144th Infantry Brigade
2nd Bn Royal Warwick's

5th Bn Gloucestershire Regiment
8th Bn Worcestershire Regiment
145th Infantry Brigade
2nd Bn Gloucestershire Regiment
4th Bn Oxford & Buckinghamshire Light Infantry
1st (Buckinghamshire Bn) Oxfordshire and Buckinghamshire Light Infantry

SECOND CORPS (Lt-General A. F. Brooke)

3RD DIVISION (Major-General B. L. Montgomery)
7th Guards Brigade
1st Bn Grenadier Guards
2nd Bn Grenadier Guards
1st Bn Coldstream Guards
8th Infantry Brigade
1st Bn Suffolk Regiment
2nd Bn East Yorkshire Regiment
4th Bn Royal Berkshire Regiment
9th Infantry Brigade
2nd Bn Lincolnshire Regiment
1st Bn King's Own Scottish Borderers
2nd Bn Royal Ulster Rifles
4TH DIVISION (Major-General D. G. Johnson)
10th Infantry Brigade
2nd Bn Bedfordshire Regiment
2nd Bn Duke of Cornwall's Light Infantry
6th Bn East Surrey Regiment
11th Infantry Brigade
2nd Bn Lancashire Fusiliers
1st Bn East Surrey Regiment
5th Bn Northamptonshire Regiment
12th Infantry Brigade
2nd Bn Royal Fusiliers
1st Bn South Lancashire Regiment
6th Bn Black Watch
50TH DIVISION (Major-General Le Q. Martel)
150th Infantry Brigade
4th Bn East Yorkshire Regiment

232

4th Bn Green Howards
5th Bn Green Howards
151st Infantry Brigade
6th Bn Durham Light Infantry
8th Bn Durham Light Infantry
9th Bn Durham Light Infantry
25th Infantry Brigade
1/7th Bn Queen's Royal Regiment
2nd Bn Essex Regiment
1st Bn Royal Irish Fusiliers

THIRD CORPS (Lt-General Sir R. F. Adam)

42ND DIVISION (Major-General W. G. Holmes)
125th Infantry Brigade
1st Bn Border Regiment
5th Bn Lancashire Fusiliers
6th Bn Lancashire Fusiliers
126th Infantry Brigade
1st Bn East Lancashire Regiment
5th Bn King's Own Royal Regiment
5th Bn Border Regiment
127th Infantry Brigade
4th Bn East Lancashire Regiment
5th Bn Manchester Regiment
1st Bn Highland Light Infantry
44TH DIVISION (Major-General E. A. Osborne)
131st Infantry Brigade
2nd Bn The Buffs
5th Bn Queen's Regiment
6th Bn Queen's Regiment
132nd Infantry Brigade
1st Bn Queen's Own Royal West Kent Regiment
4th Bn Queen's Own Royal West Kent Regiment
5th Bn Queen's Own Royal West Kent Regiment
133rd Infantry Brigade
2nd Bn Royal Sussex Regiment
4th Bn Royal Sussex Regiment
5th Bn Royal Sussex Regiment

G.H.Q. RESERVE

5TH DIVISION (Major-General H. E. Franklyn
13th Infantry Brigade
2nd Bn Cameronians
2nd Bn Royal Inniskilling Fusiliers
2nd Bn Wiltshire Regiment
17th Infantry Brigade
2nd Bn Royal Scots Fusiliers
2nd Bn Northamptonshire Regiment

6th Bn Seaforth Highlanders
12TH DIVISION (Major-General R. L. Petre)
35th Infantry Brigade
2/5th Bn Queen's Royal Regiment
2/6th Bn Queen's Royal Regiment
2/7th Bn Queen's Royal Regiment
36th Infantry Brigade
5th Bn The Buffs
6th Bn Queen's Own Royal West Kent Regiment
7th Bn Queen's Own Royal West Kent Regiment
37th Infantry Brigade
2/6th Bn East Surrey Regiment
6th Bn Royal Sussex Regiment
7th Bn Royal Sussex Regiment
23RD DIVISION (Major-General A. E. Herbert)
69th Infantry Brigade
5th Bn East Yorkshire Regiment
6th Bn Green Howards
7th Bn Green Howards
70th Infantry Brigade
10th Bn Durham Light Infantry
11th Bn Durham Light Infantry
1st Bn Tyneside Scottish
46TH INFANTRY DIVISION (Major-General H. C. Curtis)
137th Infantry Brigade
2/5th Bn West Yorkshire Regiment
2/6th Bn Duke of Wellington's Regiment
2/7th Bn Duke of Wellington's Regiment
138th Infantry Brigade
6th Bn Lincolnshire Regiment
2/4th Bn King's Own Yorkshire Light Infantry
6th Bn York & Lancaster Regiment
139th Infantry Brigade
2/5th Bn Leicestershire Regiment
2/5 Bn Sherwood Foresters
9th Bn Sherwood Foresters
51ST INFANTRY DIVISION (Major-General V. M. Fortune)
(Serving on Saar Front Under French Command, 10 May 1940. Later in action south of River Somme.)
152nd Infantry Brigade
2nd Bn Seaforth Highlanders
4th Bn Seaforth Highlanders
4th Bn Queen's Own Cameron Highlanders
153rd Infantry Brigade
4th Bn Black Watch
1st Bn Gordon Highlanders
5th Bn Gordon Highlanders
154th Infantry Brigade
1st Bn Black Watch
7th Bn Argyll & Sutherland Highlanders

8th Bn Argyll & Sutherland Highlanders
1st ARMOURED DIVISION (Major-General R. Evans)
(In action south of River Somme, except one Bn at Calais)

   2nd Armoured Brigade
The Queen's Bays
9th Royal Lancers
10th Royal Hussars
   3rd Armoured Brigade
2nd Bn Royal Tank Corps
3rd Bn Royal Tank Corps
5th Bn Royal Tank Corps
   1st Support Group
101st L.A.A. Anti-Tank Regiment

The following two Brigades also joined the B.E.F. between mid-May and mid-June

   20th Guards Brigade (to Boulogne)
2nd Bn Irish Guards
2nd Bn Welsh Guards
   30th Brigade (to Calais)
2nd Bn King's Royal Rifle Corps
1st Bn Rifle Brigade
1st Bn Queen Victoria Rifles
52ND DIVISION (Major-General J. S. Drew)
   155th Infantry Brigade
7/9th Bn Royal Scots
4th Bn King's Own Scottish Borderers
5th Bn King's Own Scottish Borderers
   156th Infantry Brigade
4/5th Bn Royal Scots Fusiliers
6th Bn Queen's Own Cameron Highlanders
7th Bn Queen's Own Cameron Highlanders
   157th Infantry Brigade
1st Bn The Glasgow Highlanders
5th Bn Highland Light Infantry
6th Bn Highland Light Infantry

Appendix 2

Summary of Ships taking part in Operation Dynamo. An Assessment

The 56 destroyers (38 of them British) which lifted 102,843 men between them were the mainstay of Operation Dynamo. The 45 ferries, pressed into service as troop transports carried 87,810, minesweepers 48,472 and other naval vessels 16,674; the 40 Dutch skoots which sailed under the White Ensign carried another 22,698.

The little boats of Ramsay's 'cockleshell navy' (including the RN launches) are credited *directly* with saving only 6,029 men. But much of their work was concerned with ferrying men from the beaches to bigger vessels moored in the roadsteads. A conservative estimate of this *indirect* work would raise the figure to 80,000 and to this has to be added the liftings of the cargo vessels, the tugs, the yachts and other miscellaneous craft. The overall figure of 338,226 is a staggering measure of the success of the operation.

The statistics that have been set out have been interpreted many times before, and most of the analysts have stressed the contribution of the 'little boats'. In doing so they have helped to create and perpetuate a legend. But the facts behind the legend must not be forgotten: Operation Dynamo was a *military* operation—an operation organized and carried out by the Royal Navy, whose ships are entitled to no less than eighty per cent of the kudos.

In sum, the B.E.F. did not save France. In trying to do so it lost thirty thousand men, all its transport and all its illusions. Fortunately it did not lose heart and the Royal Navy got it away.

Summary of Ships taking part in Operation Dynamo with details of men evacuated and ships damaged or sunk

Type of Ship	Number	Troops lifted out	Losses		
			By enemy action	Other causes	Damaged
A.A. Cruiser	1	1865	—	—	1
Destroyers	56	102843	9	—	19
Sloops	6	1436	—	—	1
Patrol Vessels	7	2504	—	—	—
Pinnaces	2	3512	1	—	—
Corvettes	11	1303	—	—	—
Minesweepers	38	48472	5	1	7
Trawlers and the like	230	28709	23	6	2
Naval Transports	3	4408	—	—	—
Armed merchantmen	3	4848	1	—	2
Torpedo Boats	15	99	—	—	—
Schuyts (Skoots)	40	22698	1	3	—
Yachts	27	4895	1	2	—
Ferries	45	87810	9	—	8
Hospital Ships	8	3006	1	—	5
Cargo Vessels	13	5790	3	—	—
Tugs	40	3164	6	1	—
Landing Craft	13	118	1	7	—
Barges	48	4726	4	8	—
Little Boats:					
Motor vessels	12	96			
R.N. launches	8	579			
Private motor boats	203	5031	7	135	not known
R.N.L.I. Lifeboats	19	323			
Total:	848	338226	72	163	45

A greater number of small boats undoubtedly took part but the exact number is not known.

This information is taken from the following:
(a) Appendix L of *The War at Sea 1939–45* (S. W. Roskill), p. 603.
(b) *The War in France and Flanders 1939–40* (L. F. Ellis), p. 248. Note that Ellis quotes a figure of 765 British ships taking part.
(c) *The Second World War* (W. S. Churchill), pp. 145, 146. Churchill states that 693 British and 168 Allied ships took part.
(d) *Revue d'Histoire de la 2e Guerre Mondiale* No 10/11. Article by M. G. Saunders who states that 228 ships were sunk and 45 damaged.

Allied Troops evacuated from Dunkirk

Date	From the beaches	From the harbour	Total evacuated	Sum total
27 May	—	7669	7669	7669
28 May	5930	11874	17804	25473
29 May	13752	33558	47310	72783
30 May	29512	24311	53823	126606
31 May	22942	45072	68014	194620
1 June	7348	47081	64429	259049
2 June	6695	19561	26256	285305
3 June	1870	24876	26746	312051
4 June	622	25553	26175	338226
Grand Totals:	98671	239555	338226	

According to Churchill the above figures are taken from Admiralty records. The War Office figure is 336427 evacuated.

Vice-Admiral Sir Bertram Ramsay recorded in his despatches a total of 338682.

French Troops evacuated from Dunkirk

According to Ramsay's despatches the following number of French troops were evacuated from Dunkirk.

Date	By French vessels	By British vessels	Totals
29 May	655	—	655
30 May	5444	3272	8616
31 May	4032	10842	14874
1 June	2765	32248	35013
2 June	905	15144	16049
3 June	4235	15568	19803
4 June	2349	24640	26989
9 June	140	956	1096
Grand Totals:	20525	102570	123095

The French Navy has stated that between 21 May and 3 June 48474 troops were evacuated by French or Belgian boats or by boats manned by French crews.

Bibliography

The following are the principal published sources consulted:

MEMOIRS

BRYANT, A. *The Turn of the Tide, based on War Diaries of Field-Marshal Viscount Alanbrooke* (London 1957)

CHURCHILL, W. S. *The Second World War*, Vol. 2: *Their Finest Hour* (London 1949)

COLVILLE, J. R. *Man of Valour* (The Life of F. M. Viscount Gort, V.C.) (London 1972)

GUDERIAN, H. *Panzer Leader* (London 1951)

GUDERIAN, H. *Mit den Panzern in Ost und West* (Göttingen 1953)

KESSELRING, A. *Soldat bis zum letzten Tag* (Bonn 1953)

LIDDELL-HART, B. H. *The Memoirs of Captain Liddell-Hart* (London 1965)

MACLEOD, R. and KELLY, D. *The Ironside Diaries 1937–1940* (London 1962)

MANSTEIN, E. VON *Lost Victories* (London 1958)

PRIOUX, R. *Souvenirs de Guerre* (Paris 1947)

REYNAUD P. *Memoires* (Paris 1960)

SPEARS, Sir EDW. *Assignment to Catastrophe* (London 1954)

WEYGAND, M. *Recalled to Service* (Rappelé au Service) (London 1952)

GENERAL LITERATURE

ARMANGAUD, Gen. J. *Le Drame de Dunkerque* (Paris 1948)

BARCLAY, Brig. C. N. *On Their Shoulders* (London 1964)

BAUER, E. *Panzer-Krieg* (Bonn 1965)

BEAUFRE, A. *Le Drame de 1940* (Paris 1965)

BENOIST-MECHIN, J. *60 Jours qui Ebranlerent l'Occident* (Paris 1956)

BETHEGNIES, R. *La défense de Dunkerque* (Lille 1950)

BETHEGNIES, R. *Le sacrifice de Dunkerque* (Lille 1947)

BLANCKAERT, S. *La 2eme guerre Mondiale a Dunkerque* (Paris 1975)

BLUMENTRITT, G. *The Soldier and the Man, General von Rundstedt* (London 1952)

BUCHHEIT, G. *Hitler der Feldherr. Die Zerstörung einer Legende* (Rastatt 1958)

BUTLER, Lt-Col. EWAN and BRADFORD, Major J. SELBY. *Keep the Memory Green* (London 1950)

COLLIER, R. *The Sands of Dunkirk* (London 1961)

DARWIN, B. *War on the Line* (London 1946)

DIVINE, D. *The Nine Days of Dunkirk* (London 1967)

DIVINE, D. *Dunkirk* (London 1945)

ELLIS, Major L. F. *The War in France and Flanders 1939–1940*, The History of the Second World War (London 1953)

FULLER, J. F. C. *The Second World War 1939–1945:* a Strategical and Tactical History (London 1948)

GORT, Viscount *First Despatch of the Commander-in-Chief, British Expeditionary Force* (London 1941)

GORT *Second Despatch of the Commander-in-Chief, British Expeditionary Force* (London 1941)

HORNE, A. *To Lose a Battle: France 1940* (London 1969)

JACOBSEN, H. A. *Dünkirchen* (Heidelberg 1958)

JACOBSEN, H. A. *Fall Gelb. Der Kampf um den deutschen Operationsplan zur West-offensive 1940* (Wiesbaden 1957)

JACOBSEN, H. A. *L'Erreur du commandement allemand devant Dunkerque* in *Revue Historique de l'Armée* (Paris 1958)

KÜHN, V. *Deutsche Fallschirmjäger im Zweiten Weltkrieg* (Stuttgart 1974)

LIDDELL-HART, B. L. *The Other Side of the Hill* (London 1951)

LUGAND, Lt-Col. *Les Forces en présence au 10 mai 1940* in *Revue Historique de l'Armée* (Paris 1953)

LYALL, G. (Editor) *The War in the Air 1939–1945* (London 1968)

LYET, P. *La Bataille de France: Mai-Juin 1940* (Paris 1947)

MACKSEY, K. *Guderian, Panzer General* (London 1975)

MAROIS, A. *The Battle of France* (London 1940)

MAROIS, A. *Why France Fell* (London 1941)

PERRON, E. *Journal d'un dunkerquois* (Dunkerque 1967)

REYNAUD, P. *In the Thick of the Fight* (London 1955)

RICHARDS, D. *Royal Air Force 1939–1945*, Vol: I, *The Fight at Odds* (London 1953)

ROSKILL, Captain S. W. *The War at Sea 1939–1945* (London 1954)

SAUNDERS, M. G. *L'Evacuation par Dunkerque* (Paris 1953) in *Revue Historique de l'Armée*

TAYLOR, T. *The March of Conquest. The German Victories in Western Europe* 1940 (New York 1958)

TREVOR-ROPER, H. R. ed. *Hitler's War Directives*, 1939–1945 (London 1964)

VANWELKENHUYZEN, J. *Les parachutistes allemands en 1939–1940* in *L'Armée— La Nation* (Brussels 1954)

WHEATLY, R. *Operation Sea Lion* (Oxford 1958)

REGIMENTAL HISTORIES

COWPER, J. M. *The Kings Own* (Vol 3) (Aldershot 1957)

FERGUSSON, B. *The Black Watch and the King's Enemies* (London 1950)

Historical Records of the Queen's Own Cameron Highlanders 1932–42 (privately printed and published by Wm. Blackwood & Sons Ltd, Edinburgh 1952)

HOWARD, M. and SPARROW, J. *The Coldstream Guards 1920–1946* (Oxford 1951)

MUIR, A. *The First of Foot* (Edinburgh 1961)

NALDER, Major-General R. F. H. *The Royal Corps of Signals*, R.S.I. (London 1958)

NIGHTINGALE, P. R. *The East Yorkshire Regiment in the War of 1939–1945* (York 1952)

RISSIK, D. *The D.L.I. at War* (Durham 1952)

Index

Aa Canal 53, 55, 64
Abbeville 43, 47, 55
Abrial, Admiral Jean-Marie 56, 68, 144, 146, 201
Adam, Lt-Gen. R. 68, 144
Advanced Air Striking Force (A.A.S.F.) 14, 31, 33, 51
Aguttes, Ensgn. P. 196
Aisne River 43, 210
Albert Canal 30, 57
Alexander, Maj.-Gen. Hon. H.R.L.G. 147
Altmayer, Gen. R. 49
Amiens 22, 42, 43, 48, 57, 59
Anne-Marie (Belgian drifter) 190
Anthony H.M.S. (destroyer) 96
Ardennes 22, 23, 30
Arras 23, 43, 51, 56, 60
Barratt, Air Marshal Sir A. 32, 34
Basilisk H.M.S. (destroyer) 164, 191
Beaumann Division ('Beauforce') 39
Beaufrère, Gen. 208
B.E.F., Units and Formations:
  Units:
  12th Royal Lancers 30, 49
  1st AA. Regt R.A. 30
  2nd Bn Welsh Guards 51
  1st Bn Royal Scots 45, 134
  7th Bn Kings Own Royal Regt 45
  2nd Bn East Yorkshire Regt 140
  5th Bn East Yorkshire Regt 125
  6th Bn Green Howards 53 (footnote)
  5th Bn Gloucestershire Regt 64
  5th Bn Manchesters 131
  6th Bn Black Watch 139,189
  2nd Bn D.L.I. 31
  8th Bn D.L.I. 189
  9th Bn D.L.I. 52
  11th Bn D.L.I. 67
  1st Bn Q.O. Cameron Highlanders 122, 130, 134
  Bdes:
  1st Army Tank Bde 38
  12th Inf. Bde 53
  20th Guards Bde 53
  30th Inf. Bde 53
  150th Inf. Bde 140
  151st Inf. Bde 53
  157th Inf. Bde 140
  Divisions:
  1st Armoured 37, 209
  1st Inf. 128
  2nd Inf. 57
  3rd Inf. 128
  4th Inf. 128, 139, 188
  5th Inf. 49, 59, 128
  12th Inf. 38, 57 (footnote)
  23rd Inf. 37, 53 (footnote)
  42nd Inf. 38, 128
  44th Inf. 57
  46th Inf. 128
  48th Inf. 128

50th Inf. 49, 51, 59, 60, 128, 129, 140, 189
51st (Highland) 39, 79 (footnote)
Belgica (Belgian coaster) 194
Bergues 53, 68, 128, 129, 140
Bethune River 38, 43
Bideford H.M.S. (sloop) 157
Billotte, Gen. G. 26, 29, 31, 36, 42, 49, 57
Blanchard, Gen. G. 30, 36, 42, 49, 57, 68, 72, 147
Bock, Gen. F. von 22, 37, 58, 65, 72
Boulogne 23, 43, 53, 54, 82, 111
Bourbourg Canal 202
Brauchitsch, Field Marshal W. von 23
Bray Beach 111, 188
Brighton (hospital ship) 90
Brighton Belle (paddle minesweeper) 150
Brighton Queen (paddle minesweeper) 165
Brooke, Lt-Gen. A. F. 144, 146, 147, 222
Calais 43, 53, 68, 73, 82
Calcutta H.M.S. (cruiser) 150
Canal du Nord 37
Canterbury (S.R. ferry) 90, 92
Cap Griz Nez 85, 157
Cassel 57, 68, 128
Cervin (tug) 154
Chamberlain, Rt Hon. N. 12, 18, 19, 67
Cherbourg 39, 43, 222
Churchill, Rt Hon. W. 19, 35, 47, 56, 125, 144, 146, 183, 184, 213, 214
Ciel de France (French coaster) 191
Clan MacAlister S.S. 117
Constant Nymph (Motor Yacht) 171
Corap, Gen André-George 30, 36, 43
Cote d'Argent (French passenger ferry) 197, 199
Coxyde 68, 142
Crested Eagle (passenger steamer) 116, 162
Deal 122, 150
Deere, Flt Lt A. 184
De Gaulle, C. 213
Dendre River 37, 42, 43
Dill, Gen. Sir J. 59, 144
Dinard (hospital ship) 90
Dinky (cabin cruiser) 179
Dixmude 128, 129
Dorrien Rose S.S. (tramp) 112
Douai 52, 58
Dowding, Air Chief Marshal Sir H. 35
Duchess of Fife (minesweeper) 150
Duke (tug) 164
Dumpling (cabin cruiser) 179
Dunkirk Roads 108, 156
Dyle River 26, 29, 30, 43

'Dynamo' Operation 47, 61, 85, 104, 121, 150, 205
Eden, Rt Hon. A., Foreign Secretary 60, 217
Elbe (Belgian tug) 170
Embry, Wing Comd. B. 67
Emma (French trawler) 190
Escaut River 43
Esk H.M.S. (destroyer) 154
Express H.M.S. (destroyer) 198
Fagalde, Gen. 58, 68
Fenella (paddle steamer) 115
Fidget (drifter) 153
Fisher Boy (drifter) 153
Formidable (drifter) 153
Foudroyant (French destroyer) 165
'Frankforce' 49, 52
Frieda (Belgian coaster) 196
Furnes 68, 140
Gallant H.M.S. (destroyer) 150, 159
Gamelin, Gen. M. 26, 29, 31
George VI, King 214
Georges, Gen. J. 26, 29, 33, 37
Gerard-Leon (Belgian drifter) 190
Giraud, Gen. H. 26, 30, 36
Goliath (Belgian tug) 170
Goodwin Sands 108, 156, 158
Gort, Gen. Viscount 27, 29, 31, 35, 47, 57, 59, 147
Gracie Fields (minesweeper) 150
Grafton H.M.S. (destroyer) 159, 192
Gravelines 53, 60, 68, 87, 89
Grenade H.M.S. (destroyer) 117, 154, 159
Greyhound H.M.S. (destroyer) 159
Grive H.M.S. (steam yacht, formerly H.M.S. Narcissus) 175
Grossdeutschland Regiment 33, 213
Guderian, Gen.-Lieut H. 17, 33, 37, 47, 54, 64, 198, 222
Halcyon H.M.S. (minesweeper) 105
Havant H.M.S. (destroyer) 165
Hazebrouck 43, 53
Headcorn 123
Hitler, Adolf 22, 26, 56, 217
Icarus H.M.S. (destroyer) 170
Imogen H.M.S. (destroyer) 100
Impulsive H.M.S. (destroyer) 105, 150
Intrepid H.M.S. (destroyer) 159
Irma Marie (French coaster) 196
Ironside, Gen. Sir E. 48, 61
Isle of Guernsey (hospital ship) 90, 92
Isle of Thanet (hospital ship) 90, 92
Ivanhoe H.M.S. (destroyer) 165
Jacketa (drifter) 153
Jacqueline (Belgian coaster) 195
Jaguar (French destroyer) 95, 201
Jaguar H.M.S. (destroyer) 119, 159
Java (tug) 156
Johanna (Belgian coaster) 172
Jolie Mascotte (French coaster) 164, 191
Jolie Rose (French coaster) 191

Jutland (skoot) 172
Keith H.M.S. (destroyer) 156, 162, 164
King George V (trawler) 199
Kleist, Gen. P. von 65
Kohistan S.S. (cargo vessel) 95
La Bassée 45, 53, 130, 133
La Bourrasque (French destroyer) 192
Lady Brassey (tug) 89, 95, 156
Lady of Mann, S.S. 199
Lambert, Capt. Hon. L. 176
La Panne 68, 90, 111, 142, 150, 188
Lebrun, President of France 213
Le Coniat, Esgn. 190
Leda (British trawler) 201
Le Foudroyant (French destroyer) 192
Le Havre 38, 43, 190
Leibstandarte Regt 64
Leopard (French destroyer) 190
Leopold, King of the Belgians 31, 69
Le Siroco (French destroyer) 192
Liège 22
Locust H.M.S. (cruiser) 198
Lord Cavan (drifter) 153
Lord Southborough (Margate lifeboat) 169, 179
Louvaine 30, 43
Luxembourg 23, 25, 30, 32
Lys River 128, 139
'Macforce' 38, 45, 57
Madeleine Camille (French fishing vessel) 195
Maginot Line 14, 26, 29, 36, 43
Maid of Kent (hospital ship) 90
Maid of Orleans S.S. (transport) 92, 165
Malcolm H.M.S. (destroyer) 117, 201
Ma Joie (motor yacht) 175
Malo-les-Bains 7, 68, 150, 192
Manstein, Gen. E. von 23
Marmion (minesweeper) 150
Marne River 47
Martel, Maj.-Gen. G. le Q. 51, 60
Mavis (supply boat) 95
Max (Belgian tug) 170
Medway Queen (minesweeper) 150
Meuse River 22, 23, 29, 30, 34, 42, 48
Miranda (Cabin-cruiser) 170
Mistral (French destroyer) 117
Mona's Isle (armed boarding vessel) 89, 156
Mona's Queen (transport) 92
Money, Lt-Col. H. K. D. 134, 138
Montgomery, Maj.-Gen. B. L. 140, 144, 147, 223
Montrose H.M.S. (destroyer) 157
Mosquito H.M.S. (destroyer) 165
Namur 22, 23, 30
Newhaven (French passenger ferry) 197
Nieuwpoort 7, 58, 68, 72, 139, 157
Notre Dame des Miracles (French coaster) 196
O.K.W. (Oberkommando der Wehrmacht) 23, 129, 209, 221
Oostdunkerque 140

Orage (French destroyer) 95
Oriole (minesweeper) 150
Ostend 82, 128, 139
Paddock Wood 123
Pangbourne H.M.S. (minesweeper) 117
Paris (hospital ship) 90, 92, 158
Park, Air Vice-Marshal K. R. 73
Pas de Calais 58
Patricia (Trinity House Pilot boat) 105
Peggy (cabin cruiser) 179
Persia (tug) 156, 165
Petain, Marshal 213, 214
'Petreforce' 38, 51, 52
Pharailde (Belgian coaster) 190
Pierre (French coaster) 196
Pierre et Marie (French trawler) 190
'Polforce' 53
Polly (Cabin cruiser) 179
Polly Johnson (trawler) 119
Pownall, Lt-Gen. H. R. 31, 47, 53, 144, 146
Prague S.S. (troop carrier) 158, 165
Prioux, Gen. 68, 72, 128, 191
Princess Maud (L.M.S. passenger ferry) 193, 199
Prins Boodwin (Belgian coaster) 196
Prudential (Ramsgate lifeboat) 169, 179
Queen of the Channel (motorship) 111, 112
Racia (tug) 176
Ramsay, Vice-Admiral B. 47, 82, 101, 108, 119, 146, 150, 151, 176, 198, 223
Reichenau, Gen. W. von 30
Reims 22, 47
Reynaud, P., French Prime Minister 35, 47, 56, 59, 144, 210
Rockall (Belgian coaster) 196
Roman (tug) 89
Rommel, Gen. E. 51, 67
Roosevelt, President 210
Rouen (French passenger ferry) 197
Royal Oak H.M.S. (battleship) 18
Royal Sovereign (motorship) 199
Royalty (barge) 154
Rundstedt, Gen. G. von 23, 29, 53, 56, 57
Ruytingen Bank 87, 156
Sabre H.M.S. (destroyer) 150
Saint de Padoue (French fishing boat) 195
Sainte Isabelle (French coaster) 196
St Malo Beach 111
St Omer 53
St Pol 53
St Quentin 37
St Seiriol (pleasure steamer) 113
St Vaast la Hougue 190
St Valery 39, 79, 222
Salome (French tanker) 196
Saltash H.M.S. (minesweeper) 165
Sambre River 30, 42
Sandown (minesweeper) 150
Sarah and Emily (cabin cruiser) 179
Sarah Ann (barge) 176
Savoy (barge) 176

Scarpe River 45, 52
Scotia (L.M.S. ferry) 153, 165
Scheldt–Escaut Line 49
Seasmalter (smack) 173
Sedan 23, 34
Senne River 37, 42
Shamrock (barge) 176
Sheerness H.M.S. (destroyer) 104, 122, 171
Shikari H.M.S. (destroyer) 198
Sibyl (tug) 176
'Sichelschnitt' Operation 24, 111, 217
Siesta (barge) 176
Silver Dawn (drifter) 153
Simla (tug) 89, 95, 156
Skipjack H.M.S. (minesweeper) 105, 163
'Smoky Joes' (minesweepers) 105
Somme River 39, 43, 57
Sperrle, Marshal H. 30
Spinel (tanker) 89
Strive (minesweeper) 142
Student, Gen. K. 23, 218
Sun IV, VIII, XIII, XV (tugs) 176
Sunbeam (barge) 176
Sundowner (cabin cruiser) 179
Swiftsure (barge) 176
Tanga (tug) 176, 199
Tennant, Capt. W. G. 85, 90, 101, 150
Thames (Belgian tug) 170
Therese Compas (Belgian drifter) 190
Tides (at Dunkirk) 108
Tollesbury (barge) 176
Totenkopf Regiment 134
Tynwald (troop carrier) 151, 199
'Usherforce' 53
Vanguard (destroyer) 175
Vega H.M.S. (destroyer) 99
Verity H.M.S. (destroyer) 119
Vernon H.M.S. (minesweeper) 153
'Vickforce' 38
Vimy 52
Vimy H.M.S. (destroyer) 99
Violaines 130, 133
Vivacious H.M.S. (destroyer) 150
Vulcain (Belgian tug) 170
Waalhaven airfield 25
Wakefield H.M.S. (destroyer) 99, 159, 192
Wake-Walker, Rear-Admiral W. F. 85, 162
Waverley H.M.S. (minesweeper) 150
Weygand, Gen. M. 56, 59, 68, 144, 210
Whitehall H.M.S. (destroyer) 164
Whitshed H.M.S. (destroyer) 199
Winchester H.M.S. (destroyer) 95
Windsor H.M.S. (destroyer) 150
Wolsey H.M.S. (destroyer) 89
'Woodforce' 53
Worcester H.M.S. (destroyer) 144, 165
Worthing (hospital ship) 90, 92
Yewdale (tramp) 119
Yser River 128, 140
Yvonne (Belgian trawler) 190
Zuydcoote 150

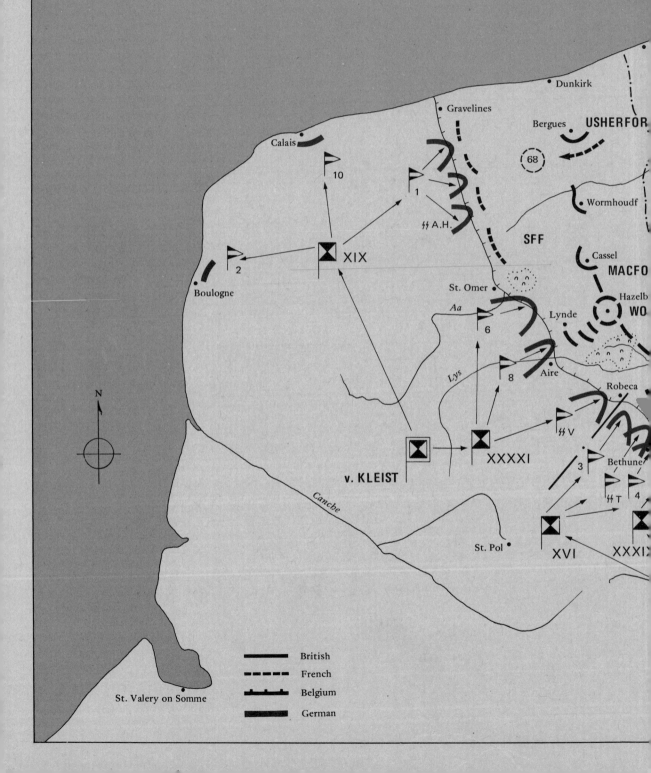

Disposition of British, French, Belgian and
German forces on the evening of 24 May 1940